W9-DAD-314

FDR & Stalin

Amos Perlmutter

University of Missouri Press

Columbia and London

FDR
& Stalin

A Not So
Grand
Alliance,
1943–1945

Library of Congress Cataloging-in-Publication Data

Perlmutter, Amos.
     FDR & Stalin : a not so grand alliance, 1943–1945 / Amos
Perlmutter
          p.   cm.
     Includes bibliographical references and index.
     ISBN 0-8262-0910-6
     1. World War, 1939–1945—Diplomatic history. 2. Roosevelt, Franklin D.
(Franklin Delano), 1882–1945. 3. Stalin, Joseph, 1879–1953.
4. United States—Foreign relations—Soviet Union. 5. Soviet Union—
Foreign relations—United States. I. Title. II. Title: FDR and Stalin.
D749.P47   1993
940.53'2—dc20   93-4866
                                                                                    CIP

Designer: Kristie Lee
Typesetter: Connell-Zeko Type & Graphics
Printer and binder:
Typefaces: Trade, Trade Extra Condensed, Helios Condensed

The material translated in Appendixes 1–4 is used with the permission of the USSR Ministry of Foreign Affairs, as are the photographs identified as courtesy the Soviet Archives.

To my beloved mother, Berta,
and my friend for life, Rosanne.
For all we share.

Other Books by Amos Perlmutter

The Life and Times of Menachem Begin
Israel: The Partitioned State
Modern Authoritarianism
Political Roles and Military Rulers
Politics and the Military in Israel: 1967–77
The Military and Politics in Modern Times
Egypt, The Praetorian State
Anatomy of Political Institutionalization:
The Case of Israel and Some Comparative Analysis
Military and Politics in Israel:
Nation Building and Role Expansion

Contents

Acknowledgments

A book is not written by a single person. Such a monumental task always leaves an author indebted. There are many institutions and persons, in the U.S. and the USSR, to which I am most grateful and without whose support this work would not have been realized. My acknowledgments must begin with two foundations that supported me generously for three years—the Bradley and the Earhart foundations. To the unfailing support of Hillel Fradkin, Dianne Monroe, and Dan Schmidt of Bradley, and to David B. Kennedy and Tony Sullivan of Earhart, I am forever in debt. Dianne, Dan, and Tony extended special understanding, patience, and generosity, for which I repeat my thanks.

In Russia, I was the first foreigner (in July, 1989) permitted access to the Soviet Foreign Ministry's archives. A variety of Americans and Russians aided me in pursuit of these previously classified materials. In the U.S. James Billington, Librarian of Congress, and Ambassador Max Kempleman were crucial in the opening of the archives to me. Vladimir Vasilevich Sokolov, Deputy Head of the USSR Ministry of Foreign Affairs, Historical-Diplomatic Department, was most helpful in releasing (by 1990) many key documents for the period 1942 to 1945 on Soviet-American relations. This access would not have been expedited without the support of former U.S. Ambassador to the USSR Jack Matlock. Andrey Shoumikhin, head of the Department of U.S. Foreign Policy of the USA-Canada Institute in Moscow, and his team of reliable, dedicated researchers and translators have done a splendid job.

Colonel General Dimitry Volkogonov, then head of military history, Soviet defense ministry, provided help, as did Rodamir Bogdanov, then Deputy Director of the USA-Canada Institute. Sergo Mikoyan, Evgeny Primakov, and Tatyana Tarasova of the Near East Institute also provided assistance. I am grateful to Adam Ulam for helping me locate a research assistant. Richard Pipes of the Harvard Department of History rendered outstanding advice on how to "get along" in the Soviet archives. His counsel was critical to my successful pursuit of the medieval Soviet archival system. From Professor Pipes I have learned more than from all Soviet historians and political scientists combined; his analyses were and continue to be most prescient.

Librarians and archivists at the Library of Congress, the National Archives in Washington, D.C., and the Franklin D. Roosevelt Library in Hyde Park were efficient, prompt, helpful, and most supportive. I offer special thanks to Suzan Elter, of the Roosevelt Library, and to Marc Renovitch, also of the Roosevelt Library, who was instrumental in helping me select the illustrations included in the book.

The sagacious advice of Robert Tucker, the Dean of American foreign policy scholarship, and Aaron Wildavsky, the leading scholar of American presidential politics, was critical. Both read different versions of the manuscript and rendered valuable help.

My coeditor of the *Journal of Strategic Studies,* John Gooch, now at the University of Leeds, read the manuscript in an earlier version and saved me from small but critical errors. I am grateful to Alex Holtzman of Cambridge University Press and my coeditor Benjamin Frankel and Gary Tischler for editing different versions of the manuscript. Also I offer very special thanks to Michael Archer of the American University Department of Government, our computer whiz. He typed, retyped, and typed again the several versions of the manuscript. David Wagner of the American University research office also merits my thanks.

Yet without the affection and dedication of Beverly Jarrett, Director and Editor-in-Chief of the University of Missouri Press, this work would not have been the same. As my editor and a wonderful friend

Beverly personally edited and expedited the preparation of the manuscript beyond the call of duty. I am humbly grateful. In my long association with university presses, only Beverly deserves the same accolades I have always bestowed on Marian Neal Ash of Yale. Jane Lago, Managing Editor of the University of Missouri Press, did a superb job of sorting out and clarifying my messy footnotes and bibliography. And Janice Smiley's heroic efforts in deciphering my handwriting and Beverly's deserves more than an honorable mention.

Last but certainly not least I acknowledge the aid of my deceased friend and most efficient administrator, Ingaborg Dim, who sorted, organized, corrected, copied, and edited the early work before her untimely death in 1990. I only wish she could have lived to see the finished product; she would have been proud of it. May her soul rest in peace.

Prologue

Mobilized for the nation's greatest foreign war—the Second World War—the American people were led to believe that the mission of a neo-Wilsonian global New Deal was to win the contest between democracy and totalitarianism. Prompted by a colossal Japanese error, the surprise attack on Pearl Harbor, and Hitler's declaration of war against the U.S., Americans entered a war their president had avoided for nearly two years. These grave mistakes of the totalitarians would serve as a blessing for humanity. But as early as August, 1941, FDR and Churchill had begun to set lofty postwar goals, however vague and emblemed in the Atlantic Charter, which committed the U.S. to a policy of self-determination for smaller states.

The Charter had clearly prohibited territorial acquisitions by states. Yet this doctrine was seriously compromised by the president, once Stalin's Soviet Union was betrayed, the Nazi-Soviet Pact was violated, and the USSR was invaded by Hitler, Stalin's ally, in 1941. Now the wily Stalin, whose war goals were clearly territorial, became the trustworthy ally of the Anglo-Americans, especially of President Roosevelt. The Charter became in effect a shell, a strategic and political burden to the president in his relations with his new ally.

Stalin's war changed after German capitulation in Stalingrad in February, 1943, from the defensive strategy to the offensive as the Red Army marched in 1944–1945 into Eastern and Central Europe, fulfilling his aspirations for territorial aggrandizement. After 1943,

President Roosevelt had at best three interrelated strategic choices: to destroy Hitler's military power in Europe in 1942–1943 and thereby achieve a powerful political realpolitik arrangement in Europe; to guard against Stalin's territorial ambitions, once Anglo-American forces invaded in 1944; or to forge, during the war, a postwar collective security arrangement under the UN with the cooperation of Stalin. FDR settled for the last of these options. This, despite Stalin's flagrant violations of the president's original goals of securing small nations and helping to establish democracy in Hitler's collapsing Europe.

This book will analyze FDR's final strategic choice, his failure either to harness Stalin or to fulfill the Atlantic Charter's principles in postwar Europe. This is the story of a president who continuously appeased Stalin, from June 22, 1941, until his death on April 12, 1945. FDR's failure to deter the rise of a Russian-Soviet empire more vast than any known since the emergence of Russia in the ninth century is examined, along with his war policy as it related to Stalin and to the USSR. Roosevelt's "not so grand alliance" with Stalin, an alliance that ultimately resulted in abandonment of the larger victory for democracy, provides a new perspective from which to view the president whose flaws have too often been overlooked or excused. This not-so-grand alliance cost Eastern and Central Europe their independence and committed America to nearly half a century of cold war.

FDR & Stalin

Chapter 1

Why Another Book on FDR?

For almost half a century the myth of FDR's far-seeing diplomacy has prevailed and remains protected by his biographical *praetorian guards* Arthur Schlesinger, Jr., James McGregor Burns, William E. Leuchtenburg, and Robert Dallek. A fresh assessment of the century's most critical years, 1943 to 1945, and the role of the free world's leader is essential. Some of the themes are new, others are not. Some arguments were heard even in FDR's time and shortly after his death. All must be put aside—the prophets, apologists, and detractors. An honest, penetrating, demythologizing, irreverent study is in order now, as we near the end of the twentieth century.

On the fiftieth anniversary of the Second World War, I propose to evaluate how the detached and parochial management style of Franklin Delano Roosevelt contributed to the postwar failure of American foreign policy in Eastern Europe and the Middle East. Much of the nature of Soviet-American relations, as well as the Soviet domination of Eastern Europe that emerged after the war, is the making of FDR, in perverse collaboration with Joseph Stalin. The Soviet alliance was the cornerstone of FDR's European policy. He hoped this alliance would replace in importance the one with Great Britain, by then a declining imperial power.

Unwilling to share Woodrow Wilson's failure in establishing a new international order, and unable alone to restructure the peace in Europe, FDR opted for an American accommodation with Stalin's

1

USSR. During the war he set in motion the foundation for an amicable U.S. policy toward totalitarian Russia.

In the pages that follow, I have challenged established orientations regarding FDR's Soviet policy. Much research in the newly opened archives has been initiated. People who were not previously consulted or who were not considered influential regarding FDR's Soviet and British policy between 1943 and 1945 have been studied. Information from archives and institutions that were not carefully researched or examined at all will become prominent herein.

Much has been written on FDR, but less so on his foreign politics. The orthodoxy today is represented by Robert Dallek, in his single-volume *Franklin Delano Roosevelt and American Foreign Policy, 1932–1945* (1979). A better source is Warren Kimball's superb three-volume *Churchill & Roosevelt: Their Complete Correspondence* (1984) with its excellent commentary. In my view, the correspondence volumes are by far the most enlightening books we have had on the FDR-Churchill failure of American foreign policy in Eastern Europe and the Middle East.

My purpose in the present study has been to analyze the consequences for subsequent American foreign policy of Roosevelt's decision to seek the dissolution of the British Empire, to decimate France's power, and to facilitate the extension of the Soviet Empire. I have reassessed the foreign policy of the Roosevelt administration in the light of recently declassified Soviet documents and newly found documents from the period. With the aid of these new references, I have been able to cast new light on the special relationship between FDR and Stalin in the critical years 1943 to 1945.

FDR, by far America's most influential twentieth-century president, has cast a long shadow over American history. That shadow is still with us. Along with Stalin and Churchill, FDR shaped the structure of world politics that came into existence after the war. Yet none of the many volumes in the five decades since FDR's death have focused on that profound influence. The liberal historians have made significant contributions to the history of FDR, but none have dealt specifically with the critical war years. Certainly none have dealt with his personal presidential style in the management of foreign affairs.

My study therefore attempts a major breakthrough in our understanding of the Rooseveltian orthodoxy. I expect this study to be controversial, but it will also have been anchored in serious, comprehensive, and substantial research into the unexamined, forgotten, or lost documents of the era. I hope that it will spark a new debate regarding FDR's impact on the nature and course of U.S.-Soviet relations, especially between 1943 and 1945.

There has been no single volume that dealt with FDR's World War II policies and activities. Different monographs have dealt with specific areas or personality issues. Yet a comprehensive analysis based on unpublished documentation had not been written. The last two years of the Second World War, 1943–1945, were the most intensive and critical for the security and foreign policy of the U.S. In fact these two years predetermined the international relations of the U.S. as it emerged as the unrivaled atomic superpower.

I will herein demonstrate that FDR, the most powerful leader of the three—U.S.-USSR-Great Britain—failed to take political advantage of the enormous U.S. economic, military, and atomic superiority. Mainly because of outdated Wilsonian ideals and personal arrogance and parochialism, FDR failed to realize or understand that the world after the war would not see an end to imperialism—only to the Western type. Stalin had already conceived of the Soviet Empire and used FDR's parochialism to advance Soviet imperial interests in Eastern Europe. Rather than neutralizing Stalin, blocking his plans and curtailing his aspirations, FDR put all his weight on Churchill and the British Empire, which was already in the process of decline. Roosevelt preferred the partnership of the cunning, machinating, and ruthless Stalin over that of the imperialist yet devotedly democratic Churchill, a leader of one of the world's greatest democracies. This book will expose the myth of New Deal war diplomacy—the only game in FDR's town. FDR, the covert agent of appeasement during the 1930s, became an ally of Joseph Stalin, the most ruthless political leader the modern world has known next to Hitler.

I have determined through documentation and incontrovertible evidence that the parochial, lackadaisical White House style in those dramatic years and the parochialism of the nation had a powerful representative in the president. The personality and policy of FDR as a world leader portray his dissembling style and enable us to confront the issue of why Roosevelt did not perceive other options than collaborating with Stalin in order to win the war and organize the peace.

FDR needed Stalin's cooperation, since the Soviet Union did indeed carry the heaviest burden of the war and suffer the heaviest casualties of the three Allies. But it was also Stalin's Soviet Union that had signed, in August, 1939, a pact with Hitler which Hitler later betrayed. What choice was left to Stalin but to fight a war of liberation from Nazi aggression? There was no reason for FDR or his advisors to fear that the USSR might make a separate deal with Hitler (who adamantly refused such overtures) or quit while the Nazi forces were deep in Russia.

FDR hoped to secure the victory with a minimum cost to the U.S., which was indeed a noble and courageous aspiration. Of course it could have been achieved without the policy of unconditional surrender of Germany and Japan, which prolonged the war, constrained U.S. moves to occupy all or most of Germany, and led to the division of Germany.

My study reveals the total absence of statecraft, as well as the diplomatic chaos that resulted from a political strategy that followed a military strategy rather than a strategy that sought political solutions first. FDR "surrendered" Eastern Europe to Stalin even before Stalin was prepared to attempt Soviet expansion into the East. I reexamined the Lend-Lease program regarding Soviet-Polish and Eastern European policies and contrasted it with Churchill's brilliant containment of Soviet ambitions in Greece in 1944 and 1945. Churchill did the opposite in Greece, supporting the anti-Communist forces. Hence Greece is a Western democracy thanks to Churchill's initiative. FDR's bitter and controversial Polish policy is reexamined here, using the new documents that demonstrate his culpability. In fact, FDR made Stalin's goals easier to achieve. He never used Lend-Lease as a bargaining chip with Stalin, even when Stalin later stood at the gates of Warsaw and let the Polish nationalists and democrats be destroyed by Hitler. In Teheran in 1943, FDR effectively surrendered Poland to Stalin. Yalta only ratified the deed.

In three key areas of the Grand Alliance dispute—the Second Front, Poland, and the dismemberment of Germany—FDR clearly colluded with Stalin against the better vision of Churchill. Both in Casablanca and Trident (May, 1943) FDR and his chiefs made a firm commitment to Stalin's pressure to open a Second Front. FDR advocated a cross-channel invasion into France, whereas Churchill had opted for an Eastern Mediterranean-Balkan invasion. Stalin opposed the latter, and FDR colluded with Stalin on a Western European-French cross-channel invasion, thus canceling an Allied invasion going east toward Southeastern and Central Europe. FDR abandoned the Poles in Teheran (actually before Teheran) and opted for Stalin's Poland solution. Some modifications were proposed by Churchill and by Roosevelt, and these were accepted by Stalin. But for FDR the Polish question in Yalta ranked third in importance after the United Nations and Russia's entry into the war with Japan. For Stalin and Churchill, Poland and the security of Eastern Europe were a first priority issue, followed by the question of German dismemberment and the role of France. In the words of Gregg Walker:

> While it is difficult to ascertain whether Roosevelt's unwillingness to get involved in the Polish-Soviet dispute reflected his personal views or was more indicative of his concern to balance political expediency with his desire to maintain Allied unity, a document found in the Map Room File of the Franklin D. Roosevelt Presidential Library provides some insight into this question. This document, a telegram the President wrote to Churchill in March, 1944 but apparently never sent—it is not included among any of the records of the Roosevelt-Churchill correspondence—may provide the best indication of Roosevelt's true attitude towards the Polish problem.
>
> "In regard to the Polish situation, I am inclined to think that the final determination of matters like boundaries can well be laid aside for awhile by the Russians, by the Polish Government, and by your Government.
>
> In other words, I think that on these particular matters we can well let nature take its course.

The main current problem is to assure the cooperation of the Polish guerrillas and population with the Russians as they advance into Poland. Most certainly we do not want any Polish opposition to the Russian armies.

In the meantime we will learn much more about Polish sentiment and the advisability of continuing or not continuing to let the Polish Government in London speak for the Poles. It is entirely possible that as the Russians advance they may recognize some other organization as more representative of the people of Poland.

The advancing Russian army will doubtless find many local Poles who will aid them as they proceed westward. This is essentially a military occupation. I still think the future government and matters like boundaries can be put on ice until we know more about it. This, in line with my general thought that we ought not cross bridges till we come to them.

If you think it would be helpful for me to wire Uncle Joe along the lines of the above, I will do so." Attached to the telegram was a note to Secretary of State Hull asking, "What would you think of my sending something like this about the Poles to the Prime Minister?"

The correspondence was never sent. Perhaps Hull dissuaded FDR from sending it. Not only might it have best reflected Roosevelt's view of the Polish problem, but it also provides support for the argument that the president was willing to consider a Polish government other than that of the London Poles. These thoughts were written on March 16th, 1944. The Soviet supported Provisional Government of Poland (the Lublin Committee) formed just a few months later. Perhaps Roosevelt privately conceded some legitimacy to the Lublin Poles, although there is certainly no public record of this.[1]

FDR finally left Yalta and abandoned Henry Morgenthau's plan for the dismemberment of Germany, and he colluded with Stalin against de Gaulle and France. The dismemberment of Germany and the weakening of France would have made Stalin's Russia the dominant power in Europe. What a disaster this could have been. Thanks to Churchill, who vehemently disagreed with FDR's policy toward de Gaulle, France was made an equal party in the division of Germany and in the stability and security of Europe against Stalin and the Soviet Union.

The most crucial questions about the FDR-Stalin relationship—taking us beyond guess work on why FDR colluded with Stalin and whether this collusion was fruitful for U.S. and Western interests—are the following:

—Did Stalin perceive FDR's overtures on the Second Front and Poland as a friendly sign or as evidence of a weak capitalist position?

—What were the bases for Stalin's position on the U.S. and FDR: a Marxist view; a pragmatist reaction; a manipulative stance, or some combination of all? Which one was the determining factor?

—Did Stalin really have dealings, feelers, thoughts of reestablishing his broken alliance with Hitler sometime after Stalingrad?

—Did Stalin negotiate over Eastern Europe, *i.e.*, Poland, from the position of a party to the Grand Alliance or that of a Soviet imperialist? Did he make FDR his ally and keep Churchill at arm's length knowing that the former either didn't understand or care for Poland? Or was all that FDR did in opposition to Churchill for the purpose of assuring the alliance and making Churchill more amenable to Stalin?

All of these questions are studied herein, using new evidence from the former Soviet Union. Students, scholars, and interested citizens concerned with the making of foreign and security policy will profit from this investigation of the impact FDR's war policy had on American political institutions as they relate to international politics. The large issues of U.S. national security and of the conduct of war from the presidential office are at issue here.

A new generation of Americans has been taught the conventional wisdom that FDR was an outstanding war strategist and that Stalin's Eastern European expansion was inevitable. This consensus must be revised to allow new generations the benefits of additional, fresh research. Public opinion-makers, writers, reporters, columnists, and other members of the media must become more knowledgeable about the "other" FDR. This study, like the recent controversial works of Paul Kennedy and Allan Bloom, seeks an audience that will make the issues raised a matter of national and public debate.

Research for the book has involved extended travel to the major repositories housing archival material from the Roosevelt years. Located in the U.S., the USSR, and Great Britain, the libraries and archives consulted included the following: the Franklin D. Roosevelt Library, Hyde Park, N.Y.; the Library of Congress and the National Archives, Washington, D.C.; the Harvard Libraries, Cambridge, Mass.; USSR Moscow Foreign Ministry Archives; London Public Records office.

Even within its specific boundaries, political biography remains a vast field. Biography at its broadest aims to shed light on the life of a particular individual. Novels, some poetry, and even anthropological studies may focus on the life of an often unknown individual, but a biography per se must deal with the life of an individual whose life has had an impact on society, on history—for good or for ill.

When approaching his subject, the biographer has no limits regarding what aspect of a person he chooses to study. Neither is he, nor should he be, limited in his approach or purpose, whether it be to explain, interpret, praise, or condemn. The biographer's approach may be telescopic, or far removed into the background. His focus may be on the subject's youth, his middle years, his old age, or all three. The biographer may explore the subject's background, environment, education, upbringing, his friends and supporters, his rivals and enemies. In pursuit of his subject, the biographer is free to make use of all fields of learning, all methods of information-gathering; he is free to explore theories and explanations of behavior, using, for example, psychohistory to delve into formative years. Likewise, cultural, anthropological, or sociological theses may be used to explain motivation in a subject. To investigate political background, the biographer must pursue all avenues to explore the political context from which his subject emerged and from which his actions evolved, anchoring him in his own time, as well as in history, and in future developments.

If the panorama of biography seems wide and extensive, it can also be deceptively so. The use of one tool as a primary means of analyzing the subject—say, using psychoanalysis to come up with a womb-to-tomb tale or steadfastly presenting a somber, basket-to-casket chronological story—is unsatisfactory and insufficient for good biography. Like literature and social science, biography is a field that, though grounded in solid scholarship, must be consistently interesting, dramatic, and compelling, capturing the essential and dispensing with detail for detail's sake. Digressions or amassing dull and unilluminating facts are hardly welcome tactics in biography. They tend to sidetrack and finally deaden a reader's interest and attention.

Readers are fascinated by the lives of significant persons. This does not mean they need or want to know everything there is to know about such persons, from their intake at meals to their daily choice of apparel, unless such information is important to the larger story. Readers are interested only in what made the person become who he or she became. If the subject was a warrior or soldier, then strategies and battles lost or won become critical. If the subject is a political figure, then the path to leadership and a person's ambitions become significant, as are his political accomplishments and failures. If the subject is an artist, a painter or composer, then his motivations, his sources of inspiration become critical. Questions arise: the subject's contributions to the world and history, or lack of them, what he offered, who listened, followed, appreciated, opposed, despised, or was in turn influenced.

It is a fact that there are no biographies, certainly no interesting ones, of insignificant persons. Those are proper subjects for the imagination, for the storyteller and novelist. But real people who make a direct and verifiable impact on our daily lives, and those who made an impact on their times and on history, these are proper subjects for the biographer. There is no question that Franklin Delano Roosevelt, as president, political leader, and war leader, is one of this century's most significant, compelling, and controversial figures.

This is not meant to be a "life and times" of FDR. We have had at least four outstanding such efforts, with one author still laboring in the chronological vineyard. Nor is my study meant to be a study of FDR's domestic politics. Rather, its focus is strictly and squarely on FDR's war aims and policies from 1943 to 1945 as they relate to Joseph Stalin and, to a lesser degree, Winston Churchill. These three leaders were the authors of and principal participants in the most important strategic summits of the war at Teheran and Yalta. Roosevelt did not actually meet personally with Stalin until 1943. Prior to that time he had employed such surrogates as Harry Hopkins, Averell Harriman, and Joseph Davies in dealing with Stalin, a method he had also used to some extent with Churchill.

The questions being posed here are fundamental: Did FDR have a grand design and strategy for the war, a political-military scheme for victory and its aftermath? If he did, what were its basic tenets, and how did it affect the course of the war? If he did not, how did he conduct the war without a grand design? What was his style of conduct, his behavior, his diplomacy, as it related to Stalin and Churchill?

My emphasis has been on the conceptual framework of FDR's war policy, his methods of operation with Stalin and the Soviet Union, and how Stalin's grand strategy for the war related to the president and the United States, and how both related to Churchill and the capitalist democracies. Even if Churchill seems to recede into the background, especially after 1943, he is not, and cannot be, marginalized. After all, these three, however unequal their respective roles in winning the war, made up what Churchill called "the Grand Alliance," a term with which I will take exception.

One of the critical concerns I have dealt with is the matter of Stalin's war aims as they affected the Soviet Union's postwar frontiers, his imposition of friendly regimes, and the territorial expansion he justified as part of his concept of security—all aims that went almost unquestioned by FDR. Stalin is not the subject of my inquiries, but his war aims, strategy, and diplomacy strongly influenced FDR's war strategy and behavior.

I have argued that the Russian entry into the war in 1941 and the grand strategies designed at Teheran in 1943 and Yalta in 1945 ended up overshadowing the early Anglo-American Casablanca strategy. Furthermore, I have demonstrated that Roosevelt's strategy eventually became linked to that of Stalin, not that of Churchill, and that FDR ultimately perceived a postwar Europe dominated by Stalin. Certainly Roosevelt believed that he could not create a new international order or an effective United Nations organization without Stalin. It is clearly demonstrated that FDR's collective security strategy, moored in a world organization, very soon collapsed, and ended in a cold war because of his indifference to Stalin's traditionally Russian strategy, a strategy anchored in the old European balance of power international political order. In short, FDR was a diplomatic and strategic failure.

I don't believe or recommend that a biographer should come to his work ignorant of his subject, lest his presuppositions or prejudices determine the outcome of his study. However, I find distasteful those claims of omnipotent objectivity, those claims maintaining a sturdy nonpartisanship in the face of the subject. The absence of passion is not necessarily a requirement for great biography. On the contrary, I think a biographer must be emotionally and intellectually involved with his subject. Familiarity, in this case, does not breed boredom, indifference, or contempt.

A passionate interest can take different forms. One may admire or love his subject, respect or despise him. Not many biographers of Hitler profess to love or admire him, but all are fascinated by him. One may be fascinated with the era, the events, and the drama, as I have been by the triumph of FDR, Stalin, and Churchill. Certainly Roosevelt himself has inspired a host of admiring and some not-so-admiring biographers. I can admire Roosevelt's vision of America without being enthralled by his war strategy. I am puzzled by and disappointed in FDR's ready admiration for Stalin, a man he never really understood.

A biographer needs what the philosopher Vico called "fantasia." Isaiah Berlin, who renders "fantasia" as "imaginative insight," has written in *The Crooked Timber of Humanity:* "We call great historians only those who not only are in full control of the factual evidence obtained by the use of the best critical methods available to them, but also possess the depth of Imaginative Insight that characterizes great novelists." Berlin continues:

> Vico's fantasia is indispensable to his conception of historical knowledge; it is unlike the knowledge that Julius Caesar is dead, or Rome was not built in a day, or that thirteen is a prime number, or that a week has seven days; nor yet is it like knowledge of how to ride a bicycle or engage in statistical research or win a battle. It is more like knowing what it is to be poor, to belong to a nation, to be a

revolutionary, to be converted to a religion, to fall in love, to be seized by nameless terror, to be delighted by a work of art. I give these examples only as analogies, for Vico is interested not in the experience of individuals but in that of entire societies. It is this kind of collective self-awareness—what men thought, imagined, felt, wanted, strove for in the face of physical nature, at a particular stage of social development, expressed by institutions, monuments, symbols, ways of writing and speech, generated by their efforts to represent and explain their condition to themselves—that he wished to analyze, and he thought he had found a path to it not trodden by others. . . . The historian who lacks "Fantasia" (and may despise it) may know the facts, and tell the story well, but somehow miss the point.[2]

My own reasons for undertaking this study stem from my teenage years during World War II. I was an avid reader of everything connected with the war. I could barely read English, but I collected pictures of the war, and one of those pictures, famous now, was of the big three at Teheran—Churchill, FDR, and Stalin seated on the porch in front of the Soviet embassy in Teheran. Of course every student of history is now familiar with that picture, and many have enjoyed the film made of that conference in the Roosevelt Library in Hyde Park, New York.

Biography has always been a staple of my reading, as have history, politics, and war strategy. And FDR captured my imagination as soon as I came to the United States, in 1951. Why not undertake a study of the great American war president during this country's most monumental war effort (outside of its Civil War)? Stalin, of course, had become for me an instant villain, as soon as I understood the fatality and unreality that led to one of this century's most despicable regimes, the Soviet Union, matched only by Hitler's Nazi regime.

In my teens, however, Stalin and the Soviet Union were seen from a different perspective. Living as I did in Palestine, when Rommel was only 120 kilometers from Alexandria, Soviet victories loomed larger and larger. Religiously, I followed the progress of the Great Patriotic War fought on huge billowing fronts in the USSR. As a graduate of the Socialist Zionist movement, I enthusiastically supported the Soviet war effort. Indoctrinated by the left and being Jewish, I firmly believed that the Soviets would destroy every Nazi alive. I doubted that the imperialist British or the Americans would or could do that.

Oddly enough, my adolescent intuitions tended to be confirmed by my studies, and by the behavior of the British and Americans after 1945. I cannot say that Stalin was a hero to us, although the photographs certainly made him look impressive, not at all like the short, pock-marked man that he was in the flesh. The Jewish community in Palestine, the Yishuv, totally supported the Soviet war effort, because the Soviets were inflicting huge losses and defeats on the Nazis. So I knew about and was fascinated by the principals in this drama—Stalin, FDR, and Churchill. But I knew nothing of their game plans and strategies; that would require maturity, study, research, and analysis.

I did considerable homework before beginning my researches for this book. Admittedly opinionated, passionate, and fascinated by my subject, I first read and reread important secondary works on World War II, FDR, Stalin, and, of course, international relations, as well as memoirs, analyses, theses, interpretations, and narratives. I read countless books on the war, especially those pertaining to the Russian front, and on American-Soviet relations before, after, but especially during the period 1943–1945. I also found a treasure in the wonderful *Foreign Relations of the United States* (*FRUS*) volumes published by the State Department. No scholar should begin researches without having access to these absolutely necessary volumes, particularly those dealing with Casablanca, Teheran, Yalta, and Potsdam. Also, the excellent *U.S. Army in World War II* series is extremely helpful, as is the superior if somewhat stuffy British Grand Strategy *History of the Second World War* (6 volumes), especially H. R. Gibbs in Volume I, J. R. M. Butler in Volume II, and Michael Howard in Volume IV.

I also made heavy use of doctoral dissertations, which often proved to be original and innovative. These unpublished dissertations are a gold mine, and I made thorough use of them. I did not miss ordering, exchanging, or rereading the original researches of young scholars, even when their arguments were not totally convincing,[3] a quality they share with many American writers.

American writers on the subject can best be put into categories of those who were close to the subject and those writing as historians, journalists, or political scientists. In the first group are members of FDR's circle: his surrogates, including his chief advisors Harry Hopkins, Averell Harriman, Cordell Hull, Joseph Davies, as well as cabinet secretaries who played advisory roles—Henry Morgenthau, Frank Knox, Henry Stimson, and Sumner Welles. The military advisors include Marshall, Leahy, King, and Eisenhower. (Incidentally, by far the best study of FDR's lieutenants is Eric Larrabee's *Commander in Chief,* published in 1987.)

I have written this book aware that there is already in existence voluminous literature representing considerable research on Franklin Delano Roosevelt. He was in office for over twelve years; his tenure encompassed the Depression and America's triumph in World War II, one of the more dramatic and eventful periods of American history.

Much has been written about the domestic aspects of Roosevelt's presidency. The bibliography issued by the Roosevelt Library lists over three thousand items, only 3 percent of which is devoted to FDR's foreign and war policy. Three of Roosevelt's authoritative biographers—Arthur Schlesinger, Jr., William Leuchtenburg, and Frank Friedel—have not written on FDR past 1936. Kenneth Davis, the most recent of the major FDR biographers, published the third volume of his study of Roosevelt's life in 1986, focusing on the New Deal years, 1933–1937. Friedel's last book, published in 1990, is an abridged version of his excellent four-volume work. One half of the book deals with the military and the war, but it is based mostly on secondary sources, relying on literature friendly to the president's war policies. Among FDR scholars, only Robert Dallek and Warren Kimball are students of his foreign policies, and Kimball focuses chiefly on FDR's relations with Winston Churchill.

These historians are members of the Roosevelt nomenclature, adherents to the Roosevelt canon. Even Davis, the most critical of the group, focuses his criticism on FDR's domestic policies. There is some criticism of Roosevelt in the vast literature on him, but most scholars have offered friendly interpretations of his career. With the exception of Dallek, whose book is devoted to Roosevelt's foreign policy between 1933 and 1945, no scholar has critically pursued Roosevelt's war years, diplomacy, and strategy.

In the U.S. archives, there is little of a factual nature to be discovered about FDR and his policies that is startling or unexpected. The contribution my book makes is not in uncovering heretofore unknown American archival material. Rather, its contribution to the assessment of Roosevelt is in demonstrating that the historical materials on which most of the Roosevelt scholarship has relied do not support the orthodox interpretations of FDR's policies. My work has been interpretation rather than digging for new facts, but the interpretation I offer will show the way for other scholars to reexamine Roosevelt's war policy.

There appears to have been an ideological and conceptual divide splitting Roosevelt scholars. FDR was secretive, manipulative, and at times deceptive; he was never open with his feelings, and he did not record his private thoughts and opinions or his thinking on policy matters. It is not surprising that there is no definitive and indisputable account of Roosevelt's war policy, of his attitude toward the Soviet Union, or of his vision of the postwar international structure. We know that he abhorred the traditional balance-of-power politics and was hostile to an imperial approach to postwar territorial and national arrangements. But beyond that, it is not possible to tell whether his preferences were with a universalist United Nations system of collective security, a two-party arrangement centering around the U.S. and the Soviet Union, or an Anglo-American economic imperium dominated by the U.S.

Warren Kimball assumes that the president based his foreign policy and postwar aspirations on a plan that called for an Anglo-American postwar imperium, a version of the Atlantic Alliance. From this view, Lend-Lease would not only prevent the collapse of Great Britain and the exposure of the east coast of the U.S. to Nazi aggression, it would also serve as an instrument by which the president might create an alliance with Great Britain. But the decision on Lend-Lease was primarily strategic, not economic. The United States did replace Great Britain as the dominant economic power, but Lend-Lease was not the cause. Kimball's assertion that Roosevelt "hedged his bets" on the Soviet Union[4] is not entirely accurate, since Roosevelt's attitude and policy toward Stalin and the Soviet Union were at the very least mixed. Roosevelt's Soviet policy begins with a variant of

Lend-Lease designed mainly to keep the Russians from being crushed by the Nazis in the early stages of the war. That policy would evolve pragmatically from event to event, but in late 1941 and early 1942 its basic considerations were military, as was demonstrated in the policy of "generosity without reciprocity." That premise could not serve as a foundation for a foreign policy. The president's fear that Stalin would strike a second deal with Hitler, which led him to adopt a policy of appeasing Stalin, was not a sound foundation for a foreign policy either.

Roosevelt's fear of a Hitler-Stalin rapprochement had less to do with any grandiose balance-of-power schemes, or "geopolitical requirements," than with winning the military campaign in the East. John Lewis Gaddis insists that FDR's "Arsenal of Democracy" was a policy that "most effectively contribute toward the maintenance of international order." It was not, however, a basis for a postwar foreign policy. It began with "aid-short-of-war" and ended in a generous Lend-Lease policy. The president's pragmatic war policy could not serve as a basis for the creation of a postwar foreign policy, "making careful use of American resources to maintain a global balance of power,"[5] as Gaddis contends.

Aid to the Soviet Union, as Kimball pointed out, was a matter of "good faith." It was not a foreign policy. The argument that Roosevelt was "leaning" toward the use of Lend-Lease as leverage on the Soviets is not convincing. Nothing the president said or did supports this argument. Gaddis admits that "none of these attempts (Lend-Lease manipulation or the monopoly over the atomic bomb) to apply leverage worked out as planned." Gaddis compares FDR with Churchill, who regarded cooperating with Stalin as making a deal with the "devil" in order to attain a higher goal. This may have been true of Churchill, who sought to defeat Hitler at any cost, but it was not true for Roosevelt, who did not have Churchill's experience with communism. It would never have occurred to Roosevelt to talk about "the Soviet Mephistopheles," as Churchill did.[6]

Thirty years after he wrote *The United States and the Origins of the Cold War,* Gaddis admits that the main reason the "United States plan for the post war world was never fully put into effect" lay in the realm of geopolitics rather than economics. It was *Stalin* and not the Soviet Union as a superpower or as an authoritarian state that made an "acceptable international order" "impossible." There was nothing "relaxed" or "consensual" about Stalin's vision of an acceptable international order. I clearly demonstrate Gaddis's discovery that FDR never perceived nor realized or even understood that it was harder "to separate any aspect of it [the Soviet Union] from the hateful and lingering influence of this remarkable but sinister figure." Thus, Gaddis now admits that the United States and its allies, at the end of World War II, "were not dealing with a normal, everyday, run-of-the-mill, statesmanlike head of government. They confronted instead a psychologically disturbed but fully functional and highly intelligent dictator who had projected his own personality not only onto those around him but onto an entire nation and had thereby, with catastrophic results, remade it in his image."[7] The president's diplomacy consciously ignored, misperceived, and misrepresented the true Stalin to the American people. In the fog of war, the well-hidden and manipulative Stalin conducted a foreign policy that contradicted American interests, purposes, and ideals.

Beginning with the Teheran summit, Roosevelt became convinced that the USSR, with each victory of the Red Army, would become a world power at the end of the war. He was right, but without a foreign policy he failed to create the U.S.-USSR relationship he wanted. Roosevelt was not "hedging"; rather he failed to achieve his goal of a postwar cooperative partnership with the Soviet Union. From 1943 on, Roosevelt had dedicated himself to that end, oblivious of Stalin's plans which, though he was personally appreciative of Roosevelt's attention, remained consistently focused on the territorial future of Russia's western boundaries. A liberal president was seeking a fruitful cooperation with a power dedicated to everything antithetical to American liberalism of the Wilsonian school.

Gaddis sees Roosevelt as well versed in balance-of-power conceptualizing, when, in fact, Roosevelt was hostile to such thinking. He was even more removed from balance-of-power thinking than his mentor Woodrow Wilson had been. The recognition of the Soviet Union in 1933 was prompted by economic interests, not by a desire to use the Soviet Union to balance the emerging Germany and Japan. Gaddis bases his reading in part on Maxim Litvinov's partisan and wishful presentations, echoed by other Soviet writers. But this hardly substantiates the case for FDR's supposed penchant for balance-of-power policies.[8]

It is not prudent to rely on Soviet writers in assessing the president's position on balance of power. FDR had no well-defined concept of international order. His thinking was idealistic, rooted in such Wilsonian principles as self-determination and laid out in the Atlantic Charter. Roosevelt believed the Soviet Union and the U.S. could play key roles in creating a stable international political order and, as a result, was willing to ignore Soviet behavior in Eastern Europe. He had no policy of "containment by integration,"[9] no policy of containment of any kind, toward the Soviet Union and international communism. His understanding of communism was rudimentary, and he knew little about the history of the movement.

It was not in Stalin's interest to cooperate with the world's largest, most powerful capitalist state, especially since, in his view, the USSR had won the war. Suspicion of capitalism and America's "ruling classes" remained central to Stalin's outlook. Because it was not part of Soviet postwar policy to make deals with the United States, FDR's efforts to anticipate postwar arrangements based on collective security principles were futile. Gaddis admits that "the major difficulty was simply the Soviet Union's imperviousness to external influences."[10] Nothing the president could have done, including the "hedging" and "stick and carrot" approach imputed to him, would have changed Stalin's mind. Any rapprochement with the U.S. would have hindered Stalin's plans for territorial and political hegemony in Eastern Europe.

In *The Juggler: Franklin Roosevelt as Wartime Statesman,* Kimball's most recent book, the author is "trying to focus on the personal foreign policy of Franklin Roosevelt, particularly the assumptions that underlay policy." Kimball asserts that "Roosevelt's image of impulsiveness usually masked a consistent pattern." But if there is a consistent pattern to be discerned in Roosevelt's foreign policy, it is the opposite of patient design or careful planning. Kimball writes that

"Roosevelt had a conscious, structured foreign policy, even if there was an enormous gap between concept and implementation,"[11] but the only thing his book proves is that the foreign policy FDR pursued—the one he "implemented"—lacked a coherent and viable conceptual pattern.

Did FDR have a foreign policy "concept" that he failed to translate into policy? Did he have a structured approach that was not implemented? On the basis of the available historical materials, including Kimball's studies, the answer must be in the negative. There is no evidence for it. And finally, it does not matter much: the United States—the world—has had to live with the consequences of the foreign policy that was implemented, not with an elusive and ethereal concept the existence of which cannot be verified. Indeed, the very title of Kimball's book captures Roosevelt's essence: he was a crafty improviser, an intuitive manipulator, an able political operator. He was a talented juggler of men and ideas and sentiments. His was not a structured, orderly mind, and his was not a structured, methodical foreign policy. He winged it.

It may be true that "the president's intuitive assessment of Soviet capabilities was, as things turned out, more accurate than that of most of his intelligence, military, and political advisers. It was an insight of crucial importance for the war." But intuition without intelligence should not be a guide to policy, even if, "as things turned out," the intuition was accurate. It could also have turned out to be the opposite. Kimball's essays rely on important documents and historical understanding, but these are insufficient to explain who was more optimistic about Soviet chances to survive in July, 1941, FDR or Hopkins. Kimball admits that "no record has surfaced of the lengthy White House discussions between Roosevelt and Hopkins on the evening of July 11, 1941." But Kimball confuses grand strategy with militarily winning the war when he says, "Roosevelt's predisposition to aid the Soviet Union fit his grand strategy." Aid to the Soviets was on the one hand designed "to boost their morale" and "at a deeper level, the aid program was always political."[12]

I will show that the aid program was hardly political and that "generosity without reciprocity," the essence of this aid program, deprived the president and the Western allies of a significant bargaining tool in negotiations with Stalin. We are told we "cannot disguise a cardinal military aid."[13] What was FDR's political advantage in his relations with Stalin if the Soviet Union won the war without American aid? "Roosevelt had bigger things in mind,"[14] that is, cooperation with Stalin. This study will show another benefit—if it can be called such—gained by cooperating with Russia, which was apparently FDR's grand strategy next to winning the war. My advantage has been access to Soviet documents, still denied to Kimball in 1990.

In Stalin's relationship with the United States and FDR, the key was that the Soviet dictator always kept his goals squarely in front of him. On the whole, Stalin respected FDR and the United States, which did not prevent him from deceiving the president. His strategy was consistent and clear. With the war against Hitler improving and likely to be won, Stalin's goals were to secure Soviet borders by direct or indirect domination of Eastern and Southeastern Europe. Before 1943, Stalin concentrated on winning the war. After Stalingrad, followed by the crucial years of 1944 and 1945, his design was if not to directly occupy Eastern Europe then at least to install friendly and, hopefully, Communist regimes in that area. Here, Churchill could see the Soviet strategy clearly developing, while Roosevelt remained blind or indifferent to it.

In the literature on Stalin before Glasnost, the works of a few writers—Robert Conquest, Vojtech Mastny, Adam Ulam, Richard Pipes, Leonard Shapiro, and the first volume of Robert Tucker—were the standards.[15] So were the older works, all highly partisan in one way or another, of Leon Trotsky, Stephan Possony, and associated rivals or victims of Stalin. Since Glasnost, new works have emerged in the United States, Great Britain, Germany, and the USSR. To mention but a few post-Glasnost works, there are Tucker's second volume, and books by Dimitry Volkogonov, Walter Laqueur, William McNeill, and Conquest again. Worthy of special attention is Richard Pipes's *The Russian Revolution,* which is nothing short of a breakthrough. It is certainly the most outstanding and comprehensive work to emerge on the Russian Revolution. The argument is only partially true that, in the absence of Soviet documents and documentation, any portrait of Stalin, Stalinism, the USSR, and particularly of Stalin's foreign policy between 1941 and 1945 and his relations with FDR and the United States, is incomplete.

This was my second book involving extensive archival and library research. I confess that I have always doubted the claims of authors who list countless pages of archival resources and private papers they claim to have examined. Maybe I'm simply not up to it, but I often suspect that no human being can read and understand all the unpublished material that some authors cite. I also have my doubts about the viewpoint and accuracy of many documents, memos, letters. Like memoirs themselves, these kinds of documents must be carefully examined in context of the times in which they were written, their sources of information, and their tendencies to deceive, persuade, dissuade, or embellish the truth.

To be sure, documentation for this book was basic, but the documents did not constitute for me the final arbiter of events and deeds. I think history has its own logic. That, and a belief that the sun never rises in the west, was my iron law in examining documents. To my mind, the authors of the documents were believable only in the context that was most appropriate for their particular judgments. When dealing with the writings of political figures and government officials, one must always keep in mind that these individuals are salesmen by nature and propagandists for their careers, their points of view if they have them. Skepticism and suspicion mixed with empathy and compassion were my guides in examining extensive American and British documentation.

However, in the Soviet material to which I gained access, as the first Western scholar privileged to examine Foreign Office and related Central Committee documents, it was not the volume of the material, but the paucity of plausible, illuminating information. There are NO Soviet diplomats of the intellectual capacity epitomized by Kennan, Thompson, Bullitt, Bohlen, and other outstanding State Department diplomats-writers-memorialists, none who had the capacity to reflect, analyze, and write with intellectual candor. One finds nothing of this sort in the writings of Litvinov, Gromyko, or other Soviet Foreign Office officials. The learned, informative, and analytical *FRUS* volumes have no counterpart in the Soviet archives and documentation.

It is impossible not to reach the conclusion that Leninist and

Bolshevist ideology, the whole system, polluted the human mind and intellect. There is an appalling poverty of thinking, a meagerness of analysis, an absence of intellectual honesty and independent thinking in these documents. They are tainted and weighted with the heavy jargon of Bolshevism and Leninism and Stalinism, making one realize why the edifices of communism crumbled so quickly and so thoroughly in recent years. If the American writers sometimes suffer from sycophancy, this seems almost a minor flaw when compared with the totalitarian Soviet mind, which was unable or unwilling to freely analyze or judge events and people. Qualitatively or quantitatively, there is no comparison between the Soviet material and the rich Anglo-American World War II documentation, not to mention the thorough and gigantic trove of German material.

Each historian and biographer has his or her villain and hero in history and examines the past from the perspective of his or her time. The panorama changes, seen from the vantage point of time, space, and imagination. One person's historical truth is another's trauma, one person's vision is another's gulag.

In this most ideological of centuries, which produced the destructive totalitarian movements of fascism, nazism, and communism, the historian and analyst and observer must take into account what is written between the lines and, more significant sometimes, what is not written at all.

Part I

Roosevelt's Style
and Strategy

Chapter 2

The President's Style and World View

How did Roosevelt arrive at decisions? What was the nature of the process? What or who influenced him? What information did he consider in making key decisions? What was his frame of reference at Teheran and Yalta? How did the president conduct the war day by day? What personal experience did he bring to the war? How did he perform as war leader, and how did he come to the decisions that shaped the postwar world?

Franklin Delano Roosevelt became a legend in his time, but beyond the legend lies an enigma. Roosevelt left little for historians to rummage through: there are no diaries, no autobiography; and the letters that exist do not reveal feelings, private observations, philosophical outlook or theories. It is doubtful that Roosevelt would have written his story even if he had lived longer. He epitomized the modern man of action—living in the moment, not inclined to introspection or reflection. He did not analyze his actions, and he offered no great theory of politics or presidential power. He was not a thoughtful man, compelled to record his thoughts on paper.

It is instructive to compare him with Winston Churchill, an equally gregarious and accessible man, but one who could never resist the invitation of a blank sheet of paper. In books, histories, diaries, reportage, fiction, and letters, Churchill wrote about anything that interested him—which was almost everything—through the prism of his own perspective. If Roosevelt continues to intrigue biographers at least partly because he left so little written material behind, Churchill achieves the same effect because he left so much. Whether writing about his ancestor the Duke of Marlborough, his tragically flawed father Lord Randolph, the English people, generals, or yeomen, Churchill's hero was always Churchill, with the wealth of material serving as a defense against understanding the man within.

A researcher will find nothing in the archives that reveals a personal Roosevelt. His letters are informational, devoid of emotions. What is striking about the fragments of communications and messages in Hyde Park is the absence of reflection on history or people. Interoffice memos to aides do not reveal strategies, goals, tactics, or his views on the meanings of the office he occupied.[1]

The man who appeared so generous with his energy, and so accessible, was also elusive. He was a friend to the whole world, but intimate with few, if any. He could inspire affection and loyalty, even though he was never really close to any person, not even the mother who adored him and lived her life for him. His relationship with his wife and fourth cousin Eleanor lacked real closeness. They admired each other's talents and intelligence, but did not provide each other with emotional fulfillment. Roosevelt was not very concerned about or affectionate toward his children. Lewis Howe and Harry Hopkins, his closest aides, could not claim personal closeness to the president.

Roosevelt resisted being known because he lacked confidence in the abilities of others. He found it difficult to delegate authority and was often frustrated by outside sources of power. In spite of the "happy warrior" face he presented to the world, his presidency was characterized by suspicion and mistrust. He made most of his decisions alone.

Operating on the strength of his personality, FDR radiated power and the joy of using it. "His habits were practical, rather than analytical."[2] Neville Chamberlain called him a "windbag," while Walter Lippmann suggested that "the trouble with Franklin D. Roosevelt is that his mind is not very clear, his purposes are not simple and his methods are not direct."[3] The consensus among those who knew him well was that he was secretive and made solitary decisions, even though he was surrounded by advisers who constituted a kind of medieval court.

Roosevelt identified with his cousin Theodore Roosevelt and, to a lesser degree, with Woodrow Wilson. Historians often compare FDR to Wilson, noting that Roosevelt was a junior member of the Wilson administration as assistant secretary of the navy and that he studied Wilson a great deal. There is something of Wilson in Roosevelt's United Nations organization, a resurrection of Wilson's League of Nations; and Wilson's moralistic international outlook is echoed in Roosevelt's approach to world affairs. Both shared a certain internationalist naiveté.

But Franklin Roosevelt resembles his great uncle Teddy the most. The resemblance is not just one of family, although this surely must have entered Franklin's mind when he compared himself to his illustrious predecessor in the presidency. FDR was born into the age of navalism, of the strategic theories of sea power and its influence upon history. America's coming of age did not at first mean that it would spread its power over the Atlantic and challenge the Old World in Europe. Power for America first meant the Far East, China, Japan, and the Pacific; and this meant sea power, a navalist orientation. China, Japan, and the Pacific caught Franklin Roosevelt's mind when he became interested in international matters; cultural nationalism, Anglo-Saxon and Pacific imperialism informed the young Roosevelt. The new American spirit was in the air that he breathed.

In 1890, Captain Alfred T. Mahan, an American naval historian, published *The Influence of Seapower in History,* emphasizing the importance of naval strategy for a continent bounded by two oceans. He viewed the oceans as strategic highways for the advancing industrial state America was becoming. Theodore Roosevelt was an enthusiastic convert to navalism, as were Henry Cabot Lodge, Henry Adams, and others.[4] Theodore also possessed an irrepressible personality, which, along with his enthusiasm for navalism and Americanism, became a tacit legacy for the young Franklin. Teddy was larger than life, even if he sometimes appeared juvenile in his poses. He was a voracious reader, a thinker, and a writer from whom FDR learned the importance of the sense of power and the relationship between power and responsibility. But Franklin never understood Theodore Roosevelt's concept of the balance of power.

It is not clear why Franklin Roosevelt joined the Democratic party, breaking family and class tradition. The influence of Wilsonianism on Roosevelt is also a subject worthy of some discussion. "Roosevelt's first administration was much less a Wilsonian restoration than might have been expected."[5] He took on only two of the party's Wilsonians, Cordell Hull and Daniel C. Roper, both of whom had little influence in his administration. Louis Brandeis, one of the old architects of Wilson's "New Freedom," was skeptical of FDR, while Wilson's critic William Bullitt became a close friend. Harold Ickes and Henry Wallace represented Republican and progressive factions, and leading New Dealer Donald Richberg also came from this group. Roosevelt remembered well Wilson's dilemma in attempting to get the American people to intervene in the Great War in Europe, and the subsequent struggle for the peace treaty that broke Wilson's spirit. With the experience of Wilson to guide him, Roosevelt became more circumspect when faced with the same dilemma in the late 1930s.

Roosevelt's legacy of the imperial presidency was "derived from a genuinely imperialist source."[6] Projecting Wilsonian idealism, Roosevelt was the offspring of the old expansionists. The Calvinist origins of Wilsonian idealism were congenial with Roosevelt's own strain of protestantism; but his instincts governed his foreign policy, and those instincts were patrician and expansionist. Roosevelt was not a disappointed Wilsonian, but rather a combination of both Wilson and Theodore Roosevelt. FDR, not Henry Luce, authored the American century; and Roosevelt's vision, centered on the Far East rather than the decaying Old World, was hardly humanitarian. It was the vision of the American mercantilists, the expansionists of the Gilded Age, the Mahans, Lodges, and Theodore Roosevelt. In the words of Protestant clergyman Josiah Strong, author of the best selling *Our Country,* God was "preparing mankind to receive our impress."[7]

FDR had had considerable administrative experience in his four years as governor of the most populous state in the Union between 1928 and 1932, and then nine years as president before the war. His administrative style combined confidence in himself and an unorthodox method of operations that shunned daily routines and detailed work. Arthur Schlesinger, Jr., claimed that "little fascinated Franklin

Roosevelt more than the tasks of presidential administration,"[8] but the opposite was the case. Roosevelt believed in executive reorganization and improving management, but his style was antithetical to all the accepted norms of classical administration. He created many agencies and bureaucracies, but his unorthodox management style prevailed, at the expense of efficient administrative practices. The president's efforts to achieve greater government efficiency were compromised by the inherent inertia of the American political system and by his own work habits.

White House decision-making was characterized by confusion and the presence of many aides who believed they had the president's ear. He received little intelligence on the development of the Munich crisis and on the events leading up to Pearl Harbor.[9] He had unfounded anxieties about the Soviet Union's loyalty to the alliance, worried needlessly about Nazi and Fascist penetrations into Latin America, and allocated military resources that were needed elsewhere to that area.[10] He overreacted to Japanese expansion without understanding that country's needs. While pursuing the war, he also pressured the British and the French to relinquish their empires. The result was chaos, indirectness, and constant overlapping of authority.[11] Friendly historians have seen touches of political genius in Roosevelt's famous habit of assigning "overlapping and competing authority and jurisdiction to his subordinates."[12] But Roosevelt's method could just as easily be seen as carelessly inefficient. It assured only that, in the end, despite the influence of others, the president made the final decision.

This method had succeeded in domestic politics, but it was not suited for the conduct of the war. Wartime decision-making suffered from a plurality of channels of information from which key advisers and assistants were at least partially blocked. Seeing himself as the ultimate poker player, Roosevelt felt that he could hold all the cards and always produce a hand that would win the game. "These methods led to frustration among his subordinates and to complaints of a lack of coordination."[13]

The conduct of the war constantly demanded that important decisions, determining crucial operations and affecting the outcome of battles, be made. Roosevelt's inclination was to wait and see, to vacillate before reaching critical decisions that required action with unpredictable outcomes. He abhorred unpredictability, and as a result avoided as much as possible making decisions on issues about which he knew little. Instinct repeatedly prevailed over long-term planning.

With Churchill and Stalin, FDR's instinct was to use his powerfully persuasive personal charm and engaging manner, hoping that his rhetoric would persuade or hypnotize. He sought to convey an image of himself as the arbitrator, the conciliator, so that he could by turns placate Stalin and mollify the increasingly despairing Churchill. Instead, what he did was engender confusion and doubt about the strength of his commitment and the direction of his strategy. Both Churchill and Stalin saw Roosevelt as indecisive, and Stalin thus believed he could use Roosevelt to advance Stalin's ends.

Internationalist, Isolationist, Reformer, or Appeaser?

Franklin Roosevelt has been portrayed as an early foe of Hitler, prevented from combating the evil that Hitler represented by an isolationist Congress. Roosevelt's rhetoric at the time may have given this impression, but his actions sought to mollify the isolationists and, in the process, sent mixed signals to European leaders. This is not surprising, as Roosevelt had essentially a nineteenth-century outlook, with no understanding of what fueled modern mass movements outside the United States, no conception of their impact on international stability. The consolidation of Nazi power in Germany and the increasing anti-Semitic legislation had little effect on Roosevelt. He remained silent when, on April 1, 1933, the Nazis boycotted all Jewish establishments, the first of many steps that would lead to the Final Solution.[14] In 1933, Hjalmar Schacht, president of the Reichsbank, met with Roosevelt, but Roosevelt's admonitions about the Nazi treatment of the Jews struck Schacht as mild.

> After dinner, exactly half an hour remained for a private conversa-
> tion between the President and me. He began with the Jewish
> question, which had undoubtedly done a great deal of harm, proba-
> bly not out of particular sympathy for the Jews, but from the old
> Anglo-Saxon sense of chivalry toward the weak. But he did not
> elaborate on this theme and said that this hurdle would be cleared
> even if its importance should not be underestimated.[15]

The president's early policy toward Nazi Germany amounted to
appeasement, though he did not pursue it with the enthusiasm of
European appeasers. Indeed, Roosevelt's slowness in formulating a
realistic and effective response to Hitler was not unusual for a time
when many Western political leaders pursued a policy of appeasement. Roosevelt's intentions in the early and middle 1930s were to
restore prosperity and protect threatened nations from military aggression, yet not upset his domestic recovery or frighten isolationists.[16] Historian Wayne Cole is right to conclude that Roosevelt
needed the support of the isolationists in Congress to realize his
domestic New Deal. They generally supported his domestic policy but
were firmly opposed to developing an internationalist, let alone an
interventionist, policy.[17] The recurrent military and political crises in
Europe and elsewhere were secondary to FDR's domestic reforms. He
found no contradictions between his commitment to economic nationalism and mild internationalism which spilled over into foreign
affairs.

The New Deal entailed an internationalist view of American interests. A global New Deal meant exporting the great American domestic
experiment abroad to inspire the yearning for a "universal democracy,
[and] for the abolition of colonialism."[18] Some of these ideas would
find their way into the Atlantic Charter of 1941 and the United
Nations charter in 1945, and be voiced strongly at Yalta. But in the
mid–1930s, Roosevelt's pronouncements about the Good Neighbor
policy and calls for international disarmament were not followed by
action. European diplomats, comparing Roosevelt's rhetoric to his
actions, concluded that he was a closet appeaser. "To the British
government," D. C. Watt writes, "especially to Premier Neville Cham-

berlain, he seemed to have appeared as an unreliable windbag in charge of a country whose friendship and support Britain simply had to have."[19]

Intellectual Roots of the New Deal and Other Domestic Policies

Cole notes that "Roosevelt's relations with American isolationists from 1932 to 1945 had enduring significance for the history of American foreign policy." He also writes that "[Roosevelt] decisively triumphed over the isolationists" and that "his victory over them marked a watershed in the history of American foreign policy."[20] The issue, however, is not who won—Roosevelt or the isolationists—but when Roosevelt finally prevailed. How much support for his domestic programs was Roosevelt willing to sacrifice for his interventionist foreign policy? This persuasive politician could have found a way to minimize such loss of support, but instead, he vacillated, procrastinated, and wavered. The combination of interventionist rhetoric and delay that amounted to inaction failed to prepare the nation for the war. It fostered a material and psychological unpreparedness which led to the prolongation of the war and to unequal postwar arrangements between the United States and the Soviet Union.

Professor Cole writes that isolationists opposed American intervention in European wars, but not necessarily in Asia, the Pacific, or Latin America, areas they considered natural American spheres of interest. They believed "the United States could more effectively lead the world to the good life by building and sustaining democracy, freedom, and prosperity at home."[21] By Cole's definition, Roosevelt was a functional isolationist. Like the isolationists, he believed in a defensive foreign policy and opposed significant military preparation. It was not until the late 1930s that Roosevelt actually supported a gradual and entirely insufficient form of military preparedness.

Historians have stressed the differences between Roosevelt and the isolationists, their differing viewpoints over legislation that created overseas entanglements. But these differences didn't show until near the end of the decade, when Roosevelt pushed legislation to help the beleaguered British.

European appeasement was motivated by the wish to satisfy Hitler in order to prevent immediate war, even if it meant the sacrifice of small Central European states. The American form of appeasement was the result of isolationism. Europeans never understood the distinction, not grasping that isolationism, which they detested, was tantamount to appeasement, which they pursued. British and German statesmen thought Roosevelt an isolationist, and, to a degree, so did the French. The policies of one's allies and potential enemies are based on such perceptions. Appeasers like Chamberlain and Lord Halifax thought they saw in the president a kindred spirit.

Differing Goals for Appeasement

The president's policy of aid short of war, projecting "positive and active roles in efforts to preserve the peace and guard security in international affairs,"[22] may have been good enough to overcome the isolationists at home. But his calls for disarmament, trade reciprocity, and conference diplomacy, along with supporting Britain's balance of trade and industrial growth, were insufficient to deter Chamberlain from his policy of appeasement. Without repealing the Neutrality Act, such talk left Chamberlain with little confidence in the president and reassured him in his impression that Roosevelt favored appeasement.

If Roosevelt intended for the British and the French to stand up to Hitler, the effect of his policies was the opposite. British historian C. A. MacDonald writes, "The United States began to use its influence to stimulate appeasement in Europe."[23] The president's globalist New Deal and his interventionist rhetoric were contributing to appeasement, not discouraging it. Washington was hoping for a final settlement of European problems through the rule of law in international affairs, through "the liberalization of world trade."[24] But the Roosevelt-Hull policy of free trade, disarmament, and the rule of law was unrealistic given the climate of the times. Somehow, Roosevelt hoped that the aggressors would be quarantined in this way. "The president was neither well informed nor very well equipped to understand what was happening in Europe."[25] Roosevelt's and Hull's idealistic and antiimperialist views meant that both men were almost naturally hostile to the British conservative ruling class in the cabinet.[26]

Although both the United States and Great Britain were inclined toward a policy of appeasement, they operated at cross purposes because they saw appeasement as a way to achieve different ends. Chamberlain hoped to rearm Great Britain by buying time, while Secretary of State Cordell Hull was simultaneously calling for a disarmament conference. The American version of appeasement was crafted by Sumner Welles who, in July of 1937, called for a revision of Versailles. "In effect, this was an implicit statement of American support for German revisionist demands."[27] It also had the effect of weakening Chamberlain's strategy of achieving appeasement with Hitler.

Roosevelt's famous 1937 Quarantine speech, hailed as the beginning of the end of American isolationism, was received with dismay in England, where it was seen as another obstacle to appeasement. The speech, according to Prime Minister Chamberlain, "by condemning the aggressors, threatened to lock the democracies into confrontation with all three 'dissatisfied' powers, Germany, Italy and Japan." Chamberlain's policy was to divide them. The speech, however, was hailed by Foreign Secretary Anthony Eden, who saw in it evidence that America was finally abandoning its "psychological withdrawal" from world affairs. This served only to irritate Chamberlain.[28]

After the speech, the Roosevelt administration continued to sound like an appeaser, with Welles, in 1938, offering an even more elaborate plan for world peace, a plan that called for an international conference to discuss new rules of international conduct, arms limitations, and tariff reductions. Welles saw the plan as providing "valuable parallel action"[29] for Anglo-German negotiations, and the president accepted Welles's recommendations. Chamberlain rejected the plan without consulting Eden, who would soon resign from the government. To the Americans, MacDonald writes, Chamberlain's rejection, which shocked Welles and the White House, meant "exclusion from all participation in European settlement."[30] But Reynolds suggests something closer to the truth when he says that Chamberlain's rejection didn't "sorely disappoint Roosevelt." The president, he argues, had never really been "very enthusiastic about Welles's plan" in the first place, and had only been giving it lip service.[31] To fill a diplomatic vacuum was one thing, but actually to coordinate a plan of action with the British was quite another. It was not the president's style to work with people he did not personally know, and he would hardly have relished the prospect of having to coordinate with Chamberlain a mutually agreeable policy.

And so, the two leaders, both favoring appeasement, failed to coordinate their policies. "Whatever F.D.R.'s private scruples, he had no alternative policy to offer, and he waited to see if Chamberlain's would succeed."[32] Chamberlain personally disliked Roosevelt, but what governed his attitude toward the president was the president's inability to match rhetoric with action. He was, as he confided to one of his trusted ministers, deeply suspicious "not indeed of American good intentions, but of American readiness to follow up inspiring words with any practical action."[33]

The Munich or Czech-Sudeten crisis, from March through September of 1938, underlined the lack of understanding or cooperation between the two men. To the active prime minister, the president was an observer who provided commentary. The president failed to articulate his concepts of deterrence or appeasement. Though disturbed about the turn of events in Czechoslovakia, he would not violate the Neutrality Act. As Chamberlain saw it, Roosevelt had adopted a position of benevolent neutrality, which constituted neither appeasement nor determined support for Chamberlain's policy. This strengthened the prime minister's view that in the absence of a clear American policy toward Europe, he must conclude a deal with Hitler himself, which meant handing Czechoslovakia over to him. Hitler's threat to Great Britain was immediate, whereas to the United States Hitler seemed removed, almost unreal. The asymmetry between the two nations, their leaders, and peoples strengthened the aggressive powers.

In retrospect the Munich crisis marked the last phase of one American policy and the beginnings of another. Roosevelt's intervention in the final stages of the crisis was a final attempt to pursue the appeasement line which had characterized policy before the an-schluss, a line based on the assumption that Hitler's aims were limited and that Germany could be reintegrated into the interna-tional system by a policy of judicious concessions. When it was revealed later in October that Hitler did not regard Munich as a final settlement, the President abandoned the policy. The failure of appeasement brought him back to the idea first evolved during the Czech crisis, of containing further German expansion by placing the economic resources of the United States behind Britain and France. This approach was based on the assumption that Hitler's aims were unlimited and that Germany could only be restrained by the threat of force. The conception of the United States as the 'arsenal of democracy', a limited liability role which envisaged the deployment of American economic rather than military power against the axis, was to characterize American policy until 1941.[34]

The object of American intervention in European affairs thereafter "would be to precipitate a movement for a general political and economic settlement which would obviate the necessity for Germany to strike out to obtain sources of raw materials in markets deemed by the German leaders necessary to maintain the living standard of the German people."[35]

Chapter 3

Roosevelt and His War Strategy

President Roosevelt brought to the war America's immense economic energy together with considerable naiveté about the implications of the task involved. He had a single purpose: to win the war. But he had no grand strategy to apply to that effort.

To evaluate Roosevelt's strengths and weaknesses as a strategist, we must first understand what strategy is. It is not the management of specific military campaigns. Strategy is not the civilian management of the military, nor is it political leaders managing military leaders. No matter how destructive or sophisticated weapons become, *strategy* has remained the same since Machiavelli and Clausewitz defined the term. Strategy is grand strategy; it is the rationale for a nation going to war, the motives behind engaging in violent struggle and/or using diplomatic means to resolve conflicts. The conduct of warfare is not the ultimate goal of grand strategy. Rather, as Machiavelli and Clausewitz have taught us, strategy encompasses the political and diplomatic struggle to resolve conflict and fulfill national aspirations. Grand strategy is not a military skill, but a political one. It speaks of both aims and reasons for diplomacy and war. It is the planning of what one intends to achieve in the execution of warfare. Grand strategy requires a set of clear goals rather than mere beliefs. The grand strategist must have a gift for timing.

The qualities required in a peacetime coalition are intensified in wartime, during which the maintenance of coalitions demands constant assessment of the changing purposes of allies and enemies. Success requires staying ahead of both rivals and allies, taking the lead in critical situations, but also exercising patience in order not to precipitate events unnecessarily. Coalition partners are likely to be more cooperative at the beginning of a crisis. But in the course of the war, alliances tend to weaken as circumstances change. Maintaining alliances requires a strategist able to perceive problems before they result in disaster or missed opportunities.

Roosevelt failed in that task because of his work habits and his disinterest in world politics before 1937 and 1938. He was further hampered by the traditions, institutions, and ideology of the country he led. The society Roosevelt represented was unsuited to negotiate the great power alliances necessitated by World War II. The United States, even as it expanded, had remained instinctively isolationist. It distrusted the Old World, subscribing to the theory that, in World War I, it had saved Europe from itself. The checks and balances inherent in the American political system, the unrestrained press, frequent elections, and the force of public opinion made it difficult for any president to adopt great strategies. Roosevelt, although the senior partner in the alliance because of his country's power, was at a disadvantage from the start when dealing with Stalin and Churchill.

Unlike Churchill, FDR was not by inclination or experience a seasoned strategist. Churchill's accomplishments as a war leader were considerable. He fought the war with the limited resources of a declining empire, an army that failed more often than it succeeded; and yet, until 1943, he was the primary mover behind the Anglo-American alliance. He prevailed over the American generals and sometimes over the president himself. But Roosevelt's relationship with Churchill was complicated by the fact that the two countries faced different problems and saw the war in different terms. England faced the threat of invasion and occupation, whereas the United States felt no such urgency and in fact did not become fully mobilized until the latter part of the war.

Stalin was different from Churchill. His country had been invaded, his regime faced with annihilation. He was deeply involved before the war, and much more so during it, with grand strategy, even though the strategy of the first years of the war, 1941 to 1943, was simply survival for his country and his regime. In domestic and party politics he was very different from either Churchill or Roosevelt. To Stalin, politics meant total political control, achieved by eliminating or exiling his political opponents. He was not hampered by an electorate, by checks and balances, or by powerful political rivals. His only restraint was the prospect of total failure. Nothing in Roosevelt's limited study of history or in his personal experience prepared him for Stalin's practice of politics. Churchill, with more experience but with less power in the alliance, took a more realistic stance toward Stalin.

When Japan attacked in 1941, the nation did not have any grand strategy to guide it in the war. The military had begun to seek policy guidance from the president only in May, 1940, after watching Germany's easy victories in France.[1] When preparations began, New Dealers headed the War Resources Board, Export Control, the Selective Services System, and some three hundred other emergency agencies run by civilians or joint civilian military officials.

Before 1940, Roosevelt had appeared committed to using his influence in Europe without having to resort to force. The United States was not a belligerent and was prevented from becoming one by the Neutrality Act. However, after Great Britain and France declared war in the wake of the Nazi invasion of Poland, the United States was perceived as a de facto belligerent by the Germans. As the threat to Great Britain became imminent, a strategy evolved. Between 1937 and 1940, President Roosevelt's goals remained unclear, except for his articulation of a search for alternatives.[2] This vagueness and vacillation over choices continued until the Japanese attack on Pearl Harbor on December 7, 1941.[3]

Roosevelt's failure of leadership might be explained by multiple factors, according to Utley: FDR was "deeply suspicious of Japanese intention"; he faced pressing matters in Europe; and he "did not have time to devote to Asian Affairs." Furthermore, "he liked to think in terms of a quarantine, naval blockades, and simple economic sanctions; the stuff of which the negotiations with Japan were made did not suit him."[4]

An examination of President Roosevelt's decision-making style and strategy formulation after 1941 requires a look at the process that led to Lend-Lease and, later, to the Allied policy of "Unconditional Surrender."

Lend-Lease: Generosity or Reciprocity?

During the summer of 1940, events forced the U.S. to consider action. The fall of France, Great Britain's isolation and the possibility of its being invaded and defeated, and the threat against the Atlantic by German U-Boats, all of these matters made the question of what to do about the war urgent for Roosevelt. Churchill looked to the United States for help. In the U.S., however, the debate was about aid to Britain, not entry into the war. This debate was a "unique crisis in the American experience."[5]

The underpinnings of America's security policy—its separation from the European and Asian powers by two oceans; the balance of power in Europe and Asia; and American free markets—were being threatened. The debate over what to do about "Britain standing alone" stirred questions about the policy of isolation that had been forged during the 1930s. America was unprepared for war and now feared what would happen if Britain should fall to the Nazis. The privileged position of the U.S. in the world seemed vulnerable.

Roosevelt understood that he could not bring America directly into the war, especially not in an election year. He moved slowly, unenthusiastically; he was reluctant to be forced into decisions by events he could not control. The debate centered on how to help Great Britain, even though it was known that an intensification of support to any extent would make the United States a de facto belligerent. The initial step on May 10, 1940, was to have American military equipment released to Great Britain and France. Roosevelt circumvented the Neutrality Act by selling the equipment back to its manufacturers, who then sold it to the Allies.

The next step, after the fall of France in June, was a strategic decision to increase aid to England to keep it from losing. The president moved to respond to Churchill's almost desperate plea for a

Harry Hopkins and Stalin meet in Moscow, 1941.
Whose advisor was he, anyway?

(Unless otherwise noted, all illustrations are courtesy of
the Franklin D. Roosevelt Library, Hyde Park, New York)

One Typewriter Strategist Who Has Made Good!

From the
Washington Star,
October 16, 1942.

From the *Des Moines Register,* January 25, 1943.

Churchill presents the sword of Stalingrad to Stalin in Teheran, February, 1943 (the sword fell a second after this photograph was taken). (Soviet Archives)

Hopkins (at left) and Stalin meet in Teheran, February, 1943. Between them is their translator, Valentin Berezhkov. To the right of Stalin, Vyacheslav Molotov and Marshal Klement Voroshilov. (Soviet Archives)

Who is the boss? Photograph by Joseph Davies of the Executive Mansion in Novosibirsk in 1943.

From the *Washington Star,* May 10, 1943.

From the *Washington Star*, May 24, 1943.

From the *Washington Star,* June 4, 1943.

From the *New York Herald-Tribune,* June 29, 1943.

"loan" of forty or fifty old destroyers, striking a deal by August. Churchill later wrote that he thought the transaction brought the two countries closer together, but there, he misread the president. "These were not the president's intentions, for the president was still hedging his bets, responding pragmatically to events and probably still hoping to avoid American belligerency if he could achieve his ends by less extreme means."[6] With the Atlantic threatened, Great Britain under attack, and Europe under Hitler's domination, it was a late date to hedge; but there simply was no American strategy for war.

In 1940, the president, without a policy or sense of direction, *was being slowly and reluctantly pushed into the war.* The turning point would be Lend-Lease, prompted by a carefully crafted letter from Churchill to Roosevelt. Churchill and Roosevelt biographer, Warren Kimball, says it "may have been the most carefully drafted and re-drafted message in the entire Churchill-Roosevelt correspondence."[7] In a plea which Churchill called one of "the most important [letters] I ever wrote," he asked Roosevelt for immediate aid in cash and sizable military supplies to offset British losses in shipping to U-Boats in the Atlantic.[8] The president never answered the letter directly,[9] but communicated his decision to help Britain through a press conference on December 17, 1940.

Lend-Lease was a characteristically Rooseveltian New Deal idea, an untraditional form of financing "to devise a give-away program that did not look like one."[10] The negotiations with Congress over the bill saw Roosevelt at his best, circumventing the isolationists and mobilizing public support. On March 11, 1941, the president signed into law the Lend-Lease Act. Lend-Lease was a key event of the war, marking the first institutionalization of the Anglo-American relation-ship. The subsidy was also taken by Hitler as a U.S. declaration of war against the Axis powers. Kimball is right when he asserts that "more than any other single event prior to the declaration of war against Germany, the Lend-Lease Act signalled that participation."[11]

Before Pearl Harbor, Roosevelt was unwilling to go beyond Lend-Lease. Lord Halifax, the British ambassador to the United States, was frustrated, writing that dealing with Roosevelt "seems like hitting wads of cotton wool." The president remained reluctant to use his powers as Commander-in-Chief "so long as national security is not imperatively compromised." The president "was attempting to work within the democratic structure as fully as he could without endangering American national security."[12]

Lend-Lease's approval by Congress demonstrated that Roosevelt could employ his political skills to great effect. "His legislative tactics in and around congress proved virtually errorless." But the short-of-war approach represented by Lend-Lease backfired. "Anyone could see that the Act (Lend-Lease) gave Hitler an excuse to declare war on the United States,"[13] but Roosevelt did not, leaving America unprepared for war.

Nevertheless, Lend-Lease helped forge one of the most enduring and successful war alliances in history, making it one of the singular achievements of the war. The Anglo-American alliance was strengthened in a series of conferences in Washington and in the Atlantic, creating a military instrument that would defeat the Axis powers by the end of 1945.

The August, 1941, Atlantic Conference typified Roosevelt's methods of operation, involving the deception and maneuverings in which he delighted. He deceived the press by appearing to go off on his pleasure yacht, the *Potomac,* then returned to the White House to board a special train at Union Station; the train took him to New London, Connecticut, where the *Potomac* was anchored, waiting to take him to the USS *Augusta,* the flagship of the U.S. Atlantic fleet. He met Churchill in Placentia Bay, Newfoundland.

The Placentia Bay conference between Churchill and Roosevelt produced what is known to history as the Atlantic Charter, which shaped the course of the war. The Charter, offering Roosevelt a forum for idealistic pronouncements, was not a plan for grand strategy.[14] In the Wilsonian tradition, it proclaimed the purpose of the war, stressing that no secret diplomacy would be conducted and that territorial arrangements and "other political bargains should await a universal peace conference."[15]

The State Department campaigned to include the abolition of "imperial preferences," a slap at the British, and the creation of a general international organization. Churchill was not too keen on a joint declaration of lofty principles, which were difficult to uphold during the course of a lengthy war; but in August, 1941, he was not in a position to argue too strongly. For the high-minded Roosevelt, though, this was not much of a concern; and he would later try, mostly unsuccessfully, committing Stalin to the Charter's "universal" principles.

The proposal that emerged from the conference came from a British working draft, and, as a result, had an "Old World outlook." The Charter was a hindrance to the successful conduct of the war, and it poisoned the Anglo-American-Soviet relationship. Its influence was "severely limited,"[16] especially when it came to Stalin, who treated the Charter with hostility. It did not serve the Grand Alliance.

Yet, the Anglo-American summits produced some remarkable results. Churchill's grand strategy undergirded the military alliance between partners unequal in strength, military capacity, and economic resources. The greatest accomplishment was the creation of a U.S.-British Combined Chiefs of Staff, headquartered in Washington, D.C., thus coming under the control of the president, but still crucial for winning the war.

The Allies remained firmly committed to a policy. Although constantly challenged, this policy was strictly adhered to throughout the war, much to the anger of American military chiefs operating in the Pacific theater, especially General Douglas MacArthur and the naval chiefs, Ernest J. King and William Leahy. But Roosevelt never wavered. He remained constant to the Europe First policy to the end of his life. The Europe First policy should not be confused with a grand strategy, though any number of historians have treated it as such.[17]

The Unconditional Surrender Formula

The Allied policy of unconditional surrender, proclaimed at Casablanca in January, 1943, applied to all the Axis belligerents, but was seen and applied differently by the Americans, British, and Soviets. The policy, an American innovation, was embraced by Stalin and supported rather indifferently by the British. It was first and foremost a typical Rooseveltian proclamation, simultaneously vague and inflexible. "The announcement," Professor Howard is quoted by A. E. Campbell as saying, "was made without any of the forethought and careful consideration which should have gone to the framing of so major an act of Allied policy."[18]

Roosevelt was motivated by memories of the outcome of World War I, when parties rushed to negotiate with each other and make secret arrangements and territorial concessions even as the war was still going on, plaguing postwar relationships. Unconditional surrender, giving the war the appearance of a moral crusade, calling the nation to a total war against enemies not deserving the usual diplomatic considerations, would avoid a repetition of post-World War I intrawar diplomacy, while offering the generals no specific strategic guidance. Unconditional surrender was successful as an inspiration, mobilizing the peoples' energies for a war of the democracies against the forces of totalitarianism. It was less successful as a strategic concept. It did not terrorize the enemy; instead it served Joseph Goebbels's propaganda machine as the massive bombings of civilian population centers stiffened German resistance. It also hampered the anti-Nazi resistance within the German military, which, faced with the Allied policy, could hope for little public support for its actions against Hitler.

As a practical policy, unconditional surrender yielded inconsistent results, often handcuffing military commanders and restricting their flexibility. The policy of not dealing with the enemy on any level was violated by Churchill, for example, when he came up with the "percentages formula" for a division of Eastern Europe between the West and the Soviets in 1944. Unconditional surrender was not applied to Italy. Churchill insisted that it apply only to Germany in order to secure the support of the Italian people, some still under German occupation after the 1943 Italian surrender.

The principal merit of unconditional surrender was that it had the president's absolute commitment even though it lacked any attention to specifics or possible consequences. As a policy, it reverberated through the postwar world, but it may have had little effect on the eventual outcome of the war itself. "With the advantage of hindsight, it may appear that the policy made little difference to the future of Italy or Japan."[19]

In my view, it also had little effect on Germany during the war. Churchill had clearly stated that he was fighting against Hitler and Hitlerism, not against Germany and Germans; but the policy of unconditional surrender did not allow for such distinctions. It aimed to punish an entire population and to destroy a country. Massive bombing did not distinguish between soldiers and civilians, Nazis and anti-Nazis, the actively ideological and the war-weary. All were killed indiscriminately, and there is no evidence that such a policy helped end the war a day sooner.

The failure to develop a policy for dealing with Germany after surrender created an occupation nightmare. As late as 1944, when the war's outcome was no longer in doubt, Roosevelt still had not made up his mind about how to deal with a defeated Germany. Policy, he suggested, depended "'on what we and the allies find when we get into Germany—and we are not there yet.'"[20] This was just another example of Roosevelt's penchant for not making decisions, and it was not challenged by Churchill or Stalin. It was another instance of the policy of muddling through, of conceiving strategy as he went along.

The Commander in Chief and the Concept of Coalition Warfare

More than anything, Roosevelt liked to be called the Commander in Chief.[21] His military staff, including Chief of the Army General George C. Marshall, acted as presidential advisers. Marshall initially had doubts about the president's unorthodox ways and secretive decision-making, but he came to trust and respect Roosevelt, a trust and respect that was mutual. Marshall believed that however undisciplined the president's methods were, he was a man of considerable political acumen.

In the crucial years of 1942 and 1943, Roosevelt was deeply involved in strategic military issues. According to Kent Roberts Greenfield, who edited many of the official U.S. war series, including the famous Green Books, the president made close to fifty crucial decisions against the advice or over the protests of his senior military advisers. Yet, as Greenfield notes, military historians and others, including, for example, Robert Sherwood and General Alan Brooke, chief of the imperial general staff, had conflicting impressions as to whether it was Roosevelt or Marshall who conducted strategy.[22]

Strategic conduct should not be confused with strategic thinking. The chief American strategic thinker was Marshall, but it was Roosevelt who conducted the coalition. In that sense, he was the supreme commander in the Lincoln tradition; but unlike Abraham Lincoln, he never carefully followed the military campaign.[23]

Roosevelt's singular contribution to the Allied war effort was adherence to the concept of a Joint Chiefs of Staff and the coordination between the American and British Joint Chiefs. But Marshall had been the originator of the Joint Chiefs concept and its guiding light. The role played by Marshall conformed to the president's preferred style. In addition to his specific command authority, Marshall acted as chief of the Joint Chiefs, a presidential surrogate in a manner similar to Harry Hopkins and other presidential staff members who acted as surrogate diplomats.

When it came to alliance strategy, Marshall, in early 1942, tried unsuccessfully to defeat the British preferred strategy in the Mediterranean. The Joint Chiefs and Marshall advocated opening a second front in Europe as early as that year, but Roosevelt at first forced Marshall to accept the British staff strategy. In April, 1942, Marshall changed his mind and persuaded Churchill to do so, a testimony to Marshall's persistence. Plans went ahead for the Second Front to alleviate pressure on the Soviets. As it turned out, this proved unnecessary after the Soviet counteroffensive late in 1942, but it showed Roosevelt's tendency to listen to his chief military adviser.

Overall, however, Roosevelt offered almost no specific strategic guidance. The president ran the war as a coalition strategist, but it was a very strange coalition, with members of unequal status and two distinct parts. One alliance was the Anglo-American, another was the American-Anglo-Soviet. The first was highly institutionalized, with a permanent military advisory body, the Anglo-American Joint Chiefs of Staff in Washington, to coordinate military effort. Stalin fought his own war, independent of his allies, not sharing military intelligence or strategic thinking with them.

Not surprisingly, most historians have taken for granted that World War II was a great coalition war against fascism and Japanese expansionism. If we keep to the loose meaning of coalition as an alliance of distinct parties combining to fight a common foe, then World War II was an example of coalition warfare. But if coalition warfare means that the parties unite their efforts into a coordinated strategy as represented in the summits, then the coalition was fragile. At best, the World War II coalition was an *entente cordiale* between Great Britain, the USSR, and America. All three participants had a common goal of defeating Germany, Italy, and Japan, but this did not amount to a Grand Alliance. The two alliances were each pursuing separate policies, and certainly Stalin never truly coordinated them. Even their separate military offensives never became a triangular military effort. For Churchill, the goal, after assuring Britain's survival, was to save the British Empire and bargain the Russians out of parts of Eastern Europe through his "percentage" deal with Stalin. Roosevelt's eye was on the Pacific, and he hoped to establish a liberal international order in Europe with Stalin's help. Stalin's larger goal was expansion into Eastern Europe at the expense of the wartime alliance. The three did not alter these basic goals at any point.

The experience of war was also different for each participant. The United States certainly suffered in the Pacific, but events such as the loss of the Philippines did not threaten U.S. survival. The territorial integrity of the United States was never at risk during any part of the war. Great Britain and the Soviet Union, however, fought for their very existence. Both desperately needed American military, political, and material support, while Roosevelt never needed his allies for material aid.

The alliance was subject to changes by developments in the military situation. Stalin was generally accommodating in 1941 and 1942, when Hitler still occupied most of European Russia. Beginning with his counteroffensive in Moscow and especially after Stalingrad, with the defeat of Hitler a given, Stalin's concept of the relationship began to change. The Soviet army's march into Eastern and Central Europe reshaped his strategy into an expansionist one.

The Churchill-Roosevelt relationship also changed after 1943, with Churchill increasingly becoming the weaker partner, a change reflected in their letters. After 1943, Churchill would, on the average, send Roosevelt two-page letters, and Roosevelt would reply by cable or through Hopkins or Harriman.[24] David Kaiser writes that "many important military questions hardly found their way into their exchanges at all."[25] In the summer of 1943, Roosevelt flatly lied to Churchill rather than admit that he had hoped to see Stalin alone before he and Churchill met.

The politics of the alliance was conducted at the great summits of Casablanca, Cairo, Teheran, and Yalta. Roosevelt and Churchill continued to pursue a global war, whereas Stalin's participation remained limited to the Soviet Union and Eastern Europe. Roosevelt did not have a strategy beyond the defeat of Germany and Japan. Roosevelt and his generals confined themselves to winning the war and did not consider the political consequences of specific military operations in their deliberations. Stalin, especially after Stalingrad, operated on two tracks—defeating Hitler and expanding the boundaries of the Soviet Union.

Part II

Roosevelt and Stalin, 1941–1943

Chapter 4

Surrogate Diplomacy
Roosevelt's Informal Government

The coming of the war did not change the president's prewar habits substantially. He continued to govern through unconventional ad hoc structures, employing procedures designed to circumvent normal channels, focusing his habitual distrust of bureaucracy on the State Department. His experience with administration of the New Deal had taught him that he was generally successful in implementing policy by bypassing the bureaucracy and creating alternative structures that he dominated.

The president surrounded himself with a court of advisers whose principal qualities were subservience and absolute loyalty. They shared the president's suspicion of bureaucracies and believed in the advantages of short-term projects that they could control directly, unburdened of complicated organizational structures and chains of command. Headed by Harry Hopkins, the group also included politicians like Wendell Willkie, Henry Wallace, and Patrick Hurley; businessmen like Averell Harriman, P. Donald Nelson, and Joseph Davies; and public servants like Robert Murphy, Sumner Welles, and William Phillips. Together and individually, they acted as personal emissaries for Roosevelt. Through them, he controlled the making and conduct of foreign policy, avoiding the foreign policy professionals at the State Department.[1]

Roosevelt wished to conduct foreign policy in a highly personal manner, using direct contacts with the principal actors—Churchill, Stalin, Chiang Kai-Shek, the Free French generals. FDR used his emissaries to achieve his goals, sending Robert Murphy as his personal ambassador to Vichy so that he could have direct contact with Philippe Pétain, and naming Harriman ambassador to the Soviet Union. Roosevelt even had Harriman communicate with him through the Navy rather than normal State Department channels.

The president's major goal in the conduct of the war was to strengthen the alliance with Great Britain and to assure at all costs that the Soviet Union remained in the alliance rather than making a separate arrangement with Nazi Germany. A secondary, but important, motivation for Roosevelt's conduct of the war was his concern with his public image. He wanted to be seen as a war leader in the same way he had been seen as leader of the New Deal. He wanted to be the Commander in Chief, the most important figure in the triple alliance.

Roosevelt's personal diplomacy, especially at the summit meetings, conveyed the image of a strong, respected, and dominant leader in control of events. The summit conferences at Casablanca, Cairo, Teheran, and Yalta provided the most visible reflections of Roosevelt's style and represented his most important diplomatic achievements. To prepare for these summits, Roosevelt employed, in addition to his advisers and emissaries, the resources of the different bureaucracies at the Treasury, State, and War departments, as well as the Joint Chiefs, including the newly created Anglo-American Joint Chiefs. But when it came to the conduct of foreign policy, the president held a monopoly. Roosevelt's foreign policy style had consequences for the conduct of the war and for the postwar world.

In addition to his surrogate diplomats, the president's foreign policy group consisted of his chief military advisers and, to a lesser extent, the departments of State and War. The president also used his intimates and friends among members of the cabinet in the field of foreign relations. Secretary of the Treasury Henry Morgenthau played a key role in Lend-Lease and in the formulation of the president's British and German policy. Morgenthau, a Jew and author of the famous "Morgenthau Plan" for the neutralization and deindustrialization of Germany, had instincts similar to those of the president.

Three Republican cabinet members were also recruited—Secretary of War Henry Stimson, Secretary of the Interior Harold Ickes, and Secretary of the Navy Frank Knox.

Roosevelt consulted them often on general war policies and sought their advice. But on Soviet policy, only Hopkins, Harriman, Davies, and later State Department Soviet Specialist Charles (Chip) Bohlen played significant roles. Finally, Admiral William D. Leahy, former Ambassador to Vichy, as a "generalist" and the president's personal chief of staff, had considerable influence on policy regarding Vichy, de Gaulle, and Churchill.[2]

The president was always eager to listen to often-contradictory advice from all sources, but he mistrusted State Department professionals for reasons reflecting his personality and experience. State Department professionals were members of Roosevelt's own patrician class, and his attitude toward them reflected his ambivalence about his aristocratic background. The president, much like his isolationist antagonists, followed a deeply traditional and provincial American approach to foreign policy; State Department professionals generally held a more pragmatic and worldly outlook. Roosevelt was also something of an antiintellectual, and the State Department professionals included people with a more academic orientation. They largely disdained Roosevelt's populist appeal and considered his internationalist idealism to be ill-considered and impractical.[3] As one researcher noted, "Franklin Roosevelt often adhered to the political aphorism that an ounce of loyalty is worth more than a pound of brains."[4]

Roosevelt, not surprisingly, selected a nonprofessional to head the State Department. Cordell Hull, who served from 1933 to 1944, was a politician like Roosevelt, with no prior experience in foreign affairs. He had been a senator from Tennessee and had served in Congress from 1906 to 1933. Roosevelt allowed Hull to concentrate on international economic problems, especially on free trade, but otherwise ignored the department. As a result, Hull was the longest-serving secretary of state in American history, and one of the least significant.

Roosevelt's hostility toward the State Department professionals was a boon to the American left, which saw the State Department as full of reactionaries and suspected it of collaborating with Vichy. The liberal and leftist press treated Roosevelt like a hero and the president reciprocated by establishing close ties with the pro-Soviet American press and its columnists before 1939, and again after Hitler invaded Russia.

In his dealings with the Soviet Union, he stretched constitutional limits without breaking them. His constant use of the American military mission in Moscow rather than embassy officials is a case in point. His relationship with Stalin was personal, based on his trust in the Soviet leader and his confidence that he could influence Stalin. This policy was pursued despite professional and unsentimental State Department advice to the contrary.

American foreign policy had always been conducted as an extension of domestic concerns. Europeans might see America's wars as imperialistic, but Americans saw them as domestic, Turneresque extensions of the concepts of free land and free trade. Thus conflicts like the Mexican War or the Indian wars were not really wars. Wars, to the United States, were European things, conducted by a Bismarck, a Wellington, or a Napoleon. America's war with Spain, its expansion into the Philippines, its challenge of Japan, its missions to China, its Open Door policies—all were really extensions of American economic enterprise. American presidents, from William McKinley to Teddy Roosevelt to Franklin Roosevelt, insisted that the United States merely wanted to spread democracy and oust the old imperial powers. It did not want colonies. Like Thomas Jefferson, FDR was an idealist in that he thought conquest could be achieved by means of free trade instead of through the imperialism he so detested.

Once the U.S. was in the war, Roosevelt characterized it as democracy against nazism. This purely American response cast the war as a project which, once successfully completed, would allow the United States to return to its prewar posture, untroubled by the potential rise of still another totalitarian system. The war would require a temporary American preoccupation with foreign policy, and this intense process would require Roosevelt's total control.

Without Ever Meeting: The Making of an American-Soviet Policy, 1941–1943

From the Nazi invasion of Russia in 1941 to the first Big Three meeting at Teheran, diplomacy between the United States and the Soviet Union constituted a form of shadow-boxing in which the two partners move separately, unobserved by each other. During this two-year period the issues that would plague the Allies at Teheran and Yalta would begin to take shape. Long before Roosevelt and Stalin met, attention was focused on the London Poles, Stalin's territorial demands, the Second Front, and the conduct of the war.

Allied policy toward Stalin at this time was mainly conducted by Churchill and his foreign secretary, Anthony Eden, who handled diplomacy independent of the United States. Churchill, however offended he was by the Nazi-Soviet Pact, also felt a tremendous sense of relief after June, 1941. The invasion meant that Great Britain was no longer isolated and the danger of Nazi invasion was past. He had a partner actively engaged in fighting Hitler. The controversial treaty of friendship with the Soviet Union signed on May 20, 1942, which split the British cabinet, was a British affair in which Roosevelt refused to participate and which he would not endorse. Stalin made his territorial demands right from the beginning, which gave the dutiful Vyacheslav M. Molotov a wedge to drive between the Allies later on.[5]

Stalin succeeded in changing the British policy that refused to legitimize the results of the 1939 Nazi-Soviet Pact. Eden, trying to allay Stalin's "supposed" anxieties,[6] portrayed the issue as the price Britain paid for an Anglo-Soviet Treaty. In violation of Churchill and cabinet guidelines (the cabinet itself was in disarray), Eden argued in favor of recognizing the disputed frontier, while Churchill preferred that "all questions of territorial frontiers must be left to the decision of the Peace Conference."[7]

The official British Foreign Office historian, Sir Lewellyn Woodward, explained British acceptance of Russian demands as follows: failure to do so might (1) "lead Stalin to consider a peace offer from Hitler"; (2) "deepen the suspicion of the Soviet government" and make it difficult "to secure real cooperation, not only during the war but after it"; and (3) foster a Russian offensive into Germany that would make it "impossible to turn them off the Baltic States."[8] This is hardly persuasive. Steven Miner was correct when he wrote that closer relations with the Soviet Union will allow greater Western influence on Soviet good will "in order to exercise as much influence as possible on the molding of their future course of action."[9] British policy toward Stalin was a portent of what would become American-Soviet war policy. Roosevelt was unreceptive to British attempts to win him over and accommodate Stalin. He only tried to deflect Stalin's demands. If in the end the British treaty with the Soviet Union did not amount to much in practical terms, it is significant for revealing Great Britain's willingness, indeed desire, to carve out an independent role in the alliance. Roosevelt's reluctance to approve Stalin's early territorial demands in the Baltics, on the other hand, stemmed not from any moral concerns, but from a desire to establish his own diplomatic relationship with Stalin, one that would not include Great Britain.

To understand the Allies' diplomacy, it is important to understand what Roosevelt and Stalin intended to achieve and how they went about it. The entire thrust of Roosevelt's diplomacy was the creation of a partnership with the Soviet Union in which the two Allies would dominate the postwar world, through a United Nations that would assure the idealistic nature of the enterprise. He trusted his personal ability to bring this off by convincing Stalin when they finally met face-to-face. American diplomacy rested on the assumption that the Allies would defeat the Axis powers, but it was also intended to dismantle the British Empire and the traditional European balance of power and the politics that entailed.

To make this work, Stalin would have to be amenable to the same postwar vision. As a result, not a discouraging word about Stalin and the Soviets would be countenanced by the president; and potential troubles—Poland, the Baltic States, the Second Front—were glossed over, avoided, or ceded to Stalin.

Roosevelt's eventual failure with Stalin was not that he "gave away" Poland and the Baltics, as critics from the right have argued. It was that his goals were unattainable, because they rested on a fundamental misunderstanding of Stalin and the Soviet system, and on Roosevelt's almost mystical faith in his personal power to persuade.

Stalin knew what he wanted and never wavered in his efforts to achieve his goals. He may have understood Roosevelt's desire for a partnership, but he never seriously entertained the notion, using it only when it served his purposes. Even in the darkest days of the Nazi invasion, when the outcome remained in doubt, Stalin insisted on the legitimization of what he had gained in the Nazi-Soviet Pact.

The decisions eventually made at Teheran and Yalta had their beginnings in the diplomacy conducted between 1941 and 1943. In the conduct of that diplomacy one can see Roosevelt and Stalin sizing each other up as they pursued their goals.

The Making and Origin of Roosevelt's Soviet Policy: Davies versus Bullitt

It is ironic that until recent times the United States was regarded in many parts of the world as an example of a successful revolutionary political system. The United States did constitute a revolutionary political system, the first federal republic in the modern world. Throughout its history, however, the United States has been inconsistent in its support of revolutions in other countries.

In modern times, the U.S. government's reaction to Marxist, Socialist, and leftist revolutions, especially the Russian Revolution, has been one of suspicion and hostility—mixed, on the popular level, with paranoia and romanticism. Writers like Jack London, Lincoln Steffens, and Upton Sinclair had extolled the virtues of the Bolshevik Revolution, creating a left-liberal political culture, expressed in magazines like *The Nation* and *New Republic*.[10] Many New Dealers saw in Stalin's collectivist experiments a mutated version of New Deal efforts and were inclined to suspend suspicion, unaware for the most part of the brutality underlying the regime. Woodrow Wilson, after expressing some initial admiration for the changes in Russia, soon grew hostile to Lenin and joined Europeans in trying to subvert the revolution. The United States government, under three successive Republican administrations during the 1920s, was aggressively hostile to the regime in Moscow. Lincoln Steffens might travel to Russia in 1921 and say "I have seen the future and it works," but less liberal citizens expressed their suspicions and fears of the Bolsheviks' witch hunts. Not until 1933 did the United States, on Roosevelt's initiative, establish formal relations with the Soviet Union. Roosevelt's motives in establishing relations with the Soviet Union were pragmatic. He hoped to increase trade while simultaneously softening the isolationist mood of Congress. "I am a good horsetrader," Roosevelt declared confidently, dismissing any apprehension over the new American-Soviet relationship.[11]

Roosevelt invested two men with the task of being America's formal representatives to the Soviet Union and with informing him about conditions in the Soviet Union. Both had enjoyed a long association with Roosevelt and had many things in common with him, but their views of the Soviet Union were diametrically opposed. The first U.S. ambassador to the Soviet Union was William Bullitt, an intelligent man with firsthand experience of both the old Russia and the new, and one who had at first sympathized with the Soviet regime. These sympathies were dispelled during his three-year term as ambassador. He was followed by Joseph E. Davies, an aggressive lawyer who had married into wealth and who ended up becoming one of the chief apologists for Stalin and the Soviet regime. Davies would become one of Roosevelt's principal advisers on the Soviet Union, and Bullitt would become an irritant to the president.

Bullitt had visited Russia for the first time in 1917 and had developed close contacts with the decadent Tsarist regime. The Bolshevik Revolution had inspired Bullitt with its utopian promise; and as a member of President Wilson's team in Paris, he gained considerable experience in negotiating with the new regime. Bullitt was an assistant secretary of state in charge of economic affairs in 1933 when Roosevelt named him to the Moscow mission. By the time his tenure in Moscow ended, he was a declared enemy of Stalin and Stalinism and had begun to bombard the president with memoranda, spelling out the real situation in the USSR. Roosevelt, however, intent on accommodating Stalin, was no longer inclined to listen. Bullitt, a strong-minded man, persisted, souring the relationship between himself and the president. He wrote in *Life Magazine* on August 30, 1948, that FDR had rejected "the urging of myself and others, to give Lend-Lease to Stalin only after the Soviet dictatorship had given formal written, public pledges to respect the eastern boundary of Europe." For Bullitt those pledges were vital because if Stalin then broke the pledges, Americans would have "been warned . . . they must take immediate precautions against Soviet imperialism."

Davies, an associate of Roosevelt since 1920 when, as a Democratic party functionary, he had seconded Roosevelt's nomination for vice-president,[12] had no experience to warrant his appointment as ambassador in 1937. His appointment was a reward for political and financial support. A successful attorney with a lucrative Washington practice, Davies had contributed heavily to Roosevelt's 1936 election campaign. He turned down a cabinet post, but accepted the ambassadorship in June of 1937.

The appointment was considered a disaster by foreign service professionals, led by George Kelly, mentor to such Sovietologists as George Kennan, Charles (Chip) Bohlen, and others.[13] He was "a novice who was sublimely ignorant of the Soviet system and of its ideology." Kennan contemptuously termed Davies "a political opportunist," or "a publicity hound."[14] Davies ignored the advice of the professionals at the embassy, relying instead on his aide Colonel Philip Faymonville, a military man of dubious reputation. Their assessment of the purges was a statement declaring that "Stalin's Russia was a prosperous experiment in industrial planning threatened on all sides by self-confessed enemies."[15] When, on July 13, 1937, sixty-one Trotskyites were charged with "spying" for Hitler, Davies wrote that "Stalin and the party leaders acted with great speed and ruthless severity. They hit first."[16] "It is believed by most competent observers," Davies wrote Hull on November 16, "that the number of party and government employees executed since the beginning of the present purge runs into the thousands, and arrests into the tens of thousands." We know now that Davies' figures were low, but he certainly had the idea.[17]

Robert Williams concludes that Davies was "at best, a reluctant ambassador, but an energetic collector of Russian art." He failed as an ambassador; and in spite of his close relations with Soviet officials, he failed to secure U.S.-USSR trade relations. His stay in Moscow nevertheless proved invaluable to him when the war came, when his benign view of the Soviets and Stalin dovetailed with that of the president. "Russian art proved a small price to pay for the future dividends of his 'Mission to Moscow.'"[18]

Davies' real importance emerged in his extraordinary role as Roosevelt's éminence grise in Soviet matters once the war started. In 1942 and 1943, he became known unofficially as an "intermediary" between the president and the Soviets. When Hitler invaded the Soviet Union, Davies became the conduit to establish close relations with Stalin. Davies also preyed on Roosevelt's concern about losing Stalin to Hitler, lobbying the administration constantly on behalf of aid to the Soviet Union. He launched "a vigorous campaign in the summer of 1941 to convince the administration to send aid to the Red Army,"[19] warning that "failure to take action [in favor of the Red Army] might force Stalin into signing a separate peace with Hitler."[20] In a conversation with Hopkins, recorded in Davies' diary (September 25, 1943), Davies did his best to "warn" the administration that "there was grave danger that just as Britain and France drove him into making terms with Hitler in 1939, there was danger that we would do it again, only this time, convince him that for the Russians the only safe way was to go it alone."[21] In a conference with Major General Josiah Strong, head of military intelligence in Russia, Davies repeated his talk about "Russia making separate peace with Hitler."

This was exactly the line Litvinov had pursued in talking with Davies. Stalin encouraged American anxieties in the absence of direct American support, in order to increase the chances for American aid. This misinformation campaign was taken seriously in the White House. Davies' claim to influence was his close relationship with the Soviets. His advice that Stalin could be trusted, that U.S. confidence in the Soviet Union must be complete, that Stalin had no real territorial expansionist plans, and that the Soviet system was bound to become more liberal—these were all things Roosevelt wanted to hear. There was no evidence to support Davies' claims, but they mirrored the president's own thoughts.

Perhaps the most influential book being read in the United States during 1942–1943 was Davies' *Mission to Moscow* (1941), which went through five printings in October of 1942 and five more in a paperback edition in 1943. Davies was encouraged in his effort by Roosevelt himself, who felt the book would help the war effort. Almost immediately after the Nazi invasion of Russia, Davies had started to work on the book with the help of ghost writers and the use of confidential State Department files. In the book, Davies saw no danger in Stalin and discounted any territorial ambition on the part of the dictator. "Russia's contribution to the war," he wrote, "speaks for itself." "I hope," he concludes, "that *Mission to Moscow* will fortify that United Nations 'great and noble cause.'"[22]

Davies was also directly responsible for Roosevelt's ill-advised 1942 promise to launch a second front. Meanwhile, Litvinov complained to Davies about Britain's policies. He insisted that Churchill opposed a cross-channel operation "for political and empire reasons." Davies relayed this information to the president, bolstering Roosevelt's "confidence in his own ability to win Stalin's trust, which paralleled that of Davies." Davies, acting as a go-between, also afforded Stalin insight into the Roosevelt-Churchill relationship, including the comment that the two leaders disagreed on "several issues."[23] In a briefing session with the Soviet dictator, Davies fed "him [Stalin] with most valuable information while to the President he was re-enforcing the ideas he had gained from the Russians."

Davies lobbied for a Roosevelt-Stalin meeting which resulted in the Teheran conference. Believing in both Roosevelt's personal magic and Stalin's personal power, Davies headed the well-wishers as Roosevelt set off for Teheran. In a talk with the president, recorded in his diary, Davies wrote:

> I told him what I had told Hopkins; that Stalin welcomes a meeting with him; but was not keen on Churchill; they 'got into each others hair'. In addition, it was quite clear to me that there would be no meeting of the three agreed upon, until by preliminary exploration,

he, STALIN, would feel reasonably sure that he would not be confronted with two against one on the matters of the security of his
western frontier, Poland, and similar matters, affecting his vital
interests. We had quite a discussion on that.[24]

Davies' tactics heightened Anglo-American tensions, while strengthening Roosevelt's conviction that "personal diplomacy had succeeded."[25]

While Davies advised that Stalin was to be trusted, Bullitt continued to advise the opposite. In another memo to the president dated
January 29, 1943, Bullitt argued that "Stalin is not a changed man
. . . no Saul on the Road to Damascus." Bullitt cautioned that the
suffering Soviet people and the Red Army fighting men did not
change the fact that "Stalin's concern is the welfare of the Soviet
state," which was and remained totalitarian. To call Stalin a nationalist did not make him a "pacifist." Nor was he Peter the Great. Bullitt
saw Russian armies annexing Bessarabia, Bukovina, Eastern Poland,
Lithuania, Latvia, and Estonia, and was not afraid to say so. He
warned that these were Stalin's "minimum aims in Europe, that other
Eastern European states were in danger, that Western European
nations themselves were being infiltrated by Communists who sought
to coerce the political process."[26]

This did not make Bullitt popular in the White House. Roosevelt
and Hopkins thought Bullitt was "exaggerating." The White House
had no interest in listening to Bullitt or to the State Department
doomsayers like Kelly, Kennan, Henderson, and Bohlen. Only friendly
voices were welcome. As Harriman told George Urban, "I was appointed to represent the United States in Moscow, not to deal with Stalin's
crimes."

Lend-Lease and the Soviet Union: Harry Hopkins
and All the President's Men

Control of the war policy from the White House meant preventing
Congress from playing a vital role in policy development. Key deci-

sions would be in Roosevelt's hands alone, as the Commander in Chief, consulting only with his most trusted advisers. The issue here is not the president's constitutional responsibility to make strategic decisions, but how he executed it. Who were those key aides? What were their roles?

The policy formulated for aiding the Soviet Union after Hitler invaded Russia would become the most obvious example of Roosevelt's diplomacy. Harry Hopkins, his principal surrogate in this instance, became the president's vehicle for circumventing the State Department and for carrying out his policy.

Hopkins' enemies described him as a "sinister figure," a backstairs intriguer, an Iowan combination of Machiavelli, Svengali, and Rasputin.[27] He was hardly that, resembling rather a Joseph the Provider, who, in his dedication to provide help to the Soviet Union, would come to resemble a congressman lobbying for government projects for his constituents. Hopkins' considerable reputation in history rests heavily on Robert E. Sherwood's dual biography, *Roosevelt and Hopkins,*[28] which has been described as "a flat, one-dimensional portrait of a true believer who merely exchanged one crusade for another." His preoccupation with aid to the Soviet Union requires a closer examination.

Hopkins resembled the president in his lack of knowledge of foreign affairs. He rarely opposed the president or acted independently. Like Davies, he did not so much advise Roosevelt as reinforce his views. Roosevelt used to say "Harry is the perfect ambassador for my purpose. He doesn't even know the meaning of the word 'practical.'"[30] He was an obedient New Dealer, and in the words of a more recent biographer, "Democracy's bureaucrat."[31]

Hopkins was at the center of Roosevelt's war policy as the president's personal representative to Churchill and Stalin. When implementation of Lend-Lease was begun in January, 1941, Churchill's initial response was a quizzical "Who's Hopkins?" but very soon Hopkins gained Churchill's complete confidence.

Hopkins may have been a quiet man, but he was tenacious when it came to pursuing any task Roosevelt assigned, a quality he displayed when assigned the responsibility of keeping the Soviet Union in the war and reassuring Stalin. Hopkins' influence on the president's

Soviet policy, and his complex relationships with Churchill and Stalin, were remarkable. This is not to suggest that he emulated Colonel Edward M. House's willingness to act independently of President Wilson's instructions, but his role in encouraging the president's trust in Stalin and hope for a postwar U.S.-Soviet relationship was considerable.

Roosevelt's immediate reaction to Hitler's invasion of the Soviet Union was to send aid. Secretary of War Stimson, on the other hand, saw the invasion as an opportunity to win the battle of the Atlantic. "His reaction to Barbarossa was more action [*sic*] to aid Britain while Hitler is busy with the Russians. [It] can be our best reaction to Russia's fighting. Politically it would be wise to take this tack. Practically it would help Russia more than sending it direct aid."[32] Hopkins initially shared this view, but Roosevelt insisted otherwise. He did not, as did some professionals at State, "fear Russian domination," which had been predicted by experts who said that after Hitler was defeated, Stalin would dominate Europe. Roosevelt simply insisted that the immediate task was to "give help to the Russian people."[33]

The most direct way to pursue this policy was to take control of a special State Department committee for Russian aid, headed by Charles Curtis, and transfer it to the Lend-Lease administration. To simplify and expedite Lend-Lease procedures and spare Hopkins additional administrative responsibilities, Roosevelt appointed Edward Stettinius, an industrialist, to head the Office of Lend-Lease Administration, under the direct authority of Roosevelt and Hopkins, thus wresting control of Lend-Lease from the State Department.[34]

Hopkins now underwent an instant conversion. Before July of 1941, Hopkins had no particular interest in the Soviet Union. But when he left for his second trip to London on July 12, he had become aware of the importance the president attached to his policy of aid to Russia, and he was determined to carry out his master's wishes.

Hopkins understood the significance of the Nazi invasion of the Soviet Union. Acting as Lend-Lease supervisor, he asked the British about technical shipping details, thinking ahead to supplying the Soviet Union. On July 25, he cabled the president asking for permission to include a visit to Moscow on his itinerary,[35] a quiet bit of deviousness where personal contact might have had a different result. John Langer's research led him to speculate that "Hopkins probably left Washington with the trip to Moscow in mind at least as a possibility. When he first proposed to go to London in 1940, the president had turned him down cold. His chances of getting presidential permission for the trip were greater, if he made the request by long distance, thus limiting discussion."[36]

There is no hard evidence for this, but Hopkins was known to orchestrate complicated deceptions in the service of the president.[37] McJimsey argues that the story of Hopkins' request to go to Moscow is "buried in contradiction." Some authors write that Churchill may have suggested the idea to him "to find the truth about the Russian military situation." Maisky, the Soviet ambassador to London, claims it was his idea. The American ambassador at the time, John Winant, planned to make the trip himself, but Hopkins asked "how would it be for me to go." Sherwood believes that it was Hopkins' idea, and that Churchill actually discouraged him from going.[38]

However he managed the two day trip, he returned a wholehearted supporter of aid to the Soviet Union. He also presented himself— solely on the basis of this trip—as an expert on the Soviet Union, although the visit had consisted mostly of shopping and a short, personal conversation with Stalin. Hopkins still knew nothing about the strengths and weaknesses of the Soviet army, nothing about the sufferings of the Russian people during the Nazi invasion, yet he concluded that "the morale of the population is good."[39] He cabled the president, Hull, and Welles on the need for large-scale aid.

With no facts to back him up, no intelligence or sources of information, Hopkins was convinced that Stalin would hold out against the Germans. He saw Stalin as resolute and sensed no desperation whatsoever. He saw nothing out of the ordinary in Stalin's pleas and his "astonishing invitation to the United States to send its own troops to the Russian front entirely under American command."[40] Stalin's so-called "coolness," to which Harriman also testified,[41] was, to Hopkins, a sign of "realism and command" displayed by "a great administrator with intimate control of the war."[42] Yet, Valentin Berezhkov, one of Stalin's translators in Teheran, presents a different version of

Stalin's behavior. He maintains that Stalin was in a state of panic after Hitler's invasion on June 22, and disappeared from public view for ten days without addressing the Russian people.[43] McJimsey's biography casts Hopkins as much more independent and active than was the Hopkins portrayed by Robert Sherwood. Adopting his mentor's uncritical view of Stalin, Hopkins was adamant in his pursuit of the Soviets. Indeed, late in the war, when Polish officials complained about the murder by the Soviets of some ten thousand Polish officers in the Katyn forest, "Hopkins dismissed the Poles as trouble makers influenced by 'large Polish landlords' who wanted to make sure that their estates were not lost to the Russians."[44]

Hopkins pursued the Soviet policy at the expense of the British. "In courting the Russians, Hopkins renewed his skepticism of British grand strategy." He was not going to allow the British to restrict American aid to the Soviet Union on political grounds. Rather, he sought to reach an agreement with the Soviet Union on the postwar treatment of Germany, preempting an Anglo-American agreement on this issue. "He felt that the Russians appreciated the American contribution to the war and were friendly enough to justify hope that relations could be improved."[45] Whatever doubts he might have had about the Soviet system, he swallowed for the duration of the war, devoting himself to fulfilling the Lend-Lease program at all costs.

And the Lend-Lease administration, which came to be Roosevelt's own mini-State Department, was the most powerful instrument at Hopkins' disposal in the pursuit of the president's Soviet policy. In order to pursue his policy effectively, the president transferred his aid program from the State Department to the Lend-Lease agency. Hopkins was chosen to supervise Lend-Lease and Averell Harriman to head operations in London as a special supply mission to the Soviet Union, known as part of the Harriman-Beaverbrook mission. Roosevelt never altered this approach.

Sharp policy differences developed between the president and the State Department, resulting in a bureaucratic war that lasted throughout the shooting war and into the postwar period. The president was convinced that American generosity alone would advance American-Soviet cooperation for the duration of the war and beyond. The State

Department consistently advised that the United States insist on reciprocity with the Soviet Union, offering aid in return for political concessions. Its officials were more hard-nosed, asserting that "no capitalist nation could ever win Soviet confidence." Roosevelt's generosity, they felt, "only heightened Soviet distrust."[46] "One might just as well strike an elephant with a feather to believe that the Kremlin is responsive to gestures," Laurence Steinhardt, U.S. ambassador to Moscow, wrote to Loy Henderson, his chief of mission and dean of the anti-Soviet cadre.[47] In order to gain Stalin's respect, the U.S. must convince him of American strength and purpose. The Soviets, they insisted, appreciated and understood power, not open-ended generosity.

And so the administration stood divided, the president and Hopkins advocating generosity, the State Department adhering to reciprocity as a basis for American policy.[48] What ensued was more than a "disorderly president" at odds with a "traditionalist" foreign service; it was a struggle over the fate of U.S.-Soviet postwar relations. In the battle between the Lend-Lease administration and the State Department can be found the roots of the cold war.

I view the creation of the Lend-Lease arrangement as the first phase of the Roosevelt-Stalin war policy. The policy was directed from the White House and run by the president's surrogates—Hopkins, Harriman, and Generals James Burns and Philip Faymonville. Burns and Faymonville, like Hopkins, shared the president's viewpoint. General Burns wrote:

> I am convinced that sincere and lasting friendship between the Soviet Union and the United States is of vital importance to victory in this war and to the future peace of the world. . . . I am also convinced that such friendship can best be achieved by a general policy of generosity, sympathetic understanding of Soviet problems and objectives, frankness and sincerity and by a spirit of courtesy and democratic equality to all Soviet individuals. In other words, a genuine Good Neighbor policy should prevail.[49]

Yet Burns, like Hopkins, knew very little about the Soviet Union and less about Stalin and his repressive policies. After the war, he wrote that his job was "to help the United States and the world by helping Russia . . . in the spirit of generosity and friendliness in order to create the most effective team work during the war and after the war."[50]

To Hopkins and the men who carried out his policies, Lend-Lease amounted to a foreign policy that kept on giving no matter what. There was no reciprocity or intelligence sharing. No one really knew where American aid went, how it was used, and to what effect. This was in sharp contrast to American dealings with the British, who, for example, were required to share intelligence.[51]

The war between "Hopkins' Shop" and the State Department has been looked upon by historians as a bureaucratic sideshow, with the differences between the amateurs in the White House and the hardened professionals at the State Department seen as between the naive and the cynical viewpoints, a debate that had little impact on policy. These historians focus instead on the debates over the great summits at Teheran and Yalta, and what they produced or failed to produce. But the debate was serious, and it had serious implications. History may credit the professionals for perceiving Stalin's intentions correctly, but the amateurs won the battle. The behavior of Hopkins and his aides is a good guide to what evolved at Teheran and Yalta.

The officials who administered Lend-Lease and a policy of generosity to the Soviets were to fulfill the act to "the letter"[52] and "even to go beyond where possible." The State Department officials envisioned a foreign policy that would extend beyond short-term war cooperation. Supply to the Soviet Union should not be an open-ended effort, but should be considered in the wider context of international relations, measured against Soviet behavior and Stalin's actions. What hobbled the State Department's actions was that Roosevelt never had a clear long-term policy toward the Soviet Union, only a short-term policy toward the war. He was incapable of taking a broader view and the State Department's professionals were the last people he would listen to. "In general," wrote the historian of U.S.-Soviet Lend-Lease, "the expediency of rendering assistance to the USSR was willingly conceded, but there were persistent doubts and misgivings over the zeal and earnestness with which the White House and its agents approached the task."[53] Roosevelt, however, felt Lend-Lease played a strategic role. "He regarded economic assistance as a principal means of holding together the uneasy alliance until the common threat could be removed."[54] He was convinced that "American generosity, in assisting the Russians, would help break down the ingrained Soviet suspicion of the West, that it would convince the Russian leaders of American good will."[55] That hope formed the president's idea of a policy beyond the immediate military necessities. A quintessential New Deal instrument for corporate-state arrangements now became a global New Deal. This attitude resulted in a policy of unconditional aid. "No supporting evidence was necessary for Soviet requests."[56]

The Soviets also saw the alliance as a short-term and self-serving war project and felt no political debts toward the U.S.[57] When the cracks in the alliance began to form in 1944, Lend-Lease was never used as a lever on the Soviets.

Probably the most dependable Hopkins aide was Colonel (now General) Philip R. Faymonville, a colorful figure who had acquired the nickname of "The Red General" during the course of a checkered career. He was so blatantly pro-Russian that his enthusiasm had caused major trouble, as in early 1943, when General George C. Marshall ordered an investigation into charges that Faymonville "was so pro-Soviet as to raise questions in some persons' minds as to whether he was being 'blackmailed' by the Soviet Government."[58]

Faymonville's "Soviet career" had begun in 1936, when he became the first military attaché to a restored U.S. embassy in Moscow. General Alfred Smith cited his "faculty of getting along with the Russians," but Loy Henderson was not impressed, holding "serious doubts as to his judgment and his impartiality whenever the Soviets are concerned."[59] In his memoirs, Henderson said,

> In view of his long-established friendly interest in the Soviet Union, his knowledge of the Russian language, the fact that he was persona grata to the Soviet government, and his support by Mrs. Roosevelt, it was almost inevitable that he should have been selected as our first military attache to the Soviet Union. Faymon-

ville's attitude of distrust of the Department of State and of its members manifested itself almost immediately upon his arrival in the Soviet Union.[60]

To the State Department officials, Faymonville seemed like a loose cannon, a man who accepted Soviet propaganda at face value. In 1936, according to Chip Bohlen, who was then a third secretary in the embassy, Faymonville "would stoutly defend the purges, insisting that they were uprooting traitors and enemies of the people."[61]

Faymonville's pro-Soviet reputation endeared him to Ambassador Davies, but it destroyed his standing within the Army. Still, Roosevelt decided there was no better man for the job. Though the Army wanted Faymonville to leave Russia, Roosevelt and Hopkins decided that he "would remain in Moscow indefinitely as our Lend-Lease representative."[62] With such strong backing from the top, Faymonville was able to act independently, becoming so secretive about his activities that even Ambassador Standley could not read his reports to the War Department and the president.

Faymonville's good standing with the Soviets conformed with the president's policy even though his zealotry upset the ambassador and the professionals in Moscow, and his dedication soon brought about his promotion to general. "Faymonville merely followed existing policy. The president's definite views on aid to the Soviet Union were made known to the Lend-Lease bureaucracy, which in turn instructed Faymonville. There is no evidence that he ever acted outside of his instructions from Washington."[63] Faymonville acted as a political officer executing presidential policy.[64] Roosevelt never intended Lend-Lease to serve as a bargaining tool with the USSR. He wanted to keep the Soviet Union in the war; "Roosevelt and Faymonville both felt that it was more important to keep the Soviet Union as an effective ally than to gain intelligence information. Attaching a price tag to Lend-Lease might have caused unnecessary resentment in Moscow."[65]

It is interesting to follow Hubert D. Van Tuyll's excellent study—based on primary intelligence sources—of Lend-Lease to Russia. The Office of Strategic Services (OSS) sources indicate that Lend-Lease personnel in Moscow, who reported directly to Washington, did not share information with U.S. military and naval attachés as late as 1943, after the reorganization of Lend-Lease. The American ambassador remained isolated, unaware of Washington's war plans, ignorant of what was happening even on the Russian front, with no access to information on civilian morale, industrial capacity, and military damage. Even when Averell Harriman took over after 1943, he found it almost impossible to obtain intelligence about the Soviets because the Lend-Lease operation was still being handled in Washington.[66]

The Soviets remained as unresponsive. The Soviet Union was less than anxious to furnish specific information on its war effort or even the precise use of Lend-Lease materials. The Russians were even less enthusiastic about having large numbers of Americans travelling around the Soviet Union. Few entry visas were given, and those only after long delays. American officers with Soviet family connections were not particularly welcome (and were sometimes expelled). U.S. missions had to verify the number of members to Soviet authorities or visas would not be forthcoming. Even the head of the Persian Gulf Command, an organization dedicated almost solely to supplying the Soviet Union, was denied a visa.[67]

American pilots were not permitted to fly Lend-Lease aircraft into the Soviet Union.[68] By 1944, not a single American had come close to the fighting on the Soviet front, except for some closely monitored guided tours.[69] American analysts had no information on the Soviet industrial system, factory designs, or military installations. Maps of airfields were not provided.[70] Americans knew nothing about the devastation the Russians had suffered at the hands of the Germans.

Roosevelt's anxieties about keeping the Soviet Union in the war had no basis in real intelligence, because none was required from the Soviets. Soviet secrecy throughout the war was amazing in terms of the behavior of an ally. American analysts seemed at a loss to explain the extent of Soviet secrecy, which covered a staggering number of areas ranging from combat operations to agricultural production. Information seemed to come only directly from Stalin, which led some officials to conclude that "Stalin apparently was the only individual in the Soviet Union who had the authority to give some information." The U.S. military mission in Moscow assumed that there might be a quid pro quo that it did not know about. In analyzing the grant of certain valuable refinery equipment, the mission's official history comments that the offer "may have been an extremely valuable bargaining point, in exchange for some Soviet concession or operation not known here." Undoubtedly Soviet officials were aware that their government would look with suspicion upon any unusual collaboration with the Allies.

The Soviet Union never went to great pains to explain its secrecy. The lack of visits to the front was justified in terms of concern for the Americans' safety. More important was the Soviet attitude regarding the American desire to know more about the specific uses of Lend-Lease material. The Russians "have always felt that during this war if we gave them material, their objective was to have victories and that it was no concern of ours for what specific purpose the material was used so long as they achieved success." One authority noted dryly that there "seems not to have been the same complete and cordial effort by Soviet Russia to exchange technical aid and information as there was between the United States and the United Kingdom."[71]

Roosevelt intended Lend-Lease as a military policy. The president also wanted the Soviet Union to enter the war against Japan and hoped Lend-Lease would encourage this.[72] Since Stalin was trying to avoid just such a move, it was not very likely. What is surprising is that the Axis powers failed to work together toward such an end, that Hitler failed to try and persuade the Japanese to open a second front.

If Harry Hopkins was his master's faithful servant, W. Averell Harriman, the next most important member of the Roosevelt entourage of surrogate statesmen, was his exact opposite. In style, temperament, and background, Harriman could have been the president's twin. Something of a playboy, Harriman was a patrician who shared many of the president's inclinations, including a belief in public service. "Harriman," wrote E. J. Kahn in a 1952 *New Yorker* profile, "is an intense, nervous chain-smoking man, is exceptionally handsome but he does not always make the most of his physical attributes. He has a rather pronounced stoop." He appeared to be the Anthony Eden of American government.

Averell Harriman was the son of E. H. Harriman, one of the wealthiest men in America, an industrialist and a member of the generation of robber-barons that included Rockefeller, Morgan, and Carnegie. Averell's career in business and politics spanned seven decades, from 1915 to 1983. He was administrator and vice-president of the Union Pacific Railroad (1915–1917), director of the Illinois Central Railroad Company (1915–1947), chairman of the Illinois Central (1920–1931), chairman of the board of W. A. Harriman (1915–1946), partner in Brown Brothers and Harriman (1931–1942). He was a special presidential representative to Great Britain and headed the Harriman-Beaverbrook mission. He was the president's Lend-Lease representative, ambassador to the Soviet Union from 1943 to 1946, ambassador to Great Britain in 1946, secretary of commerce from 1946 to 1948. He made an unsuccessful bid to win the Democratic presidential nomination in 1952, was governor of New York from 1955 to 1959, and thereafter acted as adviser and emissary for Presidents Eisenhower, Kennedy, Nixon, and Johnson, on issues such as Viet Nam, the Soviet Union, and the Middle East.[73]

Like Roosevelt, Harriman was not given to reflection. Kahn writes, "Harriman does not absorb information or arrive at conclusions in an orderly fashion. He learns things by some osmosis. He loves to have people feed ideas to him, and although he is slightly deaf, he can assimilate facts served up simultaneously by several competing sources— a telephone, a memorandum. . . . Averell has antennas—he catches the short waves, a friend of his remarked recently, 'Harriman's approach to situations is pragmatic and intuitive rather than theoretical and reflective.'"[74] There was also something of FDR's working habits in Harriman's aversion to planning.

Harriman's entry into government marked a major change for him. Until age forty-nine, he had been primarily a highly successful businessman. Noted for being innovative and hard-driving, he had made a huge success out of the Sun Valley complex in Idaho. Unlike Hopkins or Roosevelt, he was a good administrator. His work with Roosevelt was the beginning of a second career that would sustain him nearly to the end of his life.

Harriman always paid great attention to the nuances of social life and was keenly aware of his social status. A great many of the Library of Congress files concerning his duties in Great Britain are filled with the social invitations for a seemingly endless round of parties even as the country suffered under bombings and war shortages. Harriman divorced his first wife, Kathleen Lanier Lawrence, in 1929. In 1930, he married Marie Norton Whitney, who died in 1970. Then in 1971, at the age of eighty, he married Pamela Digby Churchill Hayward, who had made a fair career of marrying interesting men, including Randolph Churchill—Winston's son—and the legendary theatrical producer Leland Hayward.

Harriman brought business acumen and experience to his work in the Roosevelt administration, especially to dealing with the Soviet Union. Between 1925 and 1928, Harriman had unsuccessfully invested in Soviet Georgian manganese concessions, making his first visit to the Soviet Union in 1926 to take a look at his lost investment. Thereafter, he visited the Soviet Union regularly. He was thus in a position to look at the Soviets skeptically and realistically in a way that Hopkins never could. Harriman saw the inherent difficulties in the U.S.-USSR relationship, especially in Stalin's inflexibility and penchant for secrecy. Whereas Hopkins would never say anything negative about Stalin, Harriman's assessment was sometimes more balanced and perceptive, though he, too, would choose to ignore the darker implications of Stalin's behavior.

In a revealing interview with George Urban in the November, 1981, issue of *Encounter,* the British literary and political monthly, Harriman was asked why he did not portray Stalin as particularly repulsive or horrible in his memoirs. Harriman answered:

> You must understand that my business in Moscow was not to look at Stalin with the curiosity of an historian or the questioning eye of a political philosopher. I was sent there by the president to keep Russia in the war and save American lives. And as ideology had nothing to do with Roosevelt's decision to help Russia, I was not concerned with Soviet Party history, Stalin's record as Party leader, and the like.
>
> People studying Stalin now are looking for evidence of blood and murder. I was looking for vigorous action in Stalin's war with Nazi Germany, and I did find in him a man of action and a man of

leadership. I expected him to be tough, and he was tough, although (as I have said), he was also very polite. But his blunt words did not bother me nearly as much as they did Beaverbrook, for example. I went to see him as an equal. I had met so many important men in my time that I was not going to be awed by Stalin.

Now, Alexey Tolstoy (scion of the great Tolstoy and a British writer) did not say that Stalin was like Ivan the Terrible. He merely observed that "if you want to understand the Kremlin of today . . . you must first understand the Kremlin of Ivan the Terrible." This simply means that one could not understand Stalin's Russia without understanding Russian history and appreciating some of the, for us, appalling things which the Russian people were brought up with and were prepared to put up with. It wasn't that the Kremlin I saw somehow bore traces of the court of Ivan the Terrible, for (if I am not mistaken) Ivan was the monarch who murdered his son in a fit of anger. Stalin was not like that.[!]

Harriman probably had more personal contact with Stalin than any other American official. They met on an average of once a month during Harriman's two-and-a-half-year tour of service in Moscow. Yet, while Churchill called Harriman "Averell," to Stalin he was "Mr. Garriman." And while Harriman's talks with Churchill were inevitably described as "personal," his talks with Stalin were "discussions." Still, one of Stalin's interpreters thought that Stalin in his own way respected Harriman more than any other foreigner with whom he had contact.[75] They debated often and Harriman was known to hold his ground when Stalin would go on the offensive. Arguments were often sharp and noisy, but the relationship itself appeared to be cordial. Stalin, knowing Harriman's passion for horses, gave him a spirited mount which found its way to Harriman's stables in Orange County, New York.[76]

Harriman's transformation from uncritical observer to skeptical participant turned him into what one historian has called "one of the first Cold Warriors."[77] While Harriman may have noted that Stalin "did have a softer side to him,"[78] he had no soft feelings for Stalin, and that attitude was mutual.

In mid–1943, while serving as ambassador, Harriman's approach to the USSR, according to one student, remained one of "cautious cooperation."[79] After Stalingrad, and through early 1943, when the fortunes of the Soviet Union were changing for the better, Harriman became convinced that the old Lend-Lease policy of "give, give, give" must end. He became a convert to reciprocity.

Stalin's betrayal of the Polish uprising in 1944 was muffled by the euphoria over the Normandy landings, but Harriman was concerned. He wrote the president saying that the Soviets might dictate the Polish question in ways detrimental to the Allies, and recommended that Stalin should at least agree on the Curzon Line, even if the London Polish government was unacceptable. At this time Harriman was still not quite convinced that Stalin would impose a Communist-dominated Polish government.

Harriman was becoming a frustrated critic. Urban asked him, "You didn't think you convinced the president to be firm and vigilant in dealing with the Soviets in Eastern Europe?" Harriman replied, "The president did not have as sure a grasp of the realities in Central and Eastern Europe as he did in the Far East." Harriman would not say the president's attitude was naive. He said it was a "complex issue." According to Harriman, "Roosevelt was hopeful that his personal relationship with Stalin could carry on after the war."[80]

Harriman's role in the Soviet Lend-Lease policy had begun in August, 1941. The Harriman-Beaverbrook mission to Moscow in the fall of 1942 originated when Churchill and Roosevelt told Stalin that "the needs and demands of you and your armed service can only be determined in the light of our full knowledge of the many facts which must be taken into consideration in the decisions we take,"[81] a goal that never became the policy. Churchill chose as his emissary his minister of supply, Max Aitkin, Lord Beaverbrook, a long-time supporter who turned out to be totally uncritical of the Soviet Union, a determined propagandist for unconditional aid, the Second Front, and many other of Stalin's projects.

Because Hopkins' health had worsened, Roosevelt needed to appoint someone else as his representative. Hopkins wanted either Henry Morgenthau or Frank Knox, but Roosevelt picked Harriman because he was familiar with London and Moscow and because he "belonged to the Hopkins shop."[82] The mission also included two dedicated Hopkinsites, Generals Burns and Faymonville, though Harriman was not too happy with the latter, whom he knew only by his controversial reputation. Harriman's appointment furthered the policy of keeping Lend-Lease completely outside the State Department purview.

"Lend-Lease had not, in sending the Harriman-Beaverbrook mission to Moscow, drawn a conscious line between policies of generosity or reciprocity."[83] The issue arose only after negotiations had been concluded, with the British holding the line for reciprocity, especially in getting exact information on Russian needs. Stalin stalled, worried that the Allies would learn the true extent of the disasters his armies had suffered and about the Soviet military establishment's state of unpreparedness.

Nevertheless, the protocols were signed, and Stalin was pushed to release more than minimal information. The spirit of unquestioning generosity prevailed, and the tone of Soviet-American relations was set for the rest of the war, regardless of Harriman's doubts.

Wendell Willkie's Mission to Moscow

Roosevelt reached everywhere for surrogate help. An unlikely source turned out to be Wendell Willkie, the ebullient "liberal" Republican whom Roosevelt had defeated soundly in the 1940 presidential election. Acting on the president's behalf, Willkie embarked on a 50-day around-the-world tour in 1942 that took him to the Middle East, the Soviet Union, and China.

Willkie's stay in the Soviet Union—from September 17 to September 27—was the most significant part of the trip. It was a dramatic event that resembled an extended campaign stop, with Willkie bringing his campaign rhetoric to the Kremlin, where it surely sounded fresh, if strange. Even Andrey Vyshinsky and Vyacheslav Molotov were astonished at the performance.

Stalin held a magnificent state dinner for Willkie in Catherine the Great's dining room. Present were the Kremlin elite, headed by Stalin himself, with his acolytes, Molotov, Klement Voroshilov, Admiral Nikolay Kuznetsov, Anastas Mikoyan, Lavrenty Beria, and his aide Vladimir Dekanozov, former ambassador to Berlin. Willkie toasted the glories of the Red Army and of Stalin, showering praise on the Soviet leader. He criticized his own government for failing to intensify Lend-Lease activities, praising Stalin for "how well he kept his eyes on the ball."[84] In two days, Willkie said, he had "come to realize how unfairly the Soviet Union has been represented in the past to the American people." He hinted that "false reports with regard to the Soviet Union have been circulated by certain vested interests which feared that the Soviet government was endeavoring to spread the Soviet system to the United States," that the same vested interests "caused many Americans to believe the Soviet government did not permit freedom of religion in the Soviet Union."

Willkie's biographer writes:

> Whether Willkie's appraisal of Joseph Stalin was too generous is a question that must await the verdict of history, rendered, after the passions of the present century have faded, in the light of the forces and events amid which the Soviet dictator moved. But a rash anticipation of the verdict might be that Stalin was a man of keen intelligence, the application of which was limited by his revolutionary background (and, in his last years, a growing paranoia); of great executive ability; of tremendous resolution and force of character; and of a fierce devotion to Russia, combined with but not submerged in, a lust for personal power. These qualities made him the one man that could have kept Russia from going down under the fury of Hitler's attack. He was also, obviously, in line with the long tradition of Russian autocracy, capable of total disregard of the sufferings of individual human beings and of total contempt for the human rights that are basic to Western democracy. He could nevertheless, when he chose, display great personal charm, which visitors from the West found it impossible to dismiss as a mere facade.[85]

Standley concluded that Willkie's performance was a sham. "My personal opinion is that Mr. Willkie came to Russia more to enhance his political stature than to help the allies get on with the war."[86]

To an extent, Russian observers shared that assessment. They saw Willkie as a representative of America's corporate class which was intrinsically hostile to the working class. America's liberal left might have lavished praise on Willkie's efforts, and the president himself lauded Willkie's diplomatic tour, but the Soviets were more reticent. In a memorandum on Willkie's trip prepared by Georgy Zarubin, the head of the American Department in the Soviet Foreign Office, a different picture of Willkie emerges.

The Soviet analysis, which was sent to Stalin, identified Willkie as merely another Republican, however liberal, a corporate lawyer, a wealthy man and an enemy of the Communist party who, in his election campaign, had specifically refrained from talking about his attitude toward "workers' organizations." "Willkie's companies waged struggle against workers, members of trade unions." The *New Republic* represents the view of American-liberal intellectuals. Willkie, the report states, was an "ardent exponent of big capital." Willkie was seen as nothing more than a demagogue "playing the role of supporter of democratic rights."[87]

Nevertheless, Willkie's visit had two long-term effects. It created the image of close American-Soviet relations in the United States, a perception Roosevelt wanted to cement at home. The trip also promoted the idea of the Second Front. Willkie advocated this in an interview with *Izvestia* on September 27, where he talked of the suffering of the Russian people. Sixty million people, he said, were "now slaves in Russian territory." Food was scarce, thousands were starving, five million had already been killed or were missing. "I asked myself what can be the most effective method of winning our war by helping our heroic Russian ally. There was only one answer for me—to establish together with Great Britain a real second front in Europe and within the shortest time our military leaders will approve. Perhaps the American public will have to be prodded a little."[88] Willkie's wholehearted support of the Second Front helped push the president into a corner and gave Stalin an effective bargaining tool at Teheran.

The Soviet Diplomats Look at the United States

There is a considerable body of interpretative American literature on U.S.-Soviet relations before and during the war, but little exists about Soviet perceptions of American diplomacy. There were many contacts between American and Soviet officials at the summits and ministerial meetings, and they provide some idea about official Soviet perceptions of America's war policy. Yet, the Soviet view of these developments is missing.

We know that Stalin viewed America from a Marxist revolutionary perspective and had only a rudimentary knowledge of the American political system. The views of Stalin's representatives were not crucial to Soviet decision-making; Stalin always prevailed. Roosevelt had surrogates, but the men around Stalin were less than that, though they were not the sycophants portrayed by Western historians.

Politbureau members such as Molotov, Beria, Malenkov, Mikoyan, Lazar Kaganovich, Klement Voroshilov, and working diplomats like Litvinov, Vyshinsky, S. A. Lozovsky, Zarubin, and Dekanozov had minds of their own, and those among them who dealt with the West were talented and perceptive. Molotov, who was closest to Stalin, did not impress Westerners.

> His mottled complexion, ingratiating smile and straggly moustache hid one of the most inexorably stupid men to hold the foreign ministership of any major power in this century. Beside him, Ciano, Beck, even Ribbentrop, seem masters of intelligence, quick-witted, well informed and of impeccable judgment. He was ignorant, stupid, greedy and grasping, incurably suspicious and immovably obstinate. Like many stupid men he was cranky, pedantic even and a bit of a bully in a coarse, peasant way. Stalin made fun of his vegetarianism and his abhorrence of alcohol.[89]

It was the diplomats, however, who provided Stalin with the political intelligence about the United States. The information was filtered through the Foreign Ministry and through Stalin's secretary Poskrebyshev, who summarized reports in a few paragraphs. How Stalin used the material is difficult to assess, but the knowledge and diplomatic skill he demonstrated at Teheran and Yalta show that he must have read the diplomatic reports with interest and care.

Stalin's main diplomatic source for information about Washington was his ambassador to the U.S., Maxim Litvinov. Litvinov was a Polish Jew and former Menshevik, but Stalin had shrewdly appointed him rather than a loyal Bolshevik to the Washington post. Litvinov served as ambassador to the United States from 1933 to 1936, and was foreign minister until 1939, when the Nazi-Soviet Pact made the presence of a Jewish foreign minister uncomfortable. When the Nazis invaded the Soviet Union, Litvinov returned to Washington and provided some remarkable reports on the formulation of U.S. war policy and American political forces. Married to a British woman, and culturally very much a European, Litvinov was comfortable in Washington. He shared Roosevelt's long-term vision of a postwar partnership, a vision his successor in Washington, Andrei Gromyko, also came to accept.

Litvinov detailed his views on U.S. policy and politics in a 24-page memorandum sent to Stalin and Molotov on June 2, 1943,[90] and distributed to Voroshilov, Mikoyan, Beria, Malenkov, Vyshinsky, Dekanozov, and Lozovsky. Litvinov began by analyzing the actors in America's foreign policy, pointing out that Secretary of State Cordell Hull was, because of "his age, and personal relations between Roosevelt on the one hand and the assistant secretaries on the other, not the sole master of his department."[91] Succumbing to ideological explanations, Litvinov attributed the influence of assistants like Sumner Welles, A. A. Berle, and Breckinridge Long to their wealth, noting that they were rich and personally "worth a lot of money, maybe tens of millions and are absolutely independent in their careers." This independence was significant for Litvinov, who represented a system where there were no independent careers. Wealth meant power and access. Litvinov saw only wealthy men around Roosevelt—Harriman, Bullitt, Davies, Welles, Berle, Long, Morgenthau, Stimson, Knox, Stettinius, and even Rockefeller; and like Stalin, Litvinov perceived Roosevelt as basically a liberal capitalist pursuing capitalist goals.

Litvinov, despite the ideological biases, understood Roosevelt's court, identifying Hopkins, Morgenthau, Harriman, Davies, and other New Dealers as members in good standing. He grasped Roosevelt's style and method of operation, and he recognized the president's dependence on the progressive element of "the industrial and financial bourgeoisie," the men Litvinov called "internationalists with a 'Bourgeois-radical outlook.'"

Litvinov assured Stalin that the president was "a very staunch anti-Nazi and anti-Fascist and personally hates Hitler and Mussolini. There is no doubt that as long as Roosevelt is at the helm, he will carry the war until the complete defeat of the Axis countries. And he hopes to benefit at the expense of the British empire." In describing Roosevelt's ideas of an international trusteeship and the Four Policemen, Litvinov concluded that *"it is beyond all question that later on he will be accessible to our influence."*[92]

In the absence of sound intelligence, Litvinov hesitated to comment further on U.S.-British relations, advising only that "I believe, that the less contacts we have with America, the closer they unite with the British." He therefore persistently urged a close relationship with the United States, a position also reflected in a conversation he had with Under Secretary of State Sumner Welles on May 7, 1943. He told Welles what he had already suggested to Molotov, that "the world depends very largely upon understanding and cooperation between the Soviet Union and the United States."[93] Stalin never accepted his idea.

Litvinov complained that one of the factors militating against a closer relationship was the lack of an institutional arrangement, "a body for permanent contacts between the USA and the USSR." No consultative agency resembling the Anglo-American commissions existed between the two, and there was no mechanism for U.S.-Soviet planning in "the military sphere." "Strategic planning for the allies mainly is elaborated and exchanged in London, not in Washington."[94] Litvinov recommended the creation of a permanent military-political contact with the president and the War Department in Washington and an Allied commission in Europe, as well as Soviet participation in Anglo-American military discussions. He added that "we need not discuss our strategic plans for war against Germany." Rather, such participation would increase Soviet information and would give the USSR influence on U.S.-British strategic plans, while easing American discontent about the lack of contact between the two allies. But Stalin remained indifferent.

Litvinov expressed confidence that U.S. strategy was firmly geared toward Europe, despite Congressional isolationists and elements within the Navy and War Department who preferred to "concentrate U.S. military efforts in the struggle against Japan." He reassured Stalin that the secretaries of War, Navy, and State, as well as the president, "are decisively against a Pacific priority."

Litvinov also assessed Roosevelt's friendly attitude toward the Soviet Union as one that was likely to grow stronger. He noted that as early as 1933, Roosevelt had moved away from a typical American attitude of suspicion toward the Soviet Union. He stopped insisting on the payment of Soviet debts and remained open to the idea of a Soviet relationship despite the "hostile agitation of Bullitt." "Roosevelt," Litvinov asserted, "is more friendly to us than any other prominent American and wishes to cooperate with us."[95] Litvinov saw, however, that Roosevelt was not completely confident, writing of the president's "discontent" with "our unwillingness to discuss current and post-war political problems and to establish permanent contacts." But Litvinov assured Stalin that whatever difficulties existed, they would not affect Lend-Lease deliveries.

Litvinov assessed what the Americans did and did not want. "The USA is not at all interested in the economic or foreign political aspects of the Baltic regions' problems or in the frontier issue between us and Poland." Taking into consideration the forthcoming 1944 elections, "Roosevelt cannot be indifferent, however, to the votes of those who come from the Baltic states or Poland and also of American Catholics." That situation, he felt, was temporary. "In the process of post-war settlement Roosevelt will not support their claims if he finds himself faced with a fait accompli." The president, Litvinov understood, was interested in lofty ideas, and would present his arguments in the context of "international justice" and the Atlantic Charter. Litvinov was aware of Roosevelt's dreams and his unclear plans, and Stalin used this information at Teheran and Yalta.

Litvinov (and Gromyko after him) was deeply concerned about the 1944 presidential election and a possible change in administrations which he viewed as a potential disaster for the Soviet Union. The Republicans, Litvinov concluded, were "reactionary," "isolationists," and "bitterly anti-Soviet." Litvinov feared that if the Democrats lost the Senate, there would be a replay of Wilson's League of Nations experience. He worried about return to isolationism, an issue that also worried Gromyko, Molotov, and perhaps even Stalin himself.

Litvinov said that the president's closest friends "such as Hopkins and Davies are very optimistic about a Roosevelt victory and that cooperation with the USSR would be pursued even more intensely by the president once the war was over." Interestingly, Litvinov reported that Vice-President Henry Wallace "is more realistic about the situation and assumes Roosevelt's failure" to achieve postwar cooperation with the USSR. Finally, Litvinov concluded that as long as Roosevelt remained president, there was no danger of the United States dropping out of the war. He saw no hope for an immediate second front "without serious pressure." He said that the issue of Soviet Western borders must "be settled by ourselves" and that there would be no "considerable American counteraction."

Andrei Gromyko, Litvinov's successor, was a different kind of diplomat, more constricted and less at ease in the West. He was prone to worry, and he was not as incisive or articulate as the cosmopolitan Litvinov. But he echoed Litvinov's themes of cooperation with the United States, and Gromyko's fear of the Republicans bordered on nightmare. As late as July of 1944, Gromyko still worried that the American "ruling class" was not confident of Soviet victory, a strange notion given the successes the Red Army had enjoyed.[96] He saw changes in "attitudes in the USA ruling circles to the Soviet Union concerning trade." "Among the broad public and in official U.S. circles, an opinion was dominating that the Soviet Union would be defeated several months after the beginning of the Soviet-German war." This may have been true, but it was hardly germane to the realities that existed in 1944. It was Gromyko's way of making the point indirectly that a policy of American cooperation was tied to the successes of the Red Army.

Gromyko was both aware and fearful of Polish and Catholic power in the United States. Gromyko (and Litvinov) identified the Poles and Catholics with reactionary Republicans, betraying little understanding of American political behavior. There were Catholics who had voted for Michigan Republican Senator Arthur Vandenberg because he was a great champion of Polish and ethnic Americans; but Catholics and Poles and other ethnic groups were also a loyal constituency of Roosevelt and the Democrats.

Gromyko, again misreading the American political map, saw the Catholic church as the great enemy of Soviet interests and believed it held great political influence in the United States. He reported that the Catholic church was disseminating anti-Soviet propaganda and actively fighting against a U.S.-Soviet relationship. He complained of Polish agitation and the influence of the London Poles, noting that "Roosevelt, whose position on the Polish issue is *mainly favorable to the Soviet Union,* nevertheless takes into consideration the political influence of the Polish minorities."[97]

Like Litvinov, Gromyko was optimistic about Soviet-U.S. cooperation after the war, citing the president's support in the working class and the United States' abandonment of isolationism. He felt that the "USSR and the United States would manage to find common issues for the solution of a number of problems emerging in the future in the interests of both nations." Obviously, the United States was interested in the defeat of Germany, which, to a good Marxist like Gromyko, meant that "industry and the financial bourgeoisie is not interested in serious economic competition in Europe as Germany [was]." But it is "difficult now to say how far the administration and the ruling circles will go in this direction." He did observe, though, that the Americans intended to promote Western Europe bourgeoisie regimes, but also understood that they would refrain from establishing a pro-Fascist regime at the expense of a pro-Soviet regime.

Gromyko's worst nightmare was a victory for Thomas E. Dewey and a Republican administration, with a cabinet composed of former president Herbert Hoover as secretary of state, General Douglas MacArthur as a "war minister," Nelson Aldrich of Chase Manhattan Bank who is "personally hostile to us" as secretary of the treasury, and John L. Lewis, the anti-Roosevelt labor leader, as secretary of labor. "Such a team of a Republican President will be a telling blow to Soviet-American relations." Gromyko believed that "Re-election of President Roosevelt for the fourth term would be a most important and positive phenomena in politics." Gromyko saw the future power of the United States, noting its growing economic imperialism in Canada, Latin America, the Middle East, and China, and its desire to replace Great Britain as a great naval power. He devoted much of his report to the possibilities for growing U.S.-USSR trade relations— American manufactured products for Soviet raw materials and natural resources, and he hoped for U.S. credit (through the export-import bank) and technical assistance.

Gromyko observed that the Baltic issue would not come between the U.S. and the USSR, since the problem would be resolved "by itself in the process of their liberation by the Red Army," a conclusion he drew after talking with a number of officials, including "Harry Hopkins, who quite openly said that this was not only his personal opinion, but the President's too." Gromyko also reported Hopkins as saying that the president could not recognize the Baltic States as "component parts of the USSR" until the end of the war, because of domestic considerations.

Chapter 5

The Second Front

The questions of Poland and the Second Front were important in alliance politics and played a significant role at the Teheran and Yalta conferences. These were complicated questions, and attitudes toward them changed with changes in the circumstances of the war.

The Polish problem began when the Red Army crossed the pre–1939 Soviet border into Eastern and Central Europe. Although the Second Front would cease to be a problem after the landing at Normandy, Poland remained a source of friction among the Allies.

We begin with Soviet relations with Britain, since this is where Stalin's relations with the West after 1940 began. These relations were at low ebb during the first half of 1940. The fall of France in June, 1940, and the Nazi invasion of the Soviet Union a year later, turned Stalin into an ally of the West. The British began a series of negotiations with Stalin that culminated in the British-Soviet Treaty signed on May 26, 1942, and announced on June 11, 1942. President Roosevelt, still a nonbelligerent when the negotiations over the treaty were being conducted, was not an innocent bystander. Churchill was seeking the president's support of the treaty; but Roosevelt, hoping to formulate an independent American policy toward Stalin, remained in the background. In the end the British gradually became dependent on American-Soviet policy. The initiative for the treaty negotiations was British, and so were the results.

Prelude to the Second Front: The Russians and the British

For the British, the "Grand Alliance," a result of expedience, not trust, was born on the day Hitler invaded the Soviet Union. Churchill had said he would make a pact with the devil to defeat Hitler, and alliance with the Soviet Union came very close to being just that. He never forgave Stalin's betrayal of Britain in signing the Nazi-Soviet Pact. Hitler might not have moved westward, Poland might not have fallen, France might not have come under Nazi domination, and Britain would not have been so threatened had it not been for that agreement. Whenever Stalin made a military demand that appeared excessive, Churchill would remind him of the dire consequences of the Soviet rapprochement with Hitler.[1]

British diplomatic thinking had followed closely British military planning. In 1939, the military theater was France, but memory of the traumatic losses in World War I militated against a large British continental commitment. Hitler understood the role of the USSR to be "a chink in the British blockade," and so did the British, who considered bombing the oil fields in the Caucasus as an option against a potential combined Soviet-Nazi threat.[2]

After the indecisive Russian-Finnish war, the British chose negotiations with rather than war against the USSR. Sir Stafford Cripps, a Marxist-leaning society trial lawyer who became the ambassador to Moscow, went there on May 11, 1940, trying, even at that late date, to reverse Stalin's British policy. At the time, Fitzroy Maclean, a conservative with considerable experience in Russia who later became Churchill's representative to Tito's partisans,[3] was doubtful of such an effort. He preferred war between the Nazis and the Soviets since, in his view, Stalin hoped "to prolong the war between the allies and Germans in the hope of weakening both."[4] He thought Stalin saw the collapse of the British Empire as benefiting Russia, providing opportunities for Soviet expansion in the Near East and Central Asia.[5] Cripps failed to dissuade Stalin. The fall of France convinced Stalin that Britain would have to continue to fight Germany, and thus could mount no military threat against the Soviet Union.

Everything changed with the Nazi invasion of the Soviet Union on

June 22, 1941, but Churchill and other British leaders would never trust Stalin the way Roosevelt did. This mistrust colored the Churchill-Stalin relationship to the end of the war, and would surface during the debate on aid to Russia and the Second Front.

The Nazi invasion of the Soviet Union divided the British establishment, as it exposed the difference in philosophy between Churchill and his foreign minister Anthony Eden. Churchill oriented his policies toward the Anglo-American alliance, whereas Eden sought to develop a corresponding European-centered policy, i.e., a Soviet policy.[6] The division created a serious crisis for Churchill's conduct of the war.

Eden saw Moscow as a natural ally. He understood that the Soviet Union would replace Germany in the European balance of power after the war, and felt that Russia would be beholden to British security. He engaged in clumsy diplomatic dealings with Stalin between December, 1941, and April, 1942; and while Churchill went to America, Eden went to Moscow to negotiate a proposed British-Soviet pact.[7] On December 17, he began a series of conversations with Stalin in an attempt to pacify the increasingly bellicose dictator. But Stalin startled him with a list of Soviet demands predicated on Stalin's policy for postwar Europe and elements of the now-dead Nazi-Soviet Pact.

Under Stalin's plan, Germany was to be dismembered, Austria declared an independent nation, the Sudetenland returned to Czechoslovakia, and the Soviet borders with Finland and the Baltic States restored to pre-June 22, 1941, status. Poland would be constituted along the Curzon Line of 1919, with the loss of its eastern territory to be compensated with part of eastern Prussia; there would be Soviet bases in Finland and Romania. In return, Stalin offered the British naval bases on the French coast and in Belgium and Holland, which were already British allies.[8]

The Curzon Line was named after Lord Curzon, the British foreign secretary who, during the Versailles conference in 1919–1920, tried to delineate the Russo-Polish border along ethnic lines. The Poles, victorious in their war with the Soviets, pushed the line considerably to the east in the 1921 Treaty of Riga, where it stood until 1939, when it was altered by the Soviets in accordance with the secret protocols of the Nazi-Soviet Pact. After the defeat of Poland in September of

1939, what has been called the "fourth partition of Poland" took place, and Molotov declared to the Supreme Soviet that "nothing was left of this ugly offspring of the Versailles treaty."9

Eden, though sympathetic, was bound by Roosevelt's ban against secret arrangements and could not oblige the dictator. But Stalin was not prepared to sign an agreement that did not legitimize his pre–1941 territorial claims. "Why," Stalin asked Eden, "does the restoration of our frontiers come into conflict with the Atlantic Charter?" Eden, clearly despondent, went back to London to convince the cabinet to recognize the Soviet claims. His greatest problem was Churchill, who, having forged his Atlantic policy, was not ready to appease Stalin. "We have never recognized the 1941 frontiers of Russia except *de facto*," he cabled Eden from America.10 Churchill was not prepared to accede to Eden's "stark realism."

A crucial British cabinet debate ensued, conducted against the background of unfavorable military developments in Europe and the Mediterranean. Cripps argued for Eden's plan, calling for a "new order" and lauding the "heroic feats" of the Russians; and so did Beaverbrook, Stalin's chief apologist in the cabinet. Churchill asked Roosevelt to arbitrate the disagreement, and the president and Sumner Welles quickly rejected Eden's plan. They accepted the division of Germany, but not the pre–1941 Soviet frontiers.

The argument had political overtones, because Britain's floundering military fortunes made Churchill politically vulnerable, and Cripps and Beaverbrook both entertained thoughts of replacing him. Pressure was mounted on Churchill; his "defences were exhausted, and on March 7, he gave in," sending a disjointed letter to Roosevelt in which he wrote that "the increasing gravity of the war has led me to feel that the principles of the Atlantic Charter ought not to be construed so as to deny to Russia the frontiers she occupied when Germany attacked her."11

In his memoirs, Churchill was evasive about this episode, whereas Eden, in his memoirs, calls the negotiations with Stalin a "triumph," a claim also made by Eden's recent biographer, R. J. Rhodes.12 David Carlton, an Eden biographer who, unlike Rhodes, did not have access to Eden's private papers, argues that the Eden-Churchill conflict was serious, that it had moved Churchill to try to circumvent Roosevelt and accept Stalin's territorial demands.[13]

The British-Soviet Treaty was signed. "Churchill," writes Steven Miner, "for his part, felt uneasy with the decision to accept Stalin's demands, which he nevertheless felt must be met, and he understood more easily Roosevelt's hesitation than did the foreign office."[14] Eden, on the other hand, reflected the classic view of the old order that saw the European balance of power requiring that Germany must be contained at all costs. Since Germany was geographically closer to Great Britain than the Soviet Union, a divided Germany, even if it meant Soviet territorial expansion, was preferable. Eden stuck to the traditional long view of the foreign office, even though it was already outdated for a Britain whose power was waning.

Warren Kimball is misinformed when he writes that "Churchill had originally agreed with Eden." Churchill did not agree: two months earlier he had threatened to resign rather than accept Stalin's demands, and only surrendered to pressure, some of it politically motivated, from the cabinet.[15] Roosevelt, through Cordell Hull and Ambassador John Winant in London, had made his opposition to the Eden plan known through the critical months of 1942. For Churchill, the Baltic States were important, since they had always been a buffer against a revanchist Germany.

Roosevelt never helped Eden, and he never accepted the deal of exchanging territories for the Second Front. For Roosevelt, the issue of the Second Front was related more to a genuine military consideration for the besieged Red Army. Roosevelt, who could be pragmatic at times, wrote to Lord Halifax that "if during or after the war the Russians reoccupy the Baltic States, neither the United States nor Great Britain would or could turn them out."[16] The Eastern frontiers and the Curzon Line were not issues that concerned America. The American viewpoint was consistent: no annexation, no territorial deals, certainly not until the war had been fought and won.

The effect of the treaty between Great Britain and the Soviet Union, signed after bitter negotiations between Molotov and Eden on a text that in the end contained no mention of frontiers, was negligible. But the debate added legitimacy to Stalin's territorial demands. More importantly, it also contained Roosevelt's promise for a second front. For Churchill the price of maintaining a senior role in the war was almost a metaphysical dedication to the "Grand Alliance" that would assure his place with FDR and Stalin. It also meant the end of British Empire predominance in world politics.

The Politics of Operation Torch

Political and time pressures were pushing the Anglo-American Allies to engage in the war with greater force and on a wider front. The Allies were faced with a choice: a major cross-channel invasion or a peripheral effort elsewhere.

The British, concerned about their imperial interests in the Mediterranean, still in shock over the disaster in France, and haunted by the memory of the slaughter in World War I, were reluctant to embark on a massive, costly war. By 1942, Great Britain's army and its economy had been considerably weakened relative to their 1939 capacity, and the country could no longer mobilize men and resources to match the Americans and Russians. With the Battle of Britain won and the danger of German invasion apparently over, and with both the U.S. and the Soviet Union in the war, Churchill and his military chiefs supported an indirect approach, an imperial rather than a continental approach, attacking what the prime minister called "the soft" underbelly of Europe in the Mediterranean. Roosevelt and his staff, newcomers to the war and aware of the U.S. great economic and industrial potential, were eager to mount a major attack. The Americans wanted a cross-channel plan, which would start with Bolero-Roundup, the massive Allied deployment of U.S. troops from America to Great Britain in preparation for the Second Front.[17] Roundup, the brainchild of Generals Marshall and Eisenhower, was designed to culminate in a major landing in northern France. They called it "Invasion 1942." But with Rommel still advancing in the western Saharan desert, the British were leery.

Churchill came to Washington in time to stop the American plan, at least for a while. He and the British chief of the imperial staff, General Alan Brooke, strongly argued against an immediate cross-channel crossing, stressing that failure would bring disaster.[18] Churchill, also concerned with saving his armies in North Africa, persuaded the president to pursue a Mediterranean-North African Second Front strategy.

The alliance with Stalin, who wanted a major cross-channel invasion, complicated the decision, but in the end a compromise was reached. Initially called Operation Gymnast, it foresaw a landing in French North Africa, which would be used as a launching point for sending U.S. troops to the continent via the Italian underbelly.

The plan evolved into Operation Torch, the invasion of North Africa by American troops that would link up with British troops already fighting in the western desert. The commander of the operation would be Lt. General Dwight David Eisenhower for the American forces and Lt. General Sir Harold Alexander for the British.[19] Its scale and its logistical problems were "without previous parallel in the war, indeed in the history of warfare. Never before had states collaborated in dispatching such huge armadas over thousands of miles of ocean and landing so large an expedition in hostile or potentially hostile territory."[20] Churchill's ability to convince Roosevelt to undertake Operation Torch was a remarkable political achievement, but it was the last time the Americans would underwrite British planning of strategic options. Thereafter, Roosevelt would support American strategy, formulated by Marshall, Eisenhower, the Joint Chiefs, and Secretaries Stimson and Morgenthau, to end the war.

Despite the compromise, Stalin remained unsatisfied when Churchill told him the "news" that the major Second Front was not in the offing for 1942. Stalin, according to Harriman, responded with "bluntness almost to the point of insult regarding what he considered British fear of the Germans and a refusal to take risks."[21] Stalin so infuriated Churchill, that the latter finally exploded, "I am not sure it wouldn't be better to leave him to fight his own battles."[22] In the end, Stalin had no choice but to accept the decision. Roosevelt's failure to deliver on the promise he had made, however, gave Stalin propaganda opportunities in the Soviet Union, where he found the lack of a real second front an effective weapon with which to lecture the people about the dangers of democracy and perfidious capitalism.

How the Soviet Union Became an Ally: The Uses and Practice of Propaganda and the Second Front

Stalin's pressure for the Second Front was conducted on two tracks. Initially, the need for such an effort stemmed from the Red Army's life-and-death struggle with the Germans, the outcome of which was far from certain. But the victory at Stalingrad changed Stalin's approach. With the Red Army on the offensive, he now used the Second Front as a stick with which to beat the Western Allies. More than a military necessity, it now became an effective propaganda tool.

The new American alliance with the Soviet Union necessitated a revision of popular perceptions of that country and its leader. A totalitarian and repressive state would now be portrayed as "a heroic nation" of brave peasants fighting for their lives against the fascist invader. The calculating, ruthless dictator who signed a pact with Hitler would metamorphose into Uncle Joe, father of the nation, friend of democracy, and defender of the people. This benign view of the Soviet Union and of Stalin was necessary if there was to be public acceptance of the Soviet Union as an ally of Great Britain and the United States.

The popular American view of the Soviet Union had been traditionally hostile. The Bolsheviks, who had meant to undermine the American way of life, were not to be trusted. They had been presented at various times as convenient scapegoats for domestic troubles. Soviet propaganda did not treat the West kindly. As late as November of 1941, Soviet newspapers were making references to "fat capitalists and social fascists." After December, these same fat capitalists became "our common brothers fighting against Hitler's fascist armies."

The Nazi invasion of the USSR and U.S. entry into the war did not immediately engender acceptance of either country by its new ally. That was the task of British, American, and Soviet propaganda. In the

United States, it meant using part of the American intellectual and artistic community which, in the 1930s, viewed communism through romantic eyes and saw in the Soviet Union the last best hope of mankind. That perception had probably peaked during the Spanish Civil War, during and after which even the most loyal followers found it difficult to maintain their passion in the wake of the late discovery of the purge trials and the Nazi-Soviet Pact. The events of 1941 had renewed their faith.

At its height, in 1942 and in 1943, the effort to present the Soviet Union as a valuable ally, a democracy in spirit if not in practice, was the work of a diverse group of diplomats, writers, movie-makers, newspaper columnists and reporters, motivated by a sincere desire to help the war effort. The effort required a distortion of recent history—turning the purges, for instance, into a sideshow of the war effort, and blaming the West for forcing Stalin into the pact with Hitler. Some of the most active participants in this endeavor were former ambassador to Moscow Joseph Davies, Warner Brothers studio head Jack Warner, reporter Quentin Reynolds, playwright Lillian Hellman, photographer Margaret Bourke-White, and publisher Henry Luce. Most could hardly be called Communist party sympathizers, and some, like Luce and Warner, were decidedly anti-Communist. But they nevertheless served Stalin's purpose in one way or another, especially by emphasizing the need for a second front in 1942 and 1943.

As mentioned earlier, *Mission to Moscow* was probably the single most influential book to be published at the time. Written by the president's chief Soviet apologist, former ambassador Joe Davies, the book was very successful. Roosevelt had encouraged Davies, feeling the book would help the war effort. The president also followed closely the book's transformation into a Warner Brothers movie. The creation of the book, the book itself, and the subsequent movie demonstrate how the image of the Soviet Union and Stalin was manipulated for popular consumption.

Davies was hardly alone. As might have been expected, the *Daily Worker* took a pro-Soviet line, but so did Wendell Willkie, Fiorello LaGuardia, and writers in the *New Republic*. Liberal-left politicians, including New York Congressman Emanuel Celler and Florida Senator Claude Pepper, echoed the theme. Davies merely led the way. "The Russian people are fighting on our side and we should not forget that from the time of the American Revolution," he said in a radio address, "the Russian people have never failed to be on our side in every war we have been in." Davies did not bother to elaborate on how the "Russian people" had aided the United States in the Mexican or Spanish-American wars, but few of his listeners knew enough American history to notice. Nor did anyone really take issue with Davies' assertion that "we must never lose sight of the fact that we are aiding Russia to help ourselves and helping the Russian Government to beat Hitler doesn't mean tolerance or approval of Russian Communism."[23]

Davies began work on his book almost immediately after the Nazi invasion of Russia, with the help of ghost writers and the use of confidential State Department files. Although Edmund Wilson compared its prose to that of Warren Harding, the book was a bestseller.[24]

Davies described the purges as treason trials, calling the affected officers "measly anti-Stalinists"; and he praised Stalin, arguing that he "struck with characteristic speed, boldness and strength" in instituting the purges. "The morale of the army," he wrote, was not destroyed, nor "are they alienated from Stalin. Loyalty of the Army can be achieved once Stalin has smashed all potential rivalry and leadership." To Davies, the government was merely cleaning up possible nests of "internal aggression." He explained the midnight arrests, the summary executions, the wholesale disappearance of hundreds of people as necessary "cleansing and purging."[25] He discounted any territorial ambition on the part of the dictator.

Mission to Moscow was an effective lobbying and propaganda tool for the Soviet ambassador to Washington, Maxim Litvinov. So were the efforts of other writers.

If American publishers permitted any unfavorable comments about Russia to pass through their presses during 1942, the casual reader would have had difficulty finding them. Not only was Russia our partner, but nice words about her leaders and people sold, as Davies's *Mission to Moscow* demonstrated throughout the era. But because of the inevitable time lag between the conception of a book and its appearance on the market, there was virtually no comment on the possibility of a second front in this most durable of all media. Like most Americans whose thoughts on Russia were featured in print or on radio during the first half of 1942, authors were extolling friendship, or at least sensible cooperation, with the Russians.[26]

Margaret Bourke-White took a similar approach in her 1942 bestseller *Shooting the Russian War* and she had distinguished company.

> Quentin Reynolds, a popular journalist, positively praised Stalin for conducting the purges. 'We forget the meaning of the term,' Reynolds contended. 'The dictionary defines purge as to make physically and spiritually clean. That purge eliminated Russia's Fifth Column.' Of the Soviet leader, Reynolds wrote, 'his appearance was a contradiction of everything we had ever been led to believe about Stalin.' A British correspondent once wrote of Stalin that he looks like the kindly Italian gardener you have in once a week. 'You couldn't find a better description of the Soviet leader than that.'[27]

Stalin became something of a celebrity. Reporters wrote about his fondness for American cigarettes (he liked Lucky Strikes, Camels, and Chesterfields). For Americans, Stalin began to resemble a local sheriff, cleaning up the territory and looking out for the locals, in this case the Ukrainians, Moldavians, Estonians, and Lithuanians, liberating them from the "shame and humiliation" that had been inflicted on them by the "German Fascist-blackguards."[28]

Maurice Hindus, a popular pro-Russian American journalist, was even less restrained in extracting strange and positive images from reality. In a chapter on revolutionary Poles, Jews, and Ukrainians in his book, *Hitler Cannot Conquer Russia* (Doubleday, 1941), he wrote only of Nazi persecution and murder. Stalin's execution of Poles and Ukrainians, and the pervasive Russian anti-Semitism, were not mentioned. It had disappeared, according to Hindus, and he could prove it. "The fact that Jews raise pigs, and of superior quality, testifies much to the change that the Soviets have achieved, not only in their mentality, but in their daily occupation."[29] The popular press in the United States was equally enthusiastic in its praise. *Time Magazine* made Stalin its Man of the Year in 1943, and the February 16, 1942, issue featured on its cover Soviet Chief of Staff Marshal Boris Shaposhnikov, who is described as nothing less than a modern incarnation of Clausewitz.[30] The March 29, 1943, *Life* was a special issue devoted to the Soviet Union.

> "Henry Luce's editors," Koppes and Black write, "presented Soviet history as, in effect, a chapter in modernization, Russian-style. Lenin became a normal, well-balanced man, who was dedicated to rescuing 140,000,000 people from a brutal and incompetent tyranny. . . . Whatever the cost of farm collectivization in terms of human life and individual liberty, the historic fact is that it worked."
>
> Russian farmers were "content." We should not get too excited about the state's control of information; Soviet leaders said it was necessary "to get this job done." The NKVD, successor to the GPU, was a "national police similar to the FBI," whose job was "tracking down traitors." . . . [In short], the Russians were "one hell of a people," who "look like Americans, dress like Americans, and think like Americans."[31]

To Americanize the Russians was to sidestep the issue of the Nazi-Soviet Pact. Hindus barely mentions it, except to relate Molotov's visit to Berlin on November 12, 1940. He presents Stalin and the Red Army as victims of pro-Nazi propaganda in the West. To Hindus, the Nazis attacked Russia because Molotov had refused to join the tripartite Tokyo-Berlin-Rome axis. This "dealt a death blow to the Soviet-German pact. Seven months after Molotov's refusal, Hitler invaded Russia."[32] Ambassador Davies also took an odd view of the pact, writing that it "was not unexpected." In any case, he blamed it on the Europeans' eagerness to have a peace that would leave the USSR out of "the balance of power."[33] Davies' view that the Allies forced Stalin into the pact was echoed years later by Russian historian Roy Medvedev, a Stalin dissident but a Leninist, who wrote forty-five years later that "the nonaggression pact between Germany and the Soviet Union was not the best solution for either the Soviet Union or the forces favoring peace in the world."[34] "The U.S. was keeping its distance from European affairs, while England and France were playing an insincere and dangerous political game."[35] In effect, Medvedev, like Davies, says the Nazi-Soviet Pact was a consequence of dangerous Western power games.

The movie version of *Mission to Moscow* turned out to be the most controversial of Hollywood's efforts to do its part in promoting the Soviet Union as an ally. Later, during the anti-Communist hysteria of the late 1940s and 1950s, Warner Brothers studio officials would behave as if the movie version had materialized mysteriously out of nowhere. But at the time, they had no reason not to make the film. The brothers Warner insisted that Roosevelt had appealed to them directly to make it, and the studio received government support in making the movie.[36]

The movie was produced by Robert Buckner, who would later describe it as an "expedient lie for political purposes."[37] It was a greater distortion of history than the book had been, painting Davies as an instigator of policy, transforming the purge trials into a battle of good against evil. It also attacked isolationists. While its inaccuracies and misrepresentations are too numerous to list here, it was generally well-received at the time, disowned only after the war.

Manny Farber, movie critic for the *New Republic*, was disgusted. "Now I'm ready to vote for the booby prize," he wrote. "Not one character emerged. It was the dullest imaginable. This mishmash is directly and firmly in the tradition of Hollywood politics. A while ago it was Red-baiting, now it is Red-praising in the same sense—ignorantly. To a democratic intelligence it is repulsive and insulting."[38]

Mission to Moscow, which starred Walter Huston as Davies, was not the only Hollywood effort to praise our new found ally. Most of the rest—including Samuel Goldwyn's *The North Star, Days of Glory* (with a very young Gregory Peck as a Russian soldier), and the earlier *Blockade,* concentrated on giving a stirring portrait of the Russian peasantry bravely resisting the Nazi hordes, even though, as with the Ukrainians who were the nominal heroes of *The North Star,* this was not really the case. Lillian Hellman, incidentally, wrote the initial screenplay for *The North Star,* but battled furiously with Goldwyn over the end result.

The plays, essays, movies, articles, and books lionizing the Russian war effort helped Stalin's attempt to create public support for the Second Front. In Great Britain, the effort was spearheaded by the intellectual elites of Oxford and Cambridge and by the literary journals that supported League V (For Victory). The propaganda effort, as we shall see, continued without letup through 1943 and 1944.

The Second Front, 1942–1943

The debate over the Second Front, exhibiting the difficulties inherent in the alliance, demonstrates Clausewitz's dictum that the political and military aspects of war are inseparable. While the Allies continued to fight what Churchill called the "hated" foe, they did so without a cohesive plan of action. As Mark Stoler concludes his comprehensive analysis of the politics of the Second Front, "No one within the Grand Alliance was capable of viewing the war, politically or militarily, from an allied rather than a national perspective."[39]

Ambassador Litvinov's reports explain some of the difficulties in the alliance. Although his frequent contacts with Roosevelt led him to believe that a second front might be feasible,[40] he cautioned that Roosevelt's "military advisers were gradually dissuading him from that conviction, or it may be that it was mainly Churchill's influence." Litvinov was wrong about the generals, right about the British, especially in his conclusion that Churchill had been influenced by the British failure in North Africa. Litvinov concluded that "as far as the war policy is concerned, Roosevelt is being towed by Churchill."

Litvinov identified the Casablanca meeting as the beginning of Western doubts about an immediate large-scale effort in Europe.[41] The January 14–23, 1943, meeting between the president and Prime Minister Churchill was their fourth official conference. FDR was the first president to leave the country in time of war, traveling five thousand miles across the hazardous Atlantic Ocean to the North African port of Casablanca.[42] The decisions made there were not limited to 1943; they formed the basis for Anglo-American strategy for the remainder of the war.[43]

For the Western Allies, the Battle of the Atlantic had to be won before any attempt to launch a second front in Europe could be made. Litvinov was not convinced, suspecting, as did Stalin and Molotov, that the Anglo-American strategy was detrimental to Soviet demands for a Second Front, and the three Russians were always suspicious of the potential for an Anglo-American collusion to fight an independent war while the Russian Army bled to death. "I am inclined to think that there could be no hope of opening a second front even in the south, to say nothing of Western Europe without a very strong pressure on our part." Litvinov remained convinced that the Western Allies' military plans "strive for the maximal exhaustion of the Soviet Union in order to diminish its post world war role." But he believed that "if we wish, we can greatly influence the allies' strategic plans."[44]

Stalin exploited his failure regarding the Second Front to achieve other ends. Molotov's 1942 trip to London and Washington demonstrated Stalin's diplomacy. Although Molotov's first goal was to pressure the Americans to commit themselves on the Second Front, he also knew that the Americans and the British were still reluctant to grant Soviet territorial demands in the East. Aware that Britain was not ready to open a Second Front, he used this weakness to obtain endorsements for Soviet spheres of influence after the war. Lord Beaverbrook, for instance, declared that "if Britain agreed in advance to Soviet spheres of influence, postwar problems would be enormously simplified."[45]

Stalin was a dedicated nationalist and Communist, fighting a separate war on a separate front, always demanding support without reciprocity. When it served his purposes, he would not hesitate to drive a wedge between the Allies, as he did when Molotov obtained concessions on the Eastern territories, which was an extension of the policies Stalin had pursued with Hitler. "It still would be absurd to suggest that postwar territorial matters were more important to Stalin than a second front at a time when the fate of the Soviet state was in the balance." This, contends John LeBeau, was a "sophisticated diplomatic ploy, which was at the heart of Molotov's visit."[46]

The United States was consistently more sympathetic to the Second Front, and Roosevelt had wanted one open as quickly as possible in early 1942. Marshall was more cautious, but still thought in terms of late 1942 or 1943. Roosevelt had little difficulty in giving Molotov an initial qualified "Yes" to a second front. He told Molotov to inform Stalin that "we expect the formation of a second front this year."[47] Roosevelt stopped short of promising that the front would actually be opened in 1942, or that it would necessarily be opened in northern France. But it was enough for Molotov; he "everywhere gave the impression that Roosevelt had made a pledge, thereby further increasing pressure on the President to open up a Second Front. Stalin was satisfied that he had the Americans boxed into a corner; Roosevelt would feel obliged to go through with a cross-channel attack."[48]

The debate over the Second Front illustrated the political tensions inherent within a Grand Alliance based on differing conceptions of how to fight the war and sort out the peace.[49] Stalin's goals, once the danger from the Nazis appeared to have ebbed, reverted to the aims he had pursued with Hitler, specifically, the dismemberment of Poland and the annexation of the Baltic States. In point of fact, in spite of narrowly averting military disaster, Soviet strategy had not really changed. Stalin had new allies, but he never trusted them, despite Roosevelt's hope that the Soviet leader would become his partner in restructuring the postwar world. There was a pattern in Stalin's dealings with Hitler in 1939, with Churchill in 1941, with Roosevelt and Churchill at Teheran and Yalta, and in the negotiations between the two conferences. Roosevelt's fear that Stalin would embrace Hitler again was groundless because Stalin stood to gain nothing from such a move, but Stalin still played on that fear.

Stalin used the Second Front to legitimize his developing strategy of occupying the Baltic States and eastern Poland and establishing a Soviet sphere of domination over Eastern Europe. From the start, Stalin argued that it was only proper for the Soviet Union to ask for territory since it was paying a high price to defeat the Germans; the Red Army should keep the territory from which it was ousting the Nazi invader. The Second Front, Stalin suggested, would allow the Western Allies to fulfill similar territorial or political goals in Western Europe.

Stalin was also not above using the Second Front as a bloody litmus test with which to prod his allies. A Second Front would show good faith and a willingness to share more of the military burden that was being disproportionately carried by his people. "The Second Front served Stalin in different ways," Mastny writes. "It remained the crucial test of his improbable allies' adherence to the common cause."[50]

Roosevelt realized that America's late entry into the war prevented it from launching any attacks on mainland Europe, even though Roosevelt was ready to cross the Channel in 1942 and again in 1943. And a cross-channel Anglo-American invasion of northern France, which would have the military result of diverting as much as a third of the 150 German divisions now deployed on the Eastern front, was the only action the USSR would accept as a genuine Second Front. Wisely, the president reconsidered the plan for what Churchill would call an "early cross-channel massacre of Anglo-American troops."[51]

American army planners in Washington saw the merits of a cross-channel invasion early on. "They developed the Second Front concept as a way of winning the war on American, rather than British terms."[52] The question was one of timing. Roosevelt and Churchill recognized that a second front was vital for reasons other than showing good faith toward or easing pressure on the Soviets. Anglo-American military and political leaders feared that to stay out of Europe too long would mean a Soviet-dominated Europe. Eden was warned by an American general that

> 'if we did not watch our step we could still be discussing ways and means for operating Bolero while the Russians were marching into Berlin.' On March 30, Marshall told Roosevelt that it was important for us to have at least a strong Army Corps in England because if events did suddenly culminate in an abrupt weakness of German resistance, it was very important that there should be a sizable American representation on the ground where ever a landing on the continent of Europe was made. I also gave him as my personal opinion the fear that if we were involved at the last in Western Europe and the Russian army was approaching German soil, there would be a most unfortunate diplomatic situation immediately involved, with the possibility of a chaotic condition quickly following.[53]

The linkage between Roosevelt's rejection of an immediate second front and Stalin's failure to renounce territorial expansion influenced

American and British attitudes toward Stalin. All along, the State Department had advocated taking a harsh quid pro quo approach, especially early in the war when the Soviets were desperate for U.S. assistance. "American influence over Moscow was . . . now at its height and could only decrease as the war progressed."[54] Other voices argued that superior American strength would restrain Stalin from aggressive expansion into Europe.

The Case of Poland

Poland's image in popular history is that of a nation conquered and partitioned time and again by its neighbors. It is seen as a country enjoying periods of greatness interrupted by the ambitions of despots from Napoleon to the Kaiser to Hitler and Stalin. To understand how the Polish question was played out among the Allies, the origins of the Polish tragedy must be understood.

Poland is one of the oldest countries in Europe, going back to the year 965 A.D. As early as 1200, Poland was an imperial power, dominating parts of what are now the Soviet Union and the Baltic States. It has been and remains a deeply Catholic nation—Poland was a bulwark against the Turkish threat to Christianity—with great culture, a language, and a record of achievement in the arts and sciences.[55]

Poland's tragedy is geography. It lies trapped in the middle of the North European plain, without natural borders, vulnerable to the aggressions of its neighbors—the Russians to the east, the Germans to the west. Geopolitically, writes Davies, it has been "condemned forever to lie between the rival embraces of two rapacious suitors, or, more cruelly, as 'the gap between two stools.'"[56] As a result, Poland has suffered partition and the occupation of foreign troops to an extent unknown by any other European state.

In 1634, Poland dominated East Prussia, the Baltics, and parts of the Ukraine and southern Russia. Between 1793 and 1799, it was partitioned three times among Russia, Prussia, and Austria. After the Congress of Vienna, Poland shrunk still further. Its first state of independence in over two hundred years was declared by the Treaty of Versailles in 1919; but in 1939 it was partitioned again, this time between Hitler and Stalin. In 1945, Poland's eastern territory was annexed by the Soviet Union while parts of the defeated Germany were given to Poland.

During Poland's brief twenty-year independence, there were 4.5 million Jews in the country, mostly in the urban areas, constituting the largest Jewish population in Europe. In some major cities like Warsaw, Bialystock, and Lodz, 30 percent of the population was Jewish. Independence brought with it a militant nationalism, anti-Bolshevism, and anti-Semitism. Joseph Pilsudsky, considered the founding father of post-World War I Poland, came to power in a coup in 1926; his dictatorship, which lasted from 1926 to 1935, ended the chances for a democratic Poland.

Stalin's pretext for invading and occupying the eastern part of Poland, which was his due as part of the 1939 pact with Hitler, was its liberation from "Polish reactionaries," whose purpose was to "protect" Russia's "blood brothers" in the Ukraine and Belorussia from the aggressive Poles.[57]

The annexed territories were administered by Soviet officials and the Soviet model was imposed on a hostile population. An important political and nationalist force emerged in occupied Poland, a resistance army called the Armia Krajowa (the Home Army), which had its headquarters in Nazi-ruled Warsaw. The future of this underground would also play a significant role in the tripartite Stalin-Churchill-Roosevelt negotiations over Poland at Teheran and Yalta.

The establishment in Paris, on September 30, 1939, of a new Polish government-in-exile under General Wlyadyslaw Sikorski was the formal beginning of the Polish-Anglo-French alliance. The armed struggle inside and outside Poland became its major concern, continuing after it moved to London following the fall of France.[58]

At the time France fell, Poland briefly became Churchill's principal ally, if only since there was no other army outside the British Commonwealth actively fighting the Germans. Churchill's attitude toward the Poles was personal and emotional, and it did not necessarily translate into action. He told Sikorski he could count on him "forever."[59] In addition, both Churchill and Eden saw in Sikorski the kind of Polish statesman who had not been seen since Pilsudsky, one who was ready to seek accommodation with "Enemy Number Two," the Soviet Union. Churchill and Eden would try to use the Poles to cement their own treaty with Stalin. But Poland's stay in the limelight was brief. With Hitler's invasion of the Soviet Union, the focus shifted to the USSR and to America's role as the arsenal of democracy.

The Nazi invasion changed everything. Churchill and Roosevelt declared their full support of Stalin, Churchill in a particularly emphatic manner, and Poland was pushed to the margins. The Poles, however, were not ready to accept a marginal role. They were in a tough situation, contending with three allies: Great Britain looked upon them kindly but was in no position to back its sympathy with action; America was indifferent to their fate and irritated by having to acknowledge their presence; and the Soviet Union, the traditional enemy, coveted Polish territory.

Churchill defended the Poles to the end, although the Poles of London would be a source of irritation for him and Eden. Roosevelt had two concerns with the Poles. They presented domestic political difficulties among the sizable Polish community in America that voted Democratic, which made it necessary for him occasionally to pay lip service to the Polish cause. Poland also interfered with his vision of partnership with the Soviet Union in the postwar world, and he would sacrifice Polish interests to Stalin's ambitions in order to keep Stalin in the war and to keep his own vision alive.

The result was a complex mix of Polish diplomatic efforts, often conflicting, trying to fashion a Polish future among the competing interests of their allies. A dual diplomacy developed, one geared toward Great Britain and the United States, the other toward the Soviet Union, which they approached with the mistrust reserved for an old enemy. Polish diplomats worked hard to influence Churchill's and Roosevelt's dealings with Stalin, with a predictable result. Churchill and Eden pressured the London Poles to accept a Polish-Soviet treaty in July of 1941, only a month after the Nazi invasion. Grudgingly, both parties did so, mainly to satisfy Great Britain. But Stalin never intended to surrender eastern Poland, and even in the summer of 1941, the low point in Soviet fortunes, he continued to insist that Soviet occupation of eastern Poland, the result of the Nazi-Soviet Pact, was legitimate and permanent. For Stalin, geopolitical arrangements changed and new allies replaced old ones, but his goals remained the same. Whether dealing with Hitler, Churchill, or Roosevelt, he insisted on being accommodated on Poland.

Churchill, the Poles' sole champion, was bound to a policy dictated by Roosevelt's increasing inclination to pacify Stalin. Churchill may have been personally supportive of the idea of an independent Poland, but Britain's principal goal in the war was the preservation of its empire, not the preservation of Poland. Roosevelt did not have any interest either in challenging Stalin on a peripheral issue Roosevelt considered "small detail." Roosevelt's first priority was to win the war with Stalin's cooperation. Secondly, he wanted to end British and French colonialism and encourage Wilsonian self-determination in its place. For that purpose the United Nations was necessary, and FDR needed Stalin's cooperation for that.

Roosevelt had no specific European, or Eastern European, or Polish policy. The area did not merit the attention Roosevelt lavished on China, for instance. When it came to Poland and Eastern Europe, immediate military considerations prevailed over diplomatic issues. Roosevelt's policy toward Europe was militarily and politically peripheral and essentially Atlantic in orientation.

The Polish problem had three major components—territorial, political, and military. The country's eventual boundaries were tied to the ideological nature of the Polish government. This meant a choice between the legitimate Polish government as represented by the London Poles, who demanded the pre–1939 Polish territory occupied by the Soviet Union, or the Polish Patriotic Committee, a Communist group created by Stalin that came to be called the Lublin government, which ceded Polish eastern territory to Stalin. Support for the London government meant support for the formation of a democratic-centrist, pro-Western government. The Lublin government and its predecessor represented a Sovietized, Communist-dominated Poland.

The third factor in the Polish equation was who would liberate the Poles—the Soviet army or the Polish army, and if the latter, what kind of Polish army? Competition, sometimes open and sometimes clandestine, between the London and the Lublin Poles over the question of Poles in arms was fierce.

It is important to understand what the military, and the Polish legions in particular, mean in Polish history. Legionairism was a long-standing Polish tradition. Whether independent or conquered, big Poland or little Poland, the Polish legions were emblematic of Polish nationalism and independence, as much a symbol of Polish nationhood and independence as the Polish church, the Polish language, and Polish literature. Polish legions had distinguished themselves in Napoleon's armies; they were in Russia as well as in Austro-Hungary during the First World War, fighting as independent units among their allies. Pilsudsky commanded a Polish legion in the Austro-Hungarian army before changing sides in 1917, and traditionally the most honored Polish citizens were those who served in the legions, including Jews.

General Sikorski, the leader of the Polish London government, understood the symbolic power of the Polish legions when he established a joint command of all Polish armies, east and west, thus creating a legion for all of Poland. These armies also would constitute Poland's claim for independence, its bargaining lever in negotiating for territorial claims, and the political nature of the postwar Polish regime.

Stalin understood this, and never intended to see an independent Poland emerge from the war, certainly not a Poland that was, in his terms, "reactionary." He had a different agenda for postwar settlement, one in which the Poles figured as a weak, Soviet-dependent entity dominated by the reactivated Polish Communists (which Stalin had purged as late as 1940).

Sikorski's effort for an all-Polish army failed, as Stalin saw to it that it never materialized. Although a separate Polish army fought in British, Canadian, American, and Soviet Allied Armies, it was the potential power of the Polish underground in Poland that mattered most to the war effort. Until 1944, the Polish army was in the hands of the London government, though formed under the aegis of the tenuous 1941 Polish-Soviet pact. A military organization, called Zwiazak

Walki Sberjnej (Union of Armed Resistance), later known as the Armia Krajowa, or the Home Army, soon emerged. Its political activities included a shadow parliament or council of national unity, headed by a delegate of the London Polish government in exile.[60]

By November of 1941, a rival Communist underground had been established by the Soviet government. The Polish Communist party, previously purged by Stalin and which had participated in the Home Army as long as the Nazi-Soviet Pact was in effect, now precipitated a split in the underground, creating its own military arm, Zwiazak Wacki Wyzwole Nozi, or the Union of the Struggle for Liberation, headed by the charismatic Communist Wanda Wasilewska, a Polish woman who became a Soviet citizen in 1940. The resurrected Polish army included thousands of exiles, led by Zygmunt Berling, who accepted wartime service under the Soviets, among them former Polish POWs freed by the Soviets. The Polish army in the USSR was headed by Lt. General Wladyslaw Anders, a representative of the London government who had been arrested by the Soviets in 1939, but released under the British-imposed treaty of 1941. The Soviet attitude toward the creation of a Polish army "was conciliatory,"[61] but did not welcome it, and the differences that foreshadowed the bleak future of a free Poland soon emerged.

For Roosevelt, the Poles were a problem that threatened to upset his and the Allies' relationship with the Soviet Union. Although he subordinated the Polish problem to his wider war goals, the angry charges later made by Polish-American writers that Poland had been betrayed by Roosevelt are incomplete. Secretary Hull, like Roosevelt a strong supporter of the United Nations as an instrument for a world liberal order, saw the Polish question as an impediment to that goal. He wrote in his memoirs:

> The policy of the President and me was to refrain from stretching the United States upon a bed of nettles. In our diplomatic exchanges with both sides and in our offers of good offices, we repeatedly stated we were not entering into the merits of the differences between Poland and Russia. . . . When two neighbors discontinue speaking terms, the neighbors of each unanimously desire

to urge them to find a way to get back on speaking relations. . . . It is only through this course of friendly discussion and conference that we can possibly get Polish and Russian difficulties worked out.[62]

Hopkins expressed the sentiment that the London Poles were very much like the exasperating de Gaulle. Indeed, they were perceived in Washington as reactionaries. Roosevelt, Hopkins, Judge Samuel Rosenman, William Hassett, the president's press chief, and others never quite said it out loud, but they suspected that the London Poles were disguised Fascists and anti-Semites, a remnant of the decadent nobility.

This perception was not extended to General Sikorski, whom they at first admired and respected. To them, Sikorski was honest and straightforward, a diplomat who knew how to "get along with the Russians." But Roosevelt's respect for Sikorski did not extend to pressuring Stalin for significant concessions on the Polish question.

In regard to Poland, in all probability, Roosevelt would not have concerned himself at all with Polish borders during the War, except this issue became a question threatening Allied unity, especially Russo-American unity. Thus, it affected all of Roosevelt's primary goals for the war. As Russia continued to press for Polish and Allied acceptance of her claims on Poland's eastern territory, for Roosevelt it became a question of either abandoning Poland's eastern territory or losing Soviet support for his primary goals.[63]

Roosevelt did push for the Treaty of Riga Polish boundary, established in 1921 after a successful Polish war against Lenin's fledgling Soviet Union, but this was a small concession that did not oblige the United States to protect Poland's eastern borders. "Although on the surface, Roosevelt worked half-heartedly for some small changes in Stalin's plans for absorbing one-half of Polish territory, he seemed to do this only to keep the Poles from making any more trouble in Allied relations and to keep the political situation under control at home."[64]

Increasingly, the Poles were seen as a nuisance by both the United States and the British, capable of ruining the Grand Alliance. The president did his best to minimize his dealings with the Poles and to avoid making any commitments to them. Soviet-Polish relations became a classic example of international politics in its most Machiavellian guise.

For the Poles, the relationship with the Soviets represented a series of tragedies, from the Nazi-Soviet Pact to the establishment of a Polish-Soviet regime in Warsaw in January, 1946. First, there was General Anders' refusal to send his "legions" to fight as part of the Red Army on the Russian front. Sikorski failed to persuade Roosevelt to direct some Lend-Lease assistance to the Polish army. Later came the tragedy of the Katyn Forest Massacre, followed by the Teheran conference, which ended Poland's eastern territorial hopes. Finally, after Sikorski's death, came the disastrous split between right and center factions in the London government; the Communist army and party headed by Wanda Wasilewska and General Zygmunt Berling; and the Yalta conference that sealed the fate of Poland. Only the Jews suffered a more disastrous fate than the Poles.

The fate of Anders' army is instructive. The army grew out of the Polish-Soviet treaty, created by Churchill and Eden. Churchill saw the treaty as a link in the general pattern of the Anglo-Soviet alliance; but for the Poles it was much more, the touchstone for General Sikorski's conviction "that Poland's international posture must be a realistic reflection of her geography."[65]

Sikorski, like de Gaulle and Churchill, was courageous and realistic in his diplomatic thinking. Sikorski, according to Sarah Terry, was an unlikely rebel. He was the traditional Polish officer—meticulous, steadfast, courageous, not too imaginative. His diplomatic instincts were more acute than those of his colleagues, who were implacably hostile to the Soviets. He therefore opted for what Churchill appeared to be prescribing, hoping to gain a bigger role for Poland in the Western alliance and at the same time to pursue a relationship with Stalin not based on the traditional enmity between Poland and Russia. Sikorski understood this was the wisest option open to a Poland caught between Hitler and Stalin. For him the question of an independent Poland was one of identity and politics, not necessarily territory. Unlike the rest of the London group, he was not irreconcilably wedded to a complete eastern frontier. It was not even mentioned in his treaty with Stalin, nor was it a part of the Anglo-Soviet treaty. "Poland has entered upon the path of political realism with determination," he said.[66]

Sikorski's strategy was sound, forged at a time when the London Poles had no political or military rivals within Poland and their prestige was still high. It unraveled because Stalin had no intention of even entertaining the thought of Polish independence, because the Western Allies were indifferent to Poland, and because Anders wasted the Polish army as a potential tool for the creation of an independent nation.

Stalin understood what an independent Polish army meant in real and symbolic terms. General Georgi Zhukov, then commander and coordinator of Soviet-Polish troops, approached Anders and asked him to enter the war in Russia as part of the Red Army. Anders indignantly refused, declining also an offer to become a Red Army general. Since Stalin did not want a Polish army in the Soviet Union in the first place, this gave him a pretext for exiling the Polish army from the Soviet Union altogether. Anders, in order to save the balance of his army, withdrew it to the Middle East and the Mediterranean, where Polish troops would fight and distinguish themselves in North Africa and in the battle for Monte Cassino in Italy. Stalin was thus well served by Anders.

With the departure of Anders' army, Sikorski lost a valuable tool. He set out to find new political solutions, but again received no help from his allies. His request for Lend-Lease assistance was ignored by Roosevelt. He then worked to achieve a new Central European entity, not too removed from Churchill's Danubian confederation. He attempted to convince Edward Benes, exiled president of Czechoslovakia, to create a Czech-Polish confederation, a meaningful Central European entity that might have succeeded in acting as a bulwark against Stalin. But he was talking to the wrong man. "No one among the London-based liberation movements was as inarticulately pro-Soviet and anti-British as the Czech one."

As he did with Anders' army, Stalin coopted Sikorksi, this time by blackmailing Benes in 1942 into signing a treaty that recognized

Stalin's aims in Poland. And so, Sikorski's hopes for maintaining a Soviet relationship were repeatedly frustrated; his strategy was collapsing around him.

The final break came with the Katyn Forest Massacre. The Nazis, aware of the difficulties the Polish problem created for the Western Allies, attempted to widen the gap between Stalin and his allies. On April 13, 1943, Radio Berlin announced to the world the discovery of the bodies of some 10,000 Polish officers buried in a mass grave in the Katyn Forest in the Smolensk area.[67] The Nazi radio report stated that "the Bolsheviks had perpetrated secretly a mass execution." The Soviets dismissed the charge, calling the information something "fabricated by Goebbels's slander." But for the London Poles the old anxieties about the Soviets burst forth. When they called for a Red Cross investigation of the massacre, Stalin reacted with indignation, breaking off relations with the London Poles.

If the Poles were expecting sympathetic treatment from their allies in the West, if they thought that Churchill or Roosevelt would admonish Stalin, they were mistaken. Roosevelt appears to have acted callously in the Katyn matter, in effect blaming the victims. He treated Katyn at first as if it was an example of Nazi propaganda, complaining that the Poles had no business suspecting the Soviets. But even if the Soviets had done the deed, he felt this was no reason to put pressure on the alliance and was angry when the Poles appealed to the Red Cross. In a letter to Sikorski, Roosevelt complained about Polish behavior, advising him to keep in mind the "interests of Poland and of all the united nations."[68]

When Lt. Commander George Earle, sent by Roosevelt to gather facts on Katyn, expressed his belief that the Russians were responsible for the massacre, the president tried to convince him otherwise.

Earle has related that Roosevelt told him: "George, this is entirely German propaganda and a German plot. I am absolutely convinced the Russians did not do this." When in later months Earle kept insisting that the evidence of Soviet guilt was there, Roosevelt simply ignored his accusations.

Finally in March of 1945, when Earle wrote the president informing him that unless he heard from him he was going to publish what he knew about Katyn, Roosevelt would not allow it. FDR told Earle, "I not only do not wish it, but I specifically forbid you to publish any information or opinion about an ally that you may have acquired while in the office or in the service of the United States."[69]

What the president really believed is not as important as the fact that he tried to play down the massacre and the controversy. His approach was typical of the way he approached all issues involving the Poles, and Stalin knew that Roosevelt would never pressure him about Poland.

It was obvious that the Soviet-Polish relationship was at an end. What had Stalin gained from it? The relationship, forced on him by Churchill and Eden, gained him respectability. The idea of such a relationship allowed Great Britain and the U.S. to ignore the harsher realities and to keep the Grand Alliance against Hitler. The relationship, at least until 1943, provided Stalin a means for blunting the London Poles while gradually putting in place in Poland military and political forces that he could control. Except for his consistent insistence on Soviet rights to the Baltic States and eastern Poland, Stalin had no specific plans for Poland; these evolved with the fortunes of war.

"What Stalin would later demand both from Poland and for her would depend largely on the developing political and military balance as the end of the war approached."[70] As Stalin's options increased, so did his demands. Conversely, Polish options, or those of the London Poles and Sikorski, diminished in direct relation to the Red Army's march beyond its pre–1939 boundaries. More and more, Poland's fate was linked to the progress of Soviet tanks rather than to Churchillian diplomacy. From the United States, the Poles could expect nothing more than Roosevelt's indifference.

The Moscow Conference of Foreign Ministers, which was the prelude to Teheran, demonstrated the Polish impotence that would only increase at Teheran and Yalta. By 1943, Sikorski's military strategy of "coordinated" military efforts between the Red Army and the Polish Home Army had been politely rejected by Stalin, who did not wish to strengthen the Polish claim that they had autonomously contributed to the war against the Nazis. Increasingly Poland's future became tied to the Soviet military machine.

> During 1943, the war had entered a phase of momentous victories for the Red Army. On the last day of January, Field Marshall von Paulus surrendered at Stalingrad. By the end of July the German armies were pushed back to Kursk. The consequences of these achievements was to alter, dramatically, relations between the Big Three. Particularly important in this regard was Stalin's order of the day of 23 February, 1943. He predicted that the Red Army alone would drive the Germans out of Russia, the Ukraine, Byelorussia and the Baltic States up to the Western boundary of the Soviet Union.
> To the Polish government, this suggested that the fate of Poland was increasingly open to Soviet initiatives, particularly as each Soviet military victory seemed to reduce further the will of the Western Powers to intervene on Poland's behalf.[71]

Sikorski was killed in an unsolved plane crash and Wlyadyslaw Mikolajczyk replaced him as the new leader of the London Poles. The London government adopted an unrealistic attitude, frantically increasing pressure on their Western allies to protect their territorial integrity in the East. When Mikolajczyk pressured Eden at one point on Polish security, Eden shrugged. "What can I do?" At the Moscow Conference of Foreign Ministers, Poland was not a consideration. As Hull said, "We had gone to Moscow primarily to reach an agreement between Russia and ourselves, not an agreement between Russia and Poland."[72]

At Teheran (which will be discussed in more detail in the following chapter), Stalin made it clear to the Allies, especially Churchill, that at best he was willing to accept the Curzon Line or "something like that," and left to Churchill and Roosevelt the task of handling the London Poles.[73] He refused to resume diplomatic relations with the London Poles.

"Once the Red Army has occupied Poland, it would be too late for a negotiated settlement."[74] Churchill's acceptance of the Curzon Line conformed to his realpolitik view regarding Stalin's spheres of influence, and was in marked contrast to Roosevelt's utopian vision of a world organization as an instrument of redrawing the map of Europe. Churchill and Stalin saw the ineffectiveness of the League of Nations, and both understood that world organizations were useless in settling borders or other serious disputes.

Conforming to his unpredictable style at Teheran, Roosevelt surprised Stalin by bringing up the Polish question. The motive was electoral, not diplomatic. He said he had to return home with "something" to show for his efforts. This angered Stalin, who charged that Roosevelt had no idea what would happen to Poland.[75] Stalin felt the Allies would not push the Curzon Line on the Poles if relations were resumed.[76]

Churchill entered into the fray as a pacifier. He was willing to promote the Curzon Line to the Poles. Roosevelt was not insistent, an attitude that has led one author, George Janczewski, to see a malevolent anti-Polish attitude in the president's actions. "A number of scholars studying allied diplomacy during the Second World War were, until recently, in agreement that Roosevelt made few comments and generally held back on the issue of Poland during the Teheran Conference. For practical purposes the American president had entered into an agreement with Stalin about Poland's eastern frontier, apparently without Churchill's knowledge."[77] What is known from the Teheran records is that in a meeting with Stalin, Harriman, and Bohlen, Roosevelt jokingly said that the United States "would not go to war against the Soviet Armies" for Baltic people even if there were many of their origin in the United States.[78] Roosevelt never publicly supported Churchill's Curzon Line, leaving Churchill to deal with territorial disputes.

Churchill found an unreceptive audience in the Poles. Before and after the Moscow and Teheran conferences, Mikolajczyk besieged Churchill and Roosevelt and anyone who would listen, pleading that the Curzon Line was unacceptable. In a conversation on October 14, 1944, among Mikolajczyk, Churchill, Eden, and others in Moscow, Churchill implored Mikolajczyk to accept the Curzon Line. Mikolajczyk refused. "Should I sign a death sentence against myself?" he asked emotionally. Eden tried to reason with the Polish leader, suggesting that if the Poles accepted the Curzon Line, it would be possible to gain from Stalin full guarantees for an independent Poland. Still, Mikolajczyk remained adamant.

Churchill became exasperated. "I wash my hands of it, as far as I am concerned we shall give the business up," he said. "Because of quarrels between Poles, we are not going to wreck the peace of Europe. . . . Unless you accept the frontier," he told Mikolajczyk, "you are out of business forever." "We are losing everything," Mikolajczyk said. "We [the London government] will lose all authority in Poland if we accept the Curzon Line." Eden said that "the Russians have a strong case on the Curzon line, plus there is compensation for Poland in the West," but to no avail. The Poles, by rejecting the Curzon Line, were clinging to territorial issues and throwing away whatever hopes existed for their political autonomy.[79]

Chapter 6

Stalin

The relationship between the U.S. and the USSR and between Roosevelt and Stalin was crucial to winning the war. Stalin was the Soviet Union's chief diplomat and strategist, and his leadership style merits examination. He had no surrogates like Roosevelt had; rather, Molotov, Voroshilov, Beria, Malenkov, Dekanozov, and Zhdanov mirrored Stalin's philosophy and unquestioningly executed his orders.

New light is shed on the relationship of the two heads of state by Soviet Foreign Office documents that have been opened for the first time. The assessment of the Roosevelt-Stalin relationship cannot yet be complete, as historians are still measuring the motivations, accomplishments, and failures of great historical figures. Still, it is incorrect to claim that there is not enough documentation to make a valid assessment. In addition to documents and papers, time is a valuable tool for historians, lending perspective to events. The benefit of perspective in the work by Western and some Soviet historians has given us a more definitive portrait of Stalin the man and of his strategy and diplomacy during the war.

My purpose here is to recreate the dialogue between Stalin and Roosevelt as it related to their goals. They did not enjoy a special relationship, but the summits they held can be freshly examined from the vantage point of the leaders' respective perspectives.

In a century dominated by the forces of authoritarianism, two men towered above all the rest in terms of destructiveness. The brutal qualities of Adolf Hitler and Joseph Stalin were unmatched by other twentieth-century figures. When their destinies crossed, first in their pact of 1939, then in the war for survival from 1941 to 1945, their combined legacy was forty million dead. Fifty years later, the consequences of their brutalities are still with us, in the survivors of the Holocaust, the haunted prisoners of the Gulags, and the continuing upheavals in Eastern Europe.

Stalin's crimes cannot be enumerated here,[1] but it is important to understand just what kind of ally Roosevelt and Churchill got when Hitler invaded the Soviet Union. We should remember, however, that the collaboration among the three countries never amounted to a true alliance. "Americans, Britons and Russians were compelled to join forces against Germany out of national interests and expediency."[2] Stalin fought alone against Hitler, with no direct assistance in manpower from the Americans or the British. The U.S. and Britain sometimes fought together, sometimes apart, in the different theaters of the war.

Stalin: An Overview

"There is no political issue of greater importance in the Soviet Union than the significance of the man who has been dead for thirty-six years and the legacy he left to the people he ruled so masterfully and cruelly," Adam Ulam wrote in the introduction to the expanded edition of his *Stalin: The Man and His Era.*[3] Stalin was a peasant, a revolutionary, the heir of Lenin, political commissar, General Secretary, politician, the great warrior and leader of his country in World War II. Since the end of that war, Stalin's reputation has undergone periodic revision within the Soviet Union. Yet, even in Gorbachev's denunciation of the country's Stalinist past, the image of Stalin as a great and effective war leader remains intact.

As war leader, however, Joseph Stalin does not yield a consistent image. Little is known about his panicky reaction to the Nazi invasion of the Soviet Union. For nearly two weeks, from June 22 to July 2, as his armies collapsed and the Panzer divisions swept across Russia,

Stalin did not appear in public. The few accounts that exist tell of his being shocked by the invasion, even though intelligence from a variety of reliable sources had told him that the Nazis would invade.

But very soon after July 2, Stalin emerged to become a symbol for the defense of Mother Russia, a partner in a Grand Alliance to crush the Nazi invader. The mythology that developed created the Stalin legend, in Russian as well as in Western eyes. Part of the myth that developed in the West about the war in Russia was due to the absence of outside observers in the Soviet Union. Accounts by Western apologists and Soviet propagandists about the savage war fought on the Eastern front were so skewed, the truth of that war may never be known. The problem is not the lack of documents, but the distorted nature of the evidence that does exist. Only recently, with the writing of John Erickson, Colonel Albert Seaton, and Earl Ziemke, has the picture become more accurate.

It is not surprising that John Keegan's recent *Military History of World War II* (1989) gives more space to Crete, the Pacific and Atlantic naval campaigns than to Stalingrad, or the war between Hitler and Stalin, which resulted in millions of deaths. Why did such a war pass into the realm of myth? One reason is that Stalin fought the war within an alliance in name only. In truth, he fought without allies, never sought Western alliance, and never believed in it as part of a strategic future. He used it as a means to supply the Red Army with much-needed Lend-Lease material and to initiate the Second Front as soon as possible to facilitate Soviet counteroffensives. His philosophy was crude—if they are with me, they are not against me. Throughout the war, Stalin operated from a position of mistrust.

Adam Ulam writes that Stalin's leadership during World War II and his guidance of Soviet policy in the postwar years had until recently remained "relatively exempt from the wholesale attack" on the rest of his career. Today, his generalship, diplomacy, and postwar policies have come under closer scrutiny, even in the memoirs of Soviet marshalls who fought in the war. Soviet military historians have criticized Stalin's policies. "It's no surprise," writes Ulam, "that the new materials contain a shattering evaluation of Stalin as a war leader."[4]

Soviet analyses today treat Stalinism as cruel barbarism disguised as Marxist-Leninism and clothed in deceptive ideological trappings.[5] Stalinism has been labeled a deviant version of socialism using the name of modernization, to justify the extortion of resources from the peasantry. Soviet philosopher A. Tsipko[6] considers Stalin a despot of the left, one who used violence in the Jacobin tradition to achieve revolutionary goals.

One of Stalin's most recent authorized biographers, Colonel General Dimitry Volkogonov, characterizes Stalin's leadership as *Vlast,* or the cult of personality and power. Political scientist E. E. Ambartsumov[7] calls Stalin an "evil maniac," lazy, ignorant, but an adroit intriguer. As early as 1927, Soviet psychiatrist V. M. Behtjev judged Stalin to be afflicted with paranoia and insurmountable megalomania, a judgment which cost Behtjev his life.[8]

Stalin's diplomatic conduct of the war was creative, deceptive, and shrewd, successful in the short run, but wrong in the long run. He occupied and Sovietized Eastern and Central Europe and the Balkans; but in achieving that traditional Russian goal, he alienated a potentially friendly America and locked the Soviet Union into a costly Cold War. Instead of seeking security with the Atlantic powers, he behaved like traditional European statesmen, seeking security through territorial acquisition and military preponderance but without concomitant diplomatic conciliation. His policies—imperialist, paranoid, and expansionist—assured that his country would remain isolated.

The Man and the Mind

Stalin was General Secretary, head of the Communist party, chief of the Committee on Defense, chairman of the Military Committee. He also accepted such Caesar-like titles as Father of All Nations, the Great Leader of the Soviet People, the Great Friend of Children, the Great Helmsman, the Creator of the Constitution, the Grand Strategist of the Revolution, the Supreme Military Leader, Generalissimo and Genius of Mankind, the Leading Light of Science and the Greatest Genius of All Times and Peoples.

The titles did not seem to fit the man. From a distance, he was a familiar figure, with the familiar bushy, drooping mustache, the pipe, the plain khaki with gold military braid, the black boots. He looked common, but strong. The real man was short (between 5'2" and 5'3"), with one hand shorter than the other and always hidden defensively in his sleeves. His face was pock-marked and rough. When he smiled, he revealed rotten teeth, blackened by tobacco stains. Dark, bushy eyebrows accented an intense gaze. He seemed to personify Mozart's Serraglio, the oriental despot, and he contrasted sharply with the garrulous Churchill and the elegantly expansive Roosevelt.

Stalin remained an enigma to both friend and foe. He had no close friends, but needed the company of sycophants, among whom was the slow, subservient Marshall Klement Voroshilov, an old crony who had been his comrade in the revolutionary days. He held a grandiose image of himself, which he tried to fulfill through massive works and projects; he was a builder and killer on a grand scale,[9] the father of the Five-Year Plan, the guiding force behind collectivization and forced industrialization.

Stalin was not a man of ideas beyond an obsessive lust for power. He personified the use of raw power, or *Vlast*. This was not manipulative, Machiavellian power, but brutal and naked power. Paranoid and practical, he destroyed his own party and an entire class of Bolsheviks without hesitation in order to maintain his power. In the pursuit of his policies, Stalin caused the deaths of millions of his own people, exploiting physical and human resources in the service of his own ambition. He was not a crazed megalomaniac like Hitler; rather, he had the practical sense of a machine gun operator who gets the job done. He cared little for the theories or ideology of Marx, Engels, or even Lenin, although he parroted and plagiarized Marxist-Leninism in an obligatory Marxist tract on occasion. His most famous work was on nationalism and colonial questions. The man was surely despicable, but his strategy was nevertheless brilliant.

Stalin was the ultimate *apparatchik*. He was tuned to every nuance in the power struggles and shifts that characterized the early days of the Soviet Union. According to Boris Bazhanov, his secretary from 1923 to 1926 and author of *Stalin, der Diktator* (1930), Stalin was the intellectual inferior of his political arch rivals Trotsky, Zinoviev, and Kamenev, all of whom aspired to be Lenin's successor. In meetings among the leaders of the 1920s, Stalin would be silent or tongue-tied, smoking his pipe, unable to keep up with the verbal exchanges; but his political maneuverings were astute.[10] George Urban noted that Stalin was more concerned with gaining unrestricted power and using it than with the actual business of government during the great struggle against his rivals in the Bolshevik leadership. In the end, it was Stalin who played the most decisive role in the fundamental socio-economic transformation of the Soviet Union between 1924 and 1933.

Stalin craved power for its own sake; the statues and enforced adulation reflect that. He did not enrich himself, leading an ascetic life. Volkogonov writes that after Stalin's death "he was discovered not to have any personal belongings except for a pair of lined felt boots and a patched Sheovkia coat in the peasant style."[11] Volkogonov's major revelation, at least to Russian eyes, was Stalin's obsession with *Vozhdism,* or Caesarism. The cult of one-man leadership was propagated by Stalin, who lionized Robespierre and was a careful student of Napoleon.

The Great Purges and the 1939 Nazi-Soviet Pact are crucial keys to the understanding of Stalin's behavior from the Nazi invasion on. Each episode illuminates his thinking and maneuverings. We have considerable if incomplete information on the purges. The lack in Soviet archival documentation has allowed some of the best scholarship on the purges to come from the West, a fact readily acknowledged by Soviet historians. In particular, Robert Conquest has proved to be the most reliable source for information on the purges.[12]

Stalin's purges constitute what Hannah Arendt called the essence of totalitarianism. They were an instrument of terror that became an ongoing process. The purges, more than Western pacifism and appeasement, were at the heart of the Stalin-Hitler pact, his paranoia, and his contempt for his new Western allies. Without the impact of the purges on Russia, communism, and Stalin, the history of Soviet war policy and Stalin's relationship toward his allies is incomplete.

The purges were more than a domestic concern; they provided the basis for his foreign policy. Between 1937 and 1941, over 60 percent of the Communist delegation to the 1934 Seventeenth Party Congress had been eliminated; some three thousand members of the Politbureau were dead, including one-third of the Central Committee. All of Lenin's Bolshevik generation perished or were sent to the Gulags, among them Lev Kamenev, Georgy Zinoviev, Karal Radek, Nikolay Bukharin, A. Rykov, and M. Tomsky. The majority of foreign Communist leaders were shot or exiled.[13]

Stalin's henchmen were his Security Police, the NKVD; but Stalin also killed his own assassins, first Genrikh Yagoda, then Nicolai Yezhov. The most devastating destruction was felt in the Red Army officer corps, where thirty thousand of a corps of eighty thousand officers were purged.[14] Three marshalls were killed—Mikhail Nikolaevich Thukhachevsky, Vasily Konstantin Blucher, and Veronim Petrovich Uborevich. In addition, Stalin purged the diplomatic corps and the industrial leadership.

Stalin, the Strategist: Diplomacy, 1939–1941

Stalin had only himself to blame for what seemed a disaster of massive proportions that loomed in the wake of Hitler's invasion of the Soviet Union. He had signed the 1939 pact with Nazi Germany and pursued it energetically, blinding himself to Hitler's intentions. The Soviet Union's military unpreparedness was a direct result of the purges Stalin had conducted against his own military.[15] He accepted his military vulnerability after the purges, and this together with the danger of a possible military coup—a danger Stalin exaggerated— had motivated him to seek an alliance with Germany. Stalin did not want war and knew he was not ready for it. In the late 1930s, he could pursue a preventive alliance with the West against Hitler, or he could join with Hitler, thereby delaying war and providing a chance to gain Polish territory. Stalin knew that at some point in the future Hitler would turn east. But despite warnings from his own intelligence services and from those of the Western powers, he never understood that Hitler would act sooner rather than later. The invasion caught him completely off guard.

The Nazi-Soviet Pact had startled the West, as well as the International Comintern. Yet, it should not have been so shocking. German-Russian relations had been cooperative as far back as the immediate aftermath of World War I. It is important not to forget that without German military support, Lenin would never have found himself in the sealed train that took him from Zurich to St. Petersburg. Germany also assisted in the various coups and counter-coups that ended with the storming of the Winter Palace and the overthrow of Alexander Kerensky's provisional government.[16] And in the aftermath of Versailles, both Germany and Russia became the pariah states of Europe, left out of the European arrangements made by British and French statesmen.

After the Bolshevik Revolution was consolidated, after Rapallo in 1922, Weimar Germany and Lenin's fledgling Soviet state embarked on a policy of cooperation that continued through the 1930s with Stalin. Both the Germany of Weimar and Hitler and the Soviet Union of Lenin and Stalin sought mutual restoration of influence in Central Europe. Even the conservative Catholic Weimar statesman Gustav Stressemann was not indifferent to expanding Weimar into Poland and Czechoslovakia.[17] And General Ludwig Von Beck, who served both Weimar and Hitler until 1938, advocated territorial and security arrangements on the border of Poland and Czechoslovakia.[18]

By the summer of 1939, Stalin felt he could either wait and see how appeasement of Hitler worked or take the initiative to avoid war. "In 1939," writes Sebastian Haffner, Stalin "saw a chance for averting such a war by tossing the ball to the West."[19] Stalin was impressed with Hitler's audacity. Stalin's generals, meanwhile, stressed the need for good relations with the powerful Hitler.[20] Stalin misread Nazi Germany, considering the Nazi party to be the instrument of the Reichswehr and the industrialists, not taking it seriously. "Believing that the Reichswehr had complete control of the situation and being intent on a renewal of military collaboration with Germany, he never understood the danger Nazism represented."[21] He saw Hitler's purge of Ernest Roehm's *Sturm-Abteilung* (Storm Troops) as the end of the

"Nazi period" and the beginning of the era of the "state," with the German military, which he respected and understood, in control.

Throughout 1935 and 1936, Stalin sought an agreement with Hitler despite warnings from the international section of the NKVD that "all of the Soviet attempts to appease and conciliate Hitler are doomed."[22] By 1939, there were contacts among high- and low-level Nazi and Soviet diplomats, negotiations in which feelers were being extended. Both Hitler and Stalin were on the move, Hitler toward war, Stalin away from it.

By mid-August, Stalin had made up his mind to ally with Hitler.[23] On August 23, 1939, within the walls of the Kremlin, the Devil's Pact was signed, witnessed by Stalin, Molotov, Ribbentrop, and the Soviet and German ambassadors to Berlin and Moscow. It was "the Soviet dictator who controlled the timing and fixed the terms of the pact."[24] He intended to smash the Polish state, thus reversing the humiliation of 1920, when Polish forces had defeated Soviet armies. Stalin wanted to annex the Baltic States and establish hegemony over Bessarabia and Finland, all former Tzarist domains. In the short run, Stalin drove the harder bargain and achieved the most from the pact. He gained more than he would have from an alliance with France and Great Britain. The pact also helped trigger the war, since it allowed Hitler the freedom to move against Poland and against the West. Stalin was secure. He had averted war with Hitler, bought time, and gained territory. He had protected his regime, his state, and his territory. The fourth partition of Poland since 1793 changed the balance of power in Europe in favor of the former Versailles pariahs, as Germany and the Soviet Union now commanded Central Europe. The British were isolated, and France would fall in June of 1940. The "folly" of the Versailles statesmen had now been corrected.

Yet, Soviet-Nazi relations were deceptive. The pact did not avoid war with Germany, but merely postponed it and, for the USSR, not nearly long enough. Stalin's greed made him overlook Hitler's real ambition. The imperialistic aspect of the Nazi-Soviet Pact would reappear in Stalin's dealings with his new allies after the Nazi invasion. Stalin would try to make an almost identical deal with Churchill in 1941—Soviet domination over the Baltic States and the institutionalization of the Curzon Line.

The Nazi-Soviet Pact in Retrospect

Soviet explanations for the pact have ranged from crude propaganda to more telling analysis. The propaganda argument presented Stalin as a devious sort of Machiavelli who maneuvered circumstances so as to unleash Hitler on the Western powers, avoiding Soviet entry into war for two years. This argument has been offered by Vyshinsky, Gromyko, Molotov, Lozovsky, and other official historians of the Great Patriotic War.

A modified argument for Stalin's motives has been offered by Roy Medvedev, a former dissident and since 1989 a member of the Congress of Peoples Deputies.[25] Medvedev argues that between 1936 and 1939 Stalin was "extremely ambiguous," fluctuating between Litvinov's collective security approach and his own isolationist "socialism in one state" concept. He writes that an all-European, anti-Fascist collective security arrangement would have been preferable, though European-American appeasement would not allow it. Although Medvedev was not willing to "justify Stalin's entire policy," he argued that Stalin was "compelled" to sign the pact by the British-French policy of "toleration and nonintervention." Munich, argues Medvedev, "unleashed" Hitler and forced the non-aggression pact on the Soviet Union.[26]

But what was the error? To Medvedev, "Stalin's blunder was not the pact itself, but the attendant psychological and political atmosphere that it created." Stalin put "too much trust in his pact with Hitler and failed to perceive Germany's real plan for an invasion." Stalin felt that Hitler was a reasonable man, "an adroit and calculating politician" who "understood" Stalin.[27] His "monumental error in judgement" was in thinking that he could tie Hitler to a pact of "spheres of interest," which was merely a trap Hitler had laid for Stalin, recognizing the latter's innate paranoia and his concern for Soviet security.

Hitler needed the pact so that he would be free of any danger in the East; and to assure that safety, he was willing to share Poland with Stalin. In the wake of the pact, Stalin continued to cling to the relationship. Molotov refused to believe what was happening as late as June 22. "Perhaps this is just an act of provocation by the German militarists," he suggested when news of the German military moves came. Stalin's error was one of self-deception; he believed in Hitler to the end. His error in judgment was unpardonable and disastrous.[28]

British historian D. C. Watt sees the pact as a more complex event. "By the beginning of March [1939]," he writes, "the Soviets had retreated in part into a suspicious and dilatory isolationism, with strong hints that they would like to see an agreement with Germany which would divert German expansionism westward. Behind this lay a deep and abiding distrust of Britain and France."[29] The British and French were evasive, as Hitler was between 1940 and 1941. In 1939, it was generally assumed that Poland would be Hitler's next target. Western appeasement appeared to be driving Stalin into Hitler's arms. But it can also be said that Stalin was the architect of the nonaggression pact, and that the pact seemed to favor the Soviets. In one stroke, Stalin had achieved what neither Lenin nor Trotsky had ever managed—the annexation of Eastern Poland, the Baltic States, and Bessarabia. "Most important, [he had managed to achieve] the destructive war among the capitalists."[30]

Valentin Berezhkov's analysis of the Hitler-Stalin relationship offers clues to Stalin's real error of judgment. Berezhkov participated in the 1938–1939 Nazi-Soviet negotiations as a junior counselor and translator in Berlin. Like many others, including George Kennan, William Shirer, Joachim Fest, and Albert Speer, Berezhkov argues that Stalin had an affinity for Hitler. He maintains that Stalin hoped Hitler would not die, but would disappear, like Nero, so he would haunt generations to come.[31] Stalin placed a trust in Hitler that he never extended to anyone else. It continued longer than was safe, right to the eve of the invasion. Most Soviet historians blame international relations of the 1930s for Stalin's embrace of Hitler. A. O. Tchubaryan and A. Roshchin of the Institute of World History of the USSR Academy of Sciences, without ignoring the domestic sources of "deformed" socialism, cite the Munich Agreement of 1938 as a direct cause of the Nazi-Soviet Pact.[32] They consider U.S. neutrality another factor.

A. Baydokov blames the heads of the NKVD and military intelligence for failing to alert Stalin to the approaching war. Indeed, Stalin received numerous messages from Soviet and European intelligence sources on German preparations for war, but he ignored them. The state security apparatus was busy with the purges and Stalin's methods served to isolate him from real intelligence information. Volkogonov speculates that Stalin's purges, which Hitler knew about, might have influenced the launching of the Nazi invasion. If so, it was not an important factor, since Hitler had long planned to attack the Soviet Union.

The trauma of the collapse of the nonaggression pact and the 1941 invasion guided Stalin's subsequent policy and war diplomacy. He would be guided by memories of Allied appeasement in the 1930s and his belief that the West wanted to see the Nazis and Soviets engage in a destructive war.

From Retreat to Counteroffensive

The massive Nazi invasion of the Soviet Union was a classic surprise attack. Its initial successes were so spectacular that they surprised even the Nazis themselves. Yet the offensive surprised only Stalin, who refused to believe it was actually happening. He had initiated the pact with Hitler to buy time, knowing that war would come eventually; but when it came so suddenly, he went into a shock, and his refusal to face reality paralyzed his armies, whose lack of direction and leadership assured the invasion's early success.

Stalin had ignored the continuous flow of intelligence from a variety of sources. The attack came as no surprise to Churchill, to the Czechoslovakians, to the Poles, to Japan, or to Richard Sorge, the Soviet spy in the German embassy in Tokyo.[33] Warnings had come from Washington, where State Department officials such as Hull, Welles, and Breckinridge Long had repeatedly tried to alert the Soviets to the impending German threat. The American contribution, writes Barton Whaley, historian and analyst of the surprise attack, "is particularly remarkable because it was unexpected and improbable."[34]

The American intelligence work was credited to an amateur—a Texas businessman named Sam Edison Woods, who had become a diplomat in 1928 and served in Berlin as commercial attaché between 1937 and 1941. He was one of the early and informal intelligence gatherers in the pre-OSS State Department. In that capacity, Woods sent Stalin reliable information on the German plans to attack.[35] In February of 1939, he passed this information on to Secretary Hull, who first checked with J. Edgar Hoover to determine whether Woods was a "German plant." Hoover said the information was authentic, and Hull telegraphed a summary of Woods's information to Ambassador Steinhardt in Moscow, who related it to Andrei Vyshinsky, senior deputy to Molotov.

The early signs of Nazi invasion plans were changes in the German order of battle, mobilization movements, frontier fortifications, increased German espionage activities, border violations, and violations of Soviet air space by the Luftwaffe. Molotov and his aides were made aware of this information by British ambassador Sir Stafford Cripps, for instance, whose warning to Welles was related to the Soviet ambassador in Washington, Korstantin Umansky.[36] There were warnings from the Polish and Czech undergrounds, and even from Winston Churchill himself. Molotov dealt with these warnings consistently—he dismissed them because his master did not want to hear them. Stalin also believed that the German generals would not allow Hitler to initiate a war against the Soviet Union and would move against him if he did.[37]

The Soviet intelligence services themselves were in a state of demoralization. The sources of intelligence—the Commissariat of Foreign Affairs, the Commissariat of Internal Affairs (NKVD), the Commissariat of Defense, and the Comintern—had once been known for their high degree of professionalism and the effectiveness of their agents. But what was once one of the most advanced intelligence-gathering organizations in the world had been ruined as a result of the purges.[38]

The invasion came with vengeance. By June 22, 1941, the Germans had gathered a huge invasion force—190 divisions, or 4.6 million men, including 16 tank divisions, 13 armored divisions, 50,000 cannons and mortars, 5,000 aircraft, and some 4,000 tanks. The force was 70 percent of the entire German army.[39] Against this force, the Soviet Union had 222 divisions, of which 170 were operational, and few of which were sufficiently deployed on the crucial western borders of partitioned Poland. The Soviet army was huge, with a force of 4.2 million, but it was badly led and trained. The battle commenced on the longest frontier in the history of modern warfare, some fifteen hundred miles from the Baltic to the Black Sea.

In the weeks before the invasion, Stalin had appeared lackadaisical and confused. He refused to concede that Hitler might attack and seemed incapable of making decisions. Nikita Khrushchev, if his memoirs are to be trusted, was eager to get away from Moscow and act on his belief that war was coming.

> I kept trying to get permission from him to return to Kiev. Finally, I asked him outright, 'Comrade Stalin, war could break out any hour now, and it would be very bad if I were caught here in Moscow, or in transit. I'd better leave right away and return to Kiev.' 'Yes, I guess that's true. You'd better leave.' His answer confirmed what I'd suspected: that he hadn't the slightest idea why he'd been detaining me in Moscow. He knew my proper place was in Kiev. He had kept me around simply because he needed to have company, especially when he was afraid. He couldn't stand being alone. . . . Stalin was so afraid of war that even when the Germans tried to take us by surprise, and wipe out our resistance, he convinced himself that Hitler would keep his word and wouldn't attack us.[40]

We do not know exactly what happened to Stalin once the invasion was launched, but by all appearances he was temporarily paralyzed. According to Berezhkov, Stalin all but entombed himself in his dacha outside Moscow during the first week of the war, refusing to see anyone, refusing to confront the reality of the war. Molotov's voice was the only one heard over the radio, announcing the invasion forty-eight hours after it had begun. Admiral N. G. Kuznetsov, the People's Commissar of the Navy at the time, told of going to the Kremlin to report the situation personally on June 22. In the Kremlin, everything appeared normal. The mistakes were not attributed to "Stalin's incorrect assessment of the situation."[41] N. N. Voronov wrote, "I saw Stalin seldom in the first days of the war. He was depressed, nervous and of an uneven disposition."[42] Meanwhile, the Germans moved swiftly, sweeping into the Ukraine, Belorussia, and Russia proper. Almost immediately, the European part of Russia succumbed to the Nazi onslaught. Commanders at the beleaguered and collapsing front received no help from Moscow, and received communiques and orders without Stalin's signature. "A limitless gulf separated Soviet pre-war predictions of the likely course of war from the actuality; the latter took on the dimensions of a colossal night-marish fantasy and produced a mental vacuum, a terror of the unexplainable." "The early phases of the war demonstrated Stalin's ineptitude as a strategist, which contributed to Hitler's early victories."[43]

Even when faced with this military disaster, internal politics continued in its ruthless course. Captured Russian officers were declared traitors, while the First Security Police, Cheka, and NKVD conducted military intelligence, most of it against their own men.[44] The war was run like the purges, with political policemen informing Stalin of internal "enemies," political opposition and collaboration, real or imagined. Stalin, realizing that the monumental military failures were his, feared the potential of a military coup.

The opening salvos were followed by a continuing series of disasters for the Soviet armies. The German winter offensive, which began in October and lasted through December, was launched along the whole of the eastern front, from Lake Ladoga to Leningrad to the Black Sea and the Caucasus. The situation was as critical as the early days of June, with German troops and the tanks of Field Marshalls Heinz Guderian and Fedor Von Bock all but surrounding Moscow. But there was a difference. Stalin was no longer in a state of paralysis. He had emerged to reassert control over events.[45]

On July 3, Stalin announced on national radio the program of action for the Russian population and issued his first front-line directives to his commanders; it marked the beginning of his recovery. He soon began a routine whereby he would start his working day an hour or so before noon by calling the operations directorates for briefings on the previous night's developments.[46] Marshals G. K. Zhukov and A. M. Vassilevsky, who headed the General Staff, would report personally on the progress of the campaign to Stalin.[47] By the start of Hitler's second offensive, the General Staff had finally assumed a routine. On a typical day, the members of the Politbureau would sit along one side of a long table by the wall, facing the military people and the large portraits of A. V. Suvorov and M. I. Kutuzov that hung on the opposite side of the room. Stalin would listen silently to the reports, sometimes stalking up and down on the military side of the table. Occasionally, he would go to his desk near the back of the room and take out two Hercegovina Flor cigarettes, break them up, and methodically pack the tobacco into his pipe. Lenin's grotesque white plaster death mask lay under a glass cover on a special stand beside Stalin's desk. Usually, the reports would entail a description of the activities of Soviet forces over the past twenty-four hours. The fronts, armies, and tank and mechanized corps were referred to by the names of their commanders; the divisions, by numbers, a system Stalin had established.[48]

Very quickly, Stalin proved himself to be an astute war leader. S. Bialer described Stalin's leadership as crucial to the Soviet Union's survival.[49] Stalin's ability to mobilize the Soviet people over a sustained period of time made him the equal of Roosevelt, whose most significant contribution to the American war effort had been his ability to mobilize the American people.

Like Roosevelt, Stalin had "the ability to recognize and reward superior military talent at all levels under his command."[50] His comprehension of general strategy, both political and military, and his grasp of technical detail were remarkable,[51] though in terms of operational command planning he was probably not Hitler's equal,[52] for which Khrushchev and others have criticized him.

Yet, compared to Roosevelt or Churchill, Stalin dominated these areas because of the nature of the war he was fighting. There were many good generals among his commanders, and both they and Stalin improved as the war progressed. "The improvement of Stalin's leadership was in large part a function of the Soviet military professionals."[53] He was like Roosevelt in his ability to act as arbiter among his generals, and he surpassed Roosevelt in controlling day-to-day operations.

This was a function of the conditions of the war. Stalin did not make frequent visits to the front, but the front was approaching him in the awful winter of 1941. Roosevelt's only direct contact with the war was in face-to-face talks with his generals. A better comparison to Stalin would be Abraham Lincoln, who made every major decision in the American Civil War close to the front, aware of the danger of invasion. Stalin learned strategy because he was forced to.

Stalin's strategy gradually evolved from his initial fight for survival to his developing design for imperialism. His Eastern European strategy evolved along with Soviet advances. But Roosevelt either did not notice or ignored the change in Stalin's strategy throughout most of the war. He treated the Stalin who fought for survival the same way he treated the Stalin whose triumphant armies rolled across Eastern Europe.

In 1941, Soviet strategy had failed because the political and military commanders were unprepared for the kind of war Hitler launched against the USSR. The Kremlin had always emphasized a defensive strategy, but it was unprepared for the Nazi onslaught. Despite the defensive orientation of Soviet strategy, the Red Army launched numerous offensives to regain territory before Stalingrad. Most of these failed, but the 1941–1942 winter offensive around Moscow successfully drove the German army back from the capital.

New literature, based on both German and Soviet military archives, strengthens the argument of Andreas Hillgruber[54] that Hitler's decision to attack the Soviet armies was based on both ideological and strategic considerations. The two aims were the large scale colonization of the East and the annihilation of the Bolshevik regime as part of Germanic Lebensraum. Hitler's war in Russia was of a "fundamentally different nature from that of all other German campaigns in the Second World War."[55] "A Communist is not and can never be considered a fellow-soldier. This will be a war of annihilation."[56] Hitler demanded revenge for all atrocities committed against Germans and other racially related peoples in this campaign against "sub humans."[57] This racist element was not only Hitler's, but reflected the attitudes of many Wehrmacht generals.[58]

The Germans lost in the USSR because of several serious strategic errors, and because they failed to distinguish between the war to annihilate the Bolshevik regime and the war against the Soviet citizens. Had the Germans first liberated captive nations like the Ukrainians, the Belorussians, and the Balts, they might not have lost the war in the East. The failure to rally the Soviet peoples, who passionately hated Stalin's regime, resulted from an absence of strategic purpose in the war. Strategy is the art of limits, the art of knowing how to advance one's goals by arms and by politics. Hitler's errors brought the destruction of nazism and Germany.

Some authors identify two levels of analysis of Soviet military strategy: the political-military, which defines the character and purpose of military power, and the military-technical level, which determines how Soviet military forces operate in the field. This is a misconception of political-military relations in Stalin's time and a misunderstanding of the Stalinist system. Under Stalin's rule there was only one level of strategy—the police state. Stalin's military strategy must be measured against his total domination over the military and all other organizations. This domination of the party-state-military system defined his reign.

Stalin lost control of the military for a very brief period early in the war, as Bialer demonstrated in his account of Stalin's relations with Konstantin Rokossovsky. Stalin directed the military himself and even once boasted that he could eliminate one-third of his officer corps and "in six weeks time create substitutes for the purged officers." But he courted disaster because he had had no immediate strategy for countering Hitler's attack.

Judged by the initial results, both Stalin and Roosevelt were unprepared for war, and both paid a price for that weakness. The United States and the Western powers would have been in strategically superior positions if America had entered the war against Hitler before Pearl Harbor; and Stalin's early mistakes pushed the Soviet Union to the brink of disaster. The postwar fate of Eastern Europe might have been different had the United States invaded the continents as early as 1942.

Adam Ulam is right when he says that Stalin ran "circles around people as astute as Churchill and Roosevelt." "Did he not contribute mightily to raise a Soviet Union, bloodied and exhausted at the end of the war to superpower status."[59] At least that was the view of Soviet patriots of the day, writes Ulam. But a modern Soviet patriot might see things differently.

It is interesting to note Warren Kimball's observation that both Churchill and Roosevelt were "strangely silent" about the Nazi-Soviet war.[60] Neither was optimistic about its outcome through most of 1942, because of a lack of information about the war and because the Nazis, even after their initial defeat at the gates of Moscow, continued to mount huge offensives. British and American leaders worried about the Soviet army's capacity to absorb the losses it was suffering and the prospect of a Japanese military role on the Eastern front. Thus, British and American leaders continued to worry about a Russo-German rapprochement for longer than was necessary and conducted much of their diplomacy to ward off that possibility.

No information on key issues pertaining to the "Grand Alliance" satisfies some of the most disturbing questions that arose during the Nazi-Soviet war. Stalin's ruthless tactics against Poland confused and disappointed Roosevelt, while confirming Truman's hostility toward the Soviet Union. The empire Stalin created in Eastern Europe was short-lived and hardly worth the price. It collapsed in a matter of months in 1989. Gorbachev had to deal with the legacy of Stalinism, and he could not do so while maintaining an empire in Eastern Europe. Stalin's sweep across Eastern Europe may have seemed startling at the time, but it will ultimately be seen as failure. It was a short-term success that held within it the seeds of a larger long-term failure.

Stalin's major failure stemmed from the political system he headed. Roosevelt, Harriman, Hopkins, Churchill, Eden, and others reminded Stalin of the importance of public opinion as a source of political legitimacy in democratic societies; but the concept was alien to him. This inability to appreciate the power of public opinion led to another failure: he could not comprehend how the American people could move from sharing an "overwhelming sympathy" for the Soviet Union, in the wake of the Nazi invasion, to alarm and hostility after the Soviet Union's brutal tactics in acquiring Poland, Czechoslovakia, Hungary, and other Eastern European countries.

Soviet expansion made Stalin feel more secure in the short run, because the conquests provided a territorial buffer against the West. Stalin received plaudits in the Politbureau for out-maneuvering Churchill and Roosevelt, but he was condemned by anti-Communist Poles, by isolationists, and finally by the majority of his former allies.

Part III

Roosevelt and Stalin, 1943–1945

Chapter 7

Teheran
The Road to Yalta

Stalin and His Western Allies: Looking for a Way to Win

Something of the essential Stalin is revealed in his attitude toward Roosevelt and Churchill. Especially for Churchill, there was a mutual empathy, not trust. Churchill reminded Stalin of his old nemesis Leon Trotsky, whom Churchill admired. Stalin saw in Churchill some of the characteristics he associated with the old Jewish Mensheviks, people of energy and purpose, committed ideologues, and gifted orators. Although Stalin respected Churchill, he still mistrusted the British leader, remaining ever watchful for Old World manipulation.

Roosevelt was something of a romantic, too, but in a naive, American way. Stalin did not respect Roosevelt's preference for appeasement, but he was ready to take advantage of it. Bolshevik and Leninist ideology dominated Stalin's political habits, and he held parliamentarian and democratic political practices in contempt. Stalin appreciated power that brooked no opposition.

After the Great Purges, Stalin had no real opposition; he was free to pursue Soviet and traditional Russian goals. Russia had been threatened by the great land powers of Europe from Napoleon's France to the new Germany. Stalin was seeking security for Russian territory and legitimacy for the Bolshevik regime. Churchill, aware of security needs, understood Stalin's motives better than did Roosevelt. Roosevelt was the leader of a nation with no close enemies, a country that had not been seriously threatened since the War of 1812 and whose most costly war had been an internal tragedy.

The United States could try to escape world politics, even contemplate disarmament, but Churchill and Stalin had to achieve European stability, which meant the stability of East Central Europe and the Balkans. Both saw the need to contain Germany. Churchill wanted a confederation whereas Stalin wanted a Soviet hegemony over East-Central Europe. Roosevelt was content to minimize his commitment while hoisting the banner of a free and moral world.

Churchill saw in Stalin a man who had power and knew how to use it. Roosevelt was impressed by Stalin's power to persuade and manipulate, but had no understanding of Stalin's absolute power. New Dealers like Hopkins saw a certain resemblance between the Soviet Union's massive industrialization projects and New Deal projects, missing the fundamental differences between the two and between the societies in which they took place.

For Roosevelt and Churchill, who saw the Soviet dictator as central to their vision of the political future, dealing with Stalin was a difficult task. Roosevelt saw him as a partner—each the leader of one of the two most powerful nations in the world, capable of creating a new order. Churchill saw Stalin in terms of the European balance of power; he wanted both to use Stalin and to limit his conquests, an impossible task.

Stalin's advantages over the two Western leaders were the capability of the Red Army and his own very clear goals. Churchill, realistically assessing Britain's declining position and reflecting his country's traumatic experience in World War I, was apprehensive about continental commitments and unwilling to commit Britain to shouldering a large share of the postwar European order. He tried to adapt to this reality by a nuanced approach to Stalin, at times opposing and at other times wooing him. Roosevelt wanted the postwar Germany, though divided, to act as a buffer against the Soviet Union. Churchill sought to create conditions in Europe that would obviate the need for either British or American occupation, seeking the creation of European federalism. A divided Germany, a weak France, and the remaining Central and Eastern European states not under Soviet domination would be formed into a confederation, or perhaps two confederations—one centered on the Danube, the other in the Balkans, both designed to contain the Soviet Union.

Churchill was strongly influenced by the writings of the Hungarian internationalist Count Richard Coudenhove-Kalergi, who, between the wars, had promoted a European federation as an alternative to the League of Nations.[1] Churchill thought such a federation would not be democratic. "If the Russians built it, there would be communism and squalor; if the Germans built it there would be tyranny and brute force."[2] Roosevelt and Hopkins discouraged Churchill's idea of setting up a European council—"Roosevelt asked, 'After Germany is disarmed, what is the reason for France having a big military establishment?'"[3]—but Churchill doubted that the European powers would consent to being disarmed while the Soviet Union threatened them with the potential of the largest standing army in Europe.

Churchill's hopes did not materialize. Stalin was hostile to a Danubian confederation and sabotaged the idea. Seeing he would get no help from the Atlanticist and a pacifist Roosevelt, Churchill tried to appeal to Stalin directly. On January 16, 1944, he wrote Eden about "the tremendous victories of the Russian armies, the deep-seated changes which have taken place in the character of the Russian state and government, and the new confidence which has grown in our heart towards Stalin."[4]

Churchill's diplomacy achieved mixed results. He fought Stalin on Poland, getting him to agree to the Curzon Line, but he was unable to convince the London Poles to accept it. In Greece, Churchill was helped by the OSS and a military intervention to defeat the Greek Communist guerrillas, keeping Greece out of the Stalinist orbit. It was obvious to him that Balkan and Eastern European affairs would be run by the Soviet Union, and his percentage scheme, based on the military realities that prevailed, was born out of this recognition. The Allied sweep across Western Europe represented a counter balance to the Soviet military progress in Eastern and Central Europe. Churchill wanted the West to go into Austria and Hungary, but he could not get Roosevelt to agree. On October 9, 1944, Churchill offered Stalin his percentage deal—50/50 in Hungary, 90/10 in Greece and Romania, 50/50 in Yugoslavia. These were meant to be percentages of influence and degrees of occupation. Churchill offered a division of Germany into three parts: (1) Prussia, "the root of the evil"; (2) the Ruhr and the Saar; and (3) the more liberal Germany, meaning Bavaria, Wurtenberg and Baden, along with Austria.

After victory at Stalingrad in 1943, Stalin began to turn military success into diplomatic policy and territorial accumulation. Churchill sensed the shift rather early, but Roosevelt never really did. Hopkins remained silent and reverent toward Stalin, convincing Roosevelt to accept Stalin's aims.

The battle for the future of the world was being fought in far-flung military operations on three fronts: the Mediterranean, the Soviet Union, and the Pacific. As soon as the war had reached the shores of Italy and France, Stalin's calculations became strictly political.

Prelude to Teheran: The Moscow Conference, October, 1943

FDR was not all that interested in Churchill's schemes.[5] With the occasional exception of Poland, Roosevelt consistently sought to cooperate with Stalin. He was reluctant to confront Stalin on any of the Eastern European issues, including Poland, and especially Greece and Yugoslavia. As the president made clear at Teheran, he would not participate in an anti-Soviet alliance.[6]

Until 1943, Great Britain had served as the link in the great alliance between the United States and the Soviet Union. Churchill and Eden met separately with the Soviets and the Americans to explain, interpret, and make plans.[7] Hopkins met with Stalin in July and August of 1941, as did Harriman in 1941 and 1942; and Molotov had come to Washington in the summer of 1942. But direct contact between FDR and Stalin was minimal, leaving both the Soviets and Americans feeling like strangers. Roosevelt decided to upgrade the consultations to summit-level talks.

The spring of 1943 was a low point in U.S.-Soviet relations. Am-

bassador Standley complained that "Russian authorities apparently
. . . want their people to believe that the Red Army is fighting the war
alone . . . it's not fair."[8] Stalin, meanwhile, was fulminating about
Churchill's suspension of Arctic convoys in April of 1943. This convoy
route carried a third of American supplies to the Soviet armies preparing for their spring offensive. Stalin accused the Allies of bad faith.[9]
Unhappy with the results of the 1943 Casablanca conference, Stalin
also felt the need for a meeting with the Allies. The Moscow Conference of Foreign Ministers was held from October 18 to October 30,
1943; and it was there that Roosevelt's concerns first emerged.

The American delegation to Moscow was headed by Secretary of
State Hull, who played a major role for the first time, and included
thirty-one people, among them Maxwell Hamilton, Harriman, Cecil
Grey, Harriman's assistant Lt. R. P. Meikeljohn, special agent for the
State Department Henry Thomas, and General John Deane, who led
the military mission. The Soviets were unrelenting, emphasizing their
old theme—a demand for a Second Front in the West. They wanted to
"consider measures for shortening the war against Germany and its
allies in Europe."[10] Stalin had already raised the issue in 1942, in
response to Roosevelt's promise, when he wrote to Roosevelt "I feel
confident that no time is being wasted, that the promise to open a
second front in Europe, which you, Mr. President, and Mr. Churchill
gave for 1942 or the spring of 1943 at the latest, will be kept and that
a second front in Europe will really be opened jointly by Great Britain
and the U.S.A. next spring."[11] But now Stalin was threatening to
withdraw his ambassadors from Washington and London, refusing to
consider meeting with Roosevelt, and perhaps turning to Hitler.[12]
Stalin's complaints were accompanied by a propaganda campaign in
the West which portrayed the Allies as dragging their feet while the
Russian army bled. This time Stalin's push for a Second Front was
both an effort to embarrass his Anglo-American allies and a real push
to divert Nazi troops from the Eastern to the Western front.

At the Moscow Conference, Hull, who was not a member of the
president's war council, was dependent on General Hastings Ismay,
Churchill's chief of staff, and General Deane, head of the U.S. military
mission to Moscow, as well as Eden, all of whom briefed him on

military affairs and the Second Front. "He knew of the decision of a cross-channel attack but was never told when, where and how."[13] As a result, Hull avoided giving any definite information to the Russians. Stalin was not all that disturbed, as the Second Front campaign served his propaganda purposes and allowed him to make headway on other issues. The Russian offensive was going well, and the Germans were in retreat after the Stalingrad disaster.

Efforts to achieve a tripartite agreement, to replace the Soviet-British and the British-American bilateral agreements, on the exchange of technical information and weapons inventions also came to nothing at Moscow. Old Russian territorial ambitions, which Harriman had long predicted, came into play as the victory at Stalingrad allowed Stalin to expand his thinking on such matters.[14] The Soviets now showed interest in the Far East, where the Americans were beginning to seek their help; but Stalin emphasized the Second Front, saying he needed it in exchange for Soviet participation in the war against Japan. At the time Soviet interests in the Far East might have exceeded their desire for an Allied Second Front.[15] The results of the meeting were the Four-Nation Moscow Declaration, which included U.S. support for Chiang Kai-Shek's government, and a draft for a new international organization.

Hull directed State Department thinking regarding a new system of international order as early as 1939 and headed a new advisory committee on postwar policy, which held its first meeting on February 12, 1942, with Hull serving as chairman and his deputy Welles as vice-chairman. Roosevelt's idea of the Four Policemen (U.S., USSR, Britain, China) who would become a world security council was the result of Hull's work that recommended the creation of such a council (embodied in the current UN Security Council).

At the Moscow Conference, Hull's draft received a thorough consideration. The debate was around Article 7, which specified that following the defeat of the enemy, the signatories could not use their forces within the territory of other states. This was aimed at trying to prevent the Soviets from occupying parts of Eastern Europe. Although a compromise was reached on the wording of the article, the whole thing was but an American illusion. The Soviets joined in the declaration because of their interests in the Far East.[16]

A summit was now the perfect venue for Franklin Roosevelt's diplomatic style, where he would shape the postwar world by the force of his personality. In the historic conferences at Vienna in 1815 and Berlin in 1878, decisions were made between winners and losers. The summitry of World War II was unique, because the Allies made decisions about the postwar world while the war was still being decided, excluding a possible input from their adversaries. The Allied policy of unconditional surrender had made contact or negotiation with the enemy a moot issue in any case.

Once the Soviets were in the war, Roosevelt wanted personal contact with Stalin; as early as December 14, 1941, he wrote to the Soviet leader to convey his wish to meet at the earliest possible date. In late 1942, he communicated with both Stalin and Churchill about the possibility of a meeting in January of 1943.[17] By November 28, 1943, about two years after the formation of the Grand Alliance, Roosevelt arrived at Teheran for his first meeting with Stalin. The president's principal goal in holding a summit was to get to know Stalin and to establish a close working relationship rather than continue relying on his surrogates. It is doubtful that FDR hoped to have a relationship with Stalin like the kind he enjoyed with Churchill, but he was eager to accommodate the Soviet leader. After a long working relationship with Churchill, the bigger game now for Roosevelt was a relationship with both Stalin and Churchill, and primarily Stalin.

Roosevelt was not interested in Stalin's career, ideology, and style of leadership. He remained oblivious to the purges, accepting Davies' opinion that they were necessary political cleansings of Stalin's enemies. Roosevelt was not even seriously interested in Stalin's diplomatic tactics. He came to the summits willing to rely almost solely on his own personal charm. He would maneuver Stalin just as he had maneuvered politicians, businessmen, and labor leaders in the United States. The whole purpose of the first conference, from Roosevelt's point of view, was to bring Stalin to his side.

Stalin was reluctant to meet with Roosevelt in 1941, 1942, and even in 1943. It was obvious that the Allies were not ready for a serious Second Front effort, and Roosevelt, to Stalin's annoyance, had not accepted the 1939 frontiers in the West. Molotov was sent to Washington to see what the president wanted and what he could do for Stalin. Stalin wanted to stall while minions like Molotov, Litvinoff, Gromyko, and Maisky appraised Roosevelt.[18] The slow, drawn-out negotiations among intermediaries frustrated the president, who, in addition, hated working with translators,[19] because both prevented Roosevelt from using his personal magic.

The president's principal aim for a summit meeting was to establish a personal relationship with Stalin. He also wanted to set the military requirements and strategic priorities of the Allies, but he was obstructed by Stalin and Churchill. Churchill and his chiefs refused an early cross-channel invasion while Stalin demanded such a strategy, even though an invasion by then was not entirely in his best interests. The president sent Joe Davies to convey his understanding of Stalin's need for Soviet security and his willingness to accept the Curzon defensive line on Russia's eastern borders.[20] Davies reported back that he had spoken frankly with Stalin on the cross-channel invasion and global strategy, and he also reported that Stalin asked "Why had American officials said they would fight alongside the Polish army to prevent Polish frontiers from being pushed back?"[21]

It was becoming clear that, notwithstanding the talk about the cross-channel invasion, Poland would be the real issue at Teheran. Even before the tripartite meeting at Teheran, and before the Cairo meeting between Roosevelt and Churchill, the political agenda for Teheran had been cast. At Quebec in March of 1943, Churchill stressed the importance of the Western Alliance, while the president emphasized the importance of his concept of the Four Policemen and cooperation with Moscow. Roosevelt's goal of linking the Western Alliance into a cooperative alliance with Stalin was never accepted by Churchill, who continued to pursue his European balance-of-power orientation, calling for tough diplomatic bargaining. Roosevelt had little interest in such details, dismissing them as old-power diplomacy that should be replaced by his new summitry diplomacy. The president also introduced a new actor, Chiang Kai-Shek's China, which alarmed Churchill and annoyed Stalin.

Teheran would accentuate the growing differences among the Allies. Was the trip necessary?[22] Difficulties began immediately, with the negotiations to select a meeting site. Stalin suggested Teheran, even though it had little to recommend it to the Western Allies. Characterized by foul weather, it hosted many Nazi agents and presented a security nightmare. Teheran required Roosevelt to travel six thousand miles while Stalin covered a mere six hundred.[23] "'I cannot go to Teheran,' he pleaded with Stalin not to fail him."[24] Stalin was unmoved. Churchill wired Roosevelt, "Uncle Joe will not come beyond Teheran."[25] With Davies' guarantee that Stalin would be cooperative on the issues, Roosevelt, after a halfhearted proposal to meet in Egypt, accepted, cabling Churchill "urging that they do nothing to cause Stalin to retract the agreement and asking Churchill to accept Teheran."[26] FDR did not want representatives of the great powers (meaning France) at the conference, lest it appear that the Western Allies were ganging up on Stalin. Stalin kept telegraphic and telephone communication with his front commanders, and was in charge of the meeting.[27]

Churchill, whose influence with Roosevelt was beginning to decline, proposed a preliminary Anglo-American meeting to draft a joint strategy for dealing with Stalin, but Roosevelt objected. He did agree to meet Churchill in Cairo on November 22, 1943, before meeting with Stalin; but the result was not what Churchill had had in mind, because Roosevelt included Chiang Kai-Shek in the Cairo meeting, thereby catapulting Chiang into the status of a major player. Churchill wondered about the invitation and Roosevelt cryptically said that "he had the option on Tutankhamen's tomb for Chiang."[28]

The Chinese presence in Cairo, especially that of Madame Chiang Kai-Shek, was distracting. The opening ceremonies were impressive:

> The opening of the conference was festive. Most of the statesmen and beribboned officers had met at previous conferences and their renewal of acquaintances conjured up a scene "like a mixture of Grand Central Station and a college town on the day of a class reunion." By the end of the first day, they had exhausted Cairo's supply of Scotch whisky and were airlifting in new stocks. The prime minister contributed to the early carnival atmosphere by alternating between his zip-up siren suit and a brilliant white sharkskin suit with a ten-gallon cowboy hat. The arrival of the Chinese entourage caused a sensation. British descriptions of Chiang ranged

from "small and wizened" to a "formidable looking ruffian" to "looking something like a cross between a pine marten and a ferret." Madame Chiang left an altogether different impression. She had, according to Moran, a "certain cadaverous charm" and Brooke wrote that "although not good-looking, she certainly has a good figure which she knew how to display at its best. Gifted with great charm and gracefulness, every small movement of hers arrested and pleased the eye. For instance, at one critical moment her closely clinging black dress of black satin with golden chrysanthemums displayed a slit which exposed one of the most shapely of legs. This caused a rustle amongst some of those attending the conference and I even thought I heard a suppressed neigh come from a group of the young members."[29]

The meeting was held in the Mina Hotel near the Giza Pyramids, five miles outside of Cairo. It was a crowded affair, with the president also meeting with the kings of Greece and Yugoslavia. The generals contented themselves with military discussions about Overlord, Mediterranean operations, and plans for an amphibious operation in the Bay of Bengal called Buccaneer, which Roosevelt supported to demonstrate the esteem in which he held the Chinese. Churchill and his generals were not enthusiastic about this project.

When it came to Overlord, Churchill was more successful. The British were apprehensive enough to postpone the landings to the middle of 1944. Overlord, Churchill insisted, should not "tyrannize" other activities in the Mediterranean. The Cairo conference was not a good omen for Teheran. "The British and the Americans made a poor job of bridging their differences" on the invasion, Poland, and China.[30]

Teheran: Roosevelt and the Issue at Teheran

The Moscow Conference of Foreign Ministers had raised a number of controversial issues. Hull, in a memorandum to the president on November 23, 1943, said as much when he complained that the question of resumption of Polish-Soviet relations was no nearer to a satisfactory solution.[31] The prospect of spending much of the time with Stalin over Poland irritated the president, who wanted to use the occasion primarily to cement a closer relationship between the two.

Roosevelt wanted to use the summit to propose his dream of an international postwar organization and the possibility of a postwar partnership with Stalin. Stalin was not interested in an international organization, but the discussion of it gave him an opportunity to get concessions on Poland.

Stalin came to Teheran still angry about talk at the Moscow Conference of an Allied plan for confederations of states between Germany and Russia. "The Soviet government," wrote Sainsbury, "had begun to suspect a sinister motive—the creation of a belt of states hostile to the USSR."[32] Stalin was thus adamant about Polish borders. Most of the British and American military personnel showed distaste for Stalin. Hap Arnold and George Marshall thought Stalin should not be treated as "if he were a product of the diplomatic service. 'He was a tough SOB who made his way by murder and everything else and should be talked to that way.'"[33] To the military, Stalin was "cool," "fearless," "a man of steel," "brilliant mind," "ruthless," "inscrutable," "extremely realistic." Roosevelt told Eleanor that "he felt there was a great distrust on the part of Marshal Stalin when they met first . . . (however) he added that he intended to see that we kept our promises to the letter."[34] The prime minister was interested in shortening the war.[35]

Roosevelt considered Teheran "a great success." The personal meetings he had with Stalin were "of great importance in many respects."[36] Satisfying Stalin's demands often meant making Churchill unhappy. Churchill did his utmost to circumvent Overlord because he felt that the Allies, and certainly the British, were not ready, although Hull reminds us that Churchill actually concurred with Molotov over the "sanctity" of Overlord.[37] He also tried to bring up the Polish question, which Roosevelt was trying to avoid.

On the first day of the conference, Roosevelt—the most frail of the three, but also the youngest—greeted the other two leaders with enthusiasm. He opened with a general survey of the war in the Pacific and Europe, after which Churchill launched into the cross-channel operation. This quickly became the principal topic of discussion, with most of the talking done by Churchill and Stalin. Roosevelt remained relatively silent until the end of the discussion.[38] He said little, but what he said was crucial, indicating that nothing should be done to "delay the carrying out of Overlord." This put Roosevelt in direct opposition to Churchill, a stance that would recur throughout the conference.

Roosevelt then called the various staffs together for preliminary discussions on a plan for the invasion of southern France.[39] Discussions of Overlord continued on November 29 among the staffs, including Leahy and Marshall for the United States, Alan Brooke and Charles Portal for the British, and Voroshilov for the Soviets. Stalin wanted to know who the commander-in-chief of Overlord would be, as Leahy remembered in his memoirs. "That's when Stalin probed on the c-in-c and he [Roosevelt] leaned over me and whispered to me 'That old Bolshevik is trying to force me to give him the name of our supreme commander. I just can't tell, because I have not made up my mind.'"[40]

Alanbrooke was pessimistic about the results of Teheran. "Bad from beginning to end. Winston was not good and Roosevelt was even worse! Stalin meticulous with only two arguments—Cross Channel operations on the first of May, also offensive in Southern France!"[41] Churchill's effort to postpone the timing of the operation irritated Stalin. He tried to pin Roosevelt down to schedules and details. On November 30, the chiefs met to iron out details of timing and logis-tics. Chip Bohlen didn't appreciate Stalin's constant needling of Churchill and the president's silence. "I didn't like the attitude of the President, who not only backed Stalin but seemed to enjoy the Churchill-Stalin exchanges." Bohlen concluded that "ganging up on the Russians was to be avoided at all times," an attitude caused by a "basic error" stemming from Roosevelt's lack of understanding of the Bolsheviks."[42]

In the end, Overlord was settled in Roosevelt's favor and Churchill was forced to "surrender," according to Lord Moran. Keith Eubank concluded that "by finally agreeing to the Russo-American position on *Overlord,* Churchill had accepted a policy not to his liking. His chiefs of staff, too, were not fully in agreement, and had the conduct of the war been wholly in their control, strategy might have been very different."[43] On the second day Churchill, perhaps still irritated about the first day's proceedings, brought up Poland. "Are we to draw frontier lines?" he asked explicitly. "Yes," Stalin said.[44] Churchill used three matches to demonstrate how Poland would move west while giving up eastern Poland to the Soviets. Roosevelt remained silent, pondering the reaction of Polish voters in the United States. The president was uncomfortable with the way Churchill had drawn the discussion to Poland. According to Elliott Roosevelt, the president wanted to avoid transacting business in the first few sessions.[45] He had wanted to get acquainted, to establish some common ground with Stalin, delaying the resolution of issues until the conclusion of the conference.

After a discussion on the dismemberment of Germany and suggested international zones there, Roosevelt left the room, leaving Churchill and Stalin to discuss the details, even though Churchill was suffering from a migraine headache. Realizing that Churchill was about to bring up Poland again, Roosevelt sought out Stalin and Molotov, trying to explain to them his electoral difficulties. "He seemed on the defensive, and this let Stalin know he could push on Poland, that he could expect no serious difficulties over the issues from the president. Roosevelt explained that, because of the Polish-Catholic voters in the United States, he could not participate in 'any decision on Poland.'"[46] Harriman and Bohlen were disturbed that the president was so defensive. Harriman understood that the Red Army would move into Poland, and that by then "it would be too late for a negotiated settlement."[47] Bohlen was concerned that Stalin appeared "relieved." Roosevelt, meanwhile, indicated he would not make an issue over the Baltic States, but that Stalin should make some gesture about independence. The president also made a serious tactical error when the Big Three repaired to the conference. He began by expressing his "belated" hope for resumption of Polish-Soviet relations. Stalin was annoyed. This should have been discussed in their private meetings, and it left an opening for Churchill, who "tried to pour oil over troubled waters."[48] Speaking of Great Britain's formal obligations to Poland, Churchill failed to mollify Stalin, who was happy to cut relations with Poland in the wake of the Katyn Forest Massacre controversy, and he was not about to work with the London Poles now that he had his own Communist Poles. Roosevelt's only contribution was to ask if the western area ceded to the Poles was equal to the lost territory in the east.[49] Churchill wanted to continue the debate, but Roosevelt had had enough. The discussion turned to Germany and other matters.[50]

Teheran took place two years too late for the president to establish good relations with Stalin. He might not have acted differently, but dealing with a pre-Stalingrad Stalin could possibly have yielded more positive results for the Western Allies. Roosevelt's surrogate diplomacy had failed to fulfill this mission. After Teheran, Soviet-American relations were hardly changed from what they had been in 1941. In fact, the die for Yalta 1945 was cast.

The Rise of Lublin, the Fall of London, 1943–1945

The developments at the Moscow and Teheran conferences reflected a shift in Stalin's tactics, which in turn reflected the resurgence of Polish Communists within occupied Poland and among those exiled in the Soviet Union. Together, they would come to constitute what would be called the Lublin Poles, and would serve as a weapon against postwar Polish independence.

The rise of the Polish Communist counterforce parallels the march of the Soviet military that dictated the sequential course of Stalin's strategy. London Polish disunity, Roosevelt's indifference to the future of Poland, and the fortunes of war were pivotal factors in what occurred after 1943; but the resurrection of the Polish Communists is a remarkable story in its own way, and an example of Stalin's shrewd use of the means at hand.

In 1939, led by men and women whom Stalin contemptuously called Jewish cosmopolitans, the Polish Communists had enthusiastically supported the Nazi-Soviet Pact. As he had done with other members of the international front, Stalin systematically purged the Communist Party of Poland (KPP). Its members were hunted both by the Gestapo and by the NKVD. Scattered and disorganized, it was a party in name only. The KPP found new life with the Nazi invasion of the Soviet Union, and was reactivated when Stalin ordered its Communist followers all over Europe to march in support of the motherland and Father Stalin.[51] A seed already existed under the leadership of Wanda Wasilewska and Helen Usiyevich in the Soviet zone of occupied Poland, and a new Polish party led by Wladislaw Gomulka was established.[52]

In Poland, the Home Army enjoyed support from and close ties with the London Poles, a closeness that the Polish Communists could not claim with Moscow. The KPP constituted a strange brew. Davies described it as a "blend of Nationalism and Leninist Socialism."[53] What was remarkable was the growth of its military arm, the Peoples Guard Army (AK), consisting of and led by Polish officers and graduates of Soviet prisons and Gulags. General Zygmunt Berling became head of the Polish Armed Force in the USSR, and the army fought alongside the Soviets, subordinated to the NKVD, and under the direct control of Stalin, not the KPP.

How was it possible that this conglomerate of a small, ineffective civilian party within Poland (the KPP), a group of Soviet Polish exiles, and their NKVD-led army, with no official international standing, could rise to challenge the legitimacy of the London Poles? First came the breakdown in relations between the London Poles and the Soviet Union, precipitated by the Katyn Forest Massacre. Stalin never resumed the relationship, and immediately set about creating an alternative regime. Late in 1943, the resurrection took place with the formation of what was called the Polish Democratic Front, dominated by Soviet allies. It was aimed at the Polish resistance movement (or KNR), whose most effective arm was the AK. It was the most promising free Polish force, and it would meet its destruction during the course of the Warsaw Uprising, thus opening the way to the Polish Communists from the Soviet Union, merging with those already within Poland. Their task was the Sovietization of Poland; and with the Soviet occupation of Lublin in the fall of 1944, they became the formal alternative to the London Poles.

In retrospect, it seems paradoxical that Stalin continued to engage in a fight over boundaries when his armies were triumphant everywhere. But Stalin was never sure, even as late as 1945, that his minions in Poland could succeed or consolidate their success. Thus, under the umbrella of National Liberation Fronts, he still wanted to reassure frontier revisions before the war ended. Curiously, he might have received Western legitimacy for his territorial claims. Roosevelt all but gave him his tacit blessings, and even Churchill, suspicious and fearful of Stalin's intentions, nevertheless accepted the Curzon Line. Stalin, aware that the proximity of power did not lead to "any final crystallization of strategy by the Communists," continued his diplomacy of negotiating, slicing up the boundaries of Eastern Europe.

In the summer of 1944, Stalin directly intervened on behalf of his Polish Committee for National Liberation—the Lublin government. A new pro-Communist National Council of the Homeland began its infiltration into the Polish underground. The Moscow-trained Communists, led by Boleslaw Beirut and Wanda Wasilewska, joined forces with the local Communists of Gomulka, organizing themselves along the parallel march of the Red Army into Poland. As soon as Lublin was liberated, the Committee for National Liberation was formed. Churchill, alarmed, urged the London Poles to join Lublin before the Soviets could boast a *fait accompli.* On July 26, 1944, the Soviet government formally recognized the Lublin committee (PKWN) and named General Commissar Nikolay Bulganin as the Soviet liaison. Still, Stalin did not feel secure; the Communists remained isolated and numerically weak,[54] but the Red Army made up for weaknesses in political popularity and legitimacy.

There remained one serious roadblock, and that was the still effective and popular AK Home Army in Warsaw under the command of General Tadeusz Bor-Komorowski. The Russian army neared Warsaw, accompanied by the armies of Berling and Wasilewska, not by the army of Anders. It was at the gates of Warsaw that Anders' error was revealed. Instead of representing a force that could make itself felt, Anders' remnants were fighting with Allied armies all over the European and Mediterranean theaters of war, all thus absent at this crucial time. Stalin's response to the Home Army was to mount a propaganda campaign against it, calling it Pilsudski-ite, or SANACJA, meaning it resembled the old 1936–1939 regime of the colonels. Stalin tried to detach the AK from London.[55] But Bor-Komorowski was shrewd enough to try and counter these tactics. He called for the AK to assist the Red Army, "In this way, presenting the Soviets with the dilemma of either de facto recognizing 'London' as an ally or repressing 'friendly' AK units, thereby risking friction with the Western powers."[56] Bor's maneuver, known as Operation Tempest, was not intended to "assist the Russians" but was designed to be a tool, a "means to bolster the Polish cause among Western allies."[57] Even as the Red Army pushed toward Warsaw, the political battle between Bor and the Communists continued.

Stalin did not fall into the trap, but moved cautiously, lest the Allies come to Bor's assistance. He could afford to. Mikolajczyk had once more rejected the Curzon Line, and on November 24, 1944, he resigned. In Warsaw, Bor-Komorowski and his Home Army, with the Red Army so close, ignited the Warsaw Uprising, a long, grueling battle that ended in the decimation of the Home Army by the Germans while Soviet tanks stood only hours away. The Warsaw Uprising and its results were a tragedy for Poland, a gain for Stalin, and an embarrassment for the Western Allies. When the Soviet tanks were reported east of the city, General Bor expected that "the Russians, under their own impetus . . . would be forced to take Warsaw."[58] The pressure on the Home Army was considerable. With four thousand fighters, it was preparing to "strike the Germans in Warsaw's streets." Bor knew the AK couldn't defeat the Nazi armies; the objective was to start the insurrection and pave the way for the Red Army's offensive. But the Red Army halted at the gates of Warsaw and did not move to help the Home Army as it was relentlessly and ruthlessly crushed by the Germans. The Poles in London pleaded with the Soviet embassy, with Churchill, and with Roosevelt, who actually cabled Stalin, inquiring whether Stalin could help the AK. Stalin demurred, but promised to send supplies, which turned out not to include parachutes.

The battle raged for sixty-three days, from August 1 to October 2, 1944, and neither the Soviets nor their Polish Communist allies assisted the bleeding, dying Home Army.[59] Politically, that was not surprising, since the destruction of the Home Army removed the only serious organized resistance to the Sovietization of Poland. Stalin was aware that as the AK bled to death within Warsaw he could unleash his national committee forces. The fact that the Germans would be weakened was welcomed, but that had not been his primary consideration.

Harriman and British Ambassador Sir Archibald Clark Kerr sent messages to Stalin asking for help. Harriman found that "Stalin showed understanding and concern for the Poles in Warsaw and none of his previous vindictiveness."[60] To George F. Kennan, interviewed by J. K. Zawodny years later, it was plain that neither the British nor the Americans in Moscow understood the Soviet actions in Poland. Kennan said, "Nothing could have saved Poland from Soviet domination."[61] Harriman's attitude was that the London Poles must "put suspicion aside and earnestly attempt to make a reasonable settlement."[62]

"Whose view was he [Harriman] reflecting here?" Zawodny asked Kennan, Harriman's assistant in Moscow. Here is an exchange from their interview:

> KENNAN: Mr. Harriman's views changed during the course of the war. Of course, he was a man very loyal to the President, and he tried always to reflect the President's views and policies. He was still, at that time, trying to achieve the ideal of Big Three unity. He felt that the position of the Polish Government-in-exile was an obstacle in this. I think that during the next year his opinions changed very rapidly.
>
> ZAWODNY: Are you referring to 1945?
>
> KENNAN: Yes, the time between September 1944 and September 1945, I think Mr. Harriman saw other evidence, and changed his view. This was, if I am not mistaken, two days before the final meeting that he had with Molotov over the flying-in of supplies.
>
> ZAWODNY: I think it was earlier.
>
> KENNAN: I think that meeting was the fourteenth.
>
> ZAWODNY: Yes, it could be. I don't recall now.
>
> KENNAN: And I think that perhaps even a week later he would have written a little differently.[63]

With KPP takeover of AK by October, 1944, "The party's change of direction in October 1944, meant that in Poland the foundations of Communist power were laid in conditions of virtual civil war and overt reliance on Soviet force of Arms."[64] By early 1945, the Campaign of Terror against the AK started.

Chapter 8

Yalta
The Epitome of a Rooseveltian Utopia

The Myths of Yalta

The Yalta conference, passing almost instantly into historical mythology, even today elicits emotional and partisan responses to its results. Depending on one's political views, Yalta is seen as a "betrayal" or an "inevitable outcome," either a great triumph for Roosevelt or an abandonment of Eastern Europe by a president eager to court Stalin. But its place in history has little to do with what happened at the conference; its significance for the Grand Alliance was minimal, as the course of the alliance was determined by military and political developments going back to 1943 and Stalingrad. In fact, Yalta was a part of the denouement of the war, signalling the end of the Grand Alliance. It was Old World realpolitik, as practiced by Churchill and Stalin, winning over a sick and weakened Roosevelt who was preoccupied with pursuing the vestiges of Wilsonian idealism.

By the time of Yalta, the Third Reich was in full retreat and Hitler was in his bunker awaiting the final Russian assault on Berlin. In the United States, America's traditional anti-communism was resurfacing; Yalta, and later China, were becoming rallying symbols for it.

How did the mythology of Yalta emerge? How did a conference that was first seen as a triumph of cooperation, come to be regarded as a failed conference in which Roosevelt bargained away Poland and

Eastern Europe? Athan Theoharis is correct when he writes that "this image of Yalta resulted from post-war developments, both international and domestic. The intensification of the Cold War made the assumptions of Yalta suspect."[1] The myth of Yalta proliferated in 1950s America, the winners being the resurgent conservatives, the losers heirs to Roosevelt's legacy, many of whom became victims of the McCarthyite witch-hunts. The Alger Hiss affair was a symbol of the times—beginning as a spy case, turning into an attack on the waspish State Department and the values of the Roosevelt war leadership. The attacks would extend to Truman and Secretary of State Dean Acheson, both exemplary cold warriors.

There are three different interpretations of Yalta. The supporters of Yalta saw it as the best the president could do. With the Red Army occupying Poland and moving across Eastern Europe, Soviet hegemony over the area was no longer in question by the time of the conference. Some historians, like Raymond Sontag and Herbert Feis, do not hide the fact that Roosevelt made concessions, but they contend that these concessions reflected military realities.[2] They argue that Stalin was impossible to handle, that he was psychologically unstable, "demented," "paranoid," governed by an irrational fear of Polish betrayal, and that he could feel safe only if he dominated Poland.

Revisionist writers such as Gar Alperovitz, Gabriel Kolko, William A. Williams, D. F. Fleming, and Diane Clemens, among others, see Yalta as a triumph of reasonableness. The thrust of their argument is that Stalin's expansionism stemmed from legitimate security needs he had consistently pursued since 1941. For Stalin, Roman Catholic Poland was an archaic state, vulnerable to German challenges, oriented toward the West, and traditionally hostile to Russia. A Poland not dominated by Stalin was an unsafe Poland.

Like the Roosevelt apologists, the revisionists accept the results of Yalta as a *fait accompli,* but they go a little further, seeing it as an achievement. Diane Clemens refutes the charge that Roosevelt yielded to Stalin on Poland, Germany, and the Far East, arguing that Roosevelt made no more concessions than did Stalin. "[A]lthough the great powers differed in their initial view points, a high incidence of

Teheran, November 29, 1943, on the front portico of the Russian Embassy. Immediately behind Stalin, FDR, and Churchill, from left to right, are Harry Hopkins, Vyacheslav Molotov, Averell Harriman, and Anthony Eden.

Reporter A: Who is the man behind Stalin?
Reporter B: Probably his adviser.

Churchill and Stalin in October 1944, with Molotov, Harriman, and Eden. (Soviet Archives)

From left, Alexander Cadogan, Averell Harriman, and Anthony Eden
on board the USS *Quincy* en route to Malta, February 2, 1945.

Cadogan to Harriman: So what's next?
Harriman: Don't worry, the president will be in command.

From left, Edward Stettinius, Cadogan, and Harriman, February, 1945.

FDR's first call on Stalin after arriving at Livadia Palace for the
Yalta Conference, February 4, 1945.

Stalin: Mr. President, how about dividing the world?
FDR: You think we can do that?

FDR and Churchill meet February 4, 1945.

FDR: Listen, Winston, the Age of Imperialism is over.
Churchill: Ehmmm...

The conference of the victors at Yalta, February 3–11, 1945.

FDR and Stalin, February 9, 1945, posing in front of the Livadia Palace:
a not-so-grand alliance.

Stalin is ready to dance the Kazachok.

Stalin: The Empire has gone?
FDR: At your request.

Stalin confers with Molotov during the party marking the end of
the Yalta Conference.

Stalin: Vyatcheslav Mikhalovitch, don't you think I was in command?
Molotov: Yes, Yosif Vassiryonovitch, as expected.

The advisers and surrogates at Livadia Palace, February 28, 1945:
from left, Harry Hopkins, Steve Early, and Charles Bohlen.

consensus was reached at the conference."[3] There was no equality among the three powers at Yalta, with Great Britain the lesser partner.

The third interpretation is that of the detractors of Yalta. They are many, and their attacks come from many sides. But regardless of how hostile their feelings or how partisan their loyalties, their criticism is rooted in fact. Some thought that by the time of Yalta, Roosevelt was a sick man who thoughtlessly abandoned Poland and Eastern Europe out of weakness. Others felt Roosevelt's internationalism blinded him to the realities of what was happening. Republican Senator Arthur Vandenberg felt Roosevelt had abandoned the realism of his cousin Theodore and of Henry Cabot Lodge. To these critics, Roosevelt's neo-Wilsonianism was responsible for the "surrender" at Yalta.

Theoharis divides the conservative detractors into three groups: the "extremists," such as Senators Robert A. Taft and John W. Bricker and columnists like Westbrook Pegler and George Sokolsky; the "partisans," such as Senators Richard Nixon and Karl Mundt and the House Un-American Activities Committee; and the "moderates," such as Vandenberg, Henry Cabot Lodge, Jr., and General Eisenhower.[4] It was a curious mix: moderate Republicans who supported a bipartisan policy during the war; anti-interventionists and former isolationists; anti-Communist reactionaries who were passionately hostile to Roosevelt and the New Dealers. But they all echoed a single theme—Yalta was a failure and the price paid was too high. For many, Yalta was a betrayal of America's higher values.

Going to Yalta

By winter of 1944, the war in Europe was nearing its climax. The Red Army marched out of the Soviet Union into Eastern Europe and Germany itself, as the Allied Second Front expanded out of its beachhead and liberated Paris. Roosevelt, who had just won his fourth term, wanted another summit, despite his failing health. It would be his last opportunity to forge a better understanding for a postwar alliance with Stalin. FDR still believed in his personal magic, in his powers of persuasion; but he still needed to use that magic on his partners. Roosevelt and Churchill saw some urgency in the need for another summit. There could be no settlement on the postwar status of Europe without Stalin. There were the issues of Poland, the need for a commission on liberated Europe to settle the European international order, the division of Germany, the Far East, and the United Nations.

Stalin was hardly eager for another summit and felt little need for one. He feared that with the Allies now on the march in Europe and well on their way to defeating the Japanese in the Pacific, they would begin making demands for settlements on Poland, Germany, and on the United Nations, while offering little in the way of concessions. Stalin was in a comfortable position without a conference: Lend-Lease was continuing; he was nurturing the support of European Communists everywhere; the Polish government in London was rapidly losing its legitimacy; Edward Benes, the Czechoslovak president-in-exile, had made his deal with the Soviets. Stalin had nothing to gain from a summit in which he would very likely be put on the defensive.

Each of the Allies had different priorities. Roosevelt's number one priority was the creation of the United Nations. Next, Roosevelt wanted to ensure Soviet entry into the war against Japan and settle the issue of the division of Germany. Poland was last on his agenda, and he did not relish the prospect of discussing it, knowing its domestic political reverberations.

For Stalin, the security of Eastern Europe, represented by Poland, was the central issue. The partition of Germany came next, and the Far East last. For Great Britain, Poland was also a top priority, as it represented Britain's hope for a stable Europe. The future of France and Germany came next, followed by the future of the Balkans, Greece, Turkey, and Iran.[5]

The disparities among the three were obvious. The United States was concerned primarily with lofty goals, not balance-of-power issues. Territory and security meant everything to Stalin, which placed Soviet expansion in Poland at the center of his concerns. Churchill worried about such British imperial concerns as the balance of power in Central Europe and the Balkans. Beginning in the middle of July, 1944, until February of 1945, Roosevelt lobbied Stalin for a tripartite meeting.[6] At the Quebec conference in the fall of 1944, Roosevelt had already discussed his determination to have another summit among the three leaders. He was determined to frame the future of Europe with Stalin, not with Churchill. Roosevelt wanted to get away from Churchill's idea of spheres of influence, and thus sought a conference where he would be free to disagree with Churchill and deal directly with Stalin. When it came to Poland, Kimball points out that "Roosevelt didn't want controversy over the Polish question to turn domestic and congressional opinion against a postwar international organization or continued great-power cooperation."[7] Persuaded by many, including President Benes, that Stalin could be trusted,[8] convinced that he could personally persuade Stalin, FDR had no intention of irritating Stalin with the Polish question. For Roosevelt, what would be important about Yalta was not what was signed, but what was promised, which is the heart of the tragedy of Yalta.

Roosevelt thought that the Polish territorial issues should be incorporated into the declaration of a liberated Europe. He wanted to deal with universal principles at Yalta, not details or Churchillian map drawing. He had no patience with traditional European problems, seeing himself as a new man, like Wilson had been, a leader of a great nation untouched by war. Of course, on the issue of China, he could revert to European-style great power arrangements. But as long as the Pacific was dominated by the United States and its ally China, he could announce Atlantic universalism in Europe.

On January 25, 1945, at 8:30 A.M., Roosevelt embarked on a three-day journey of five thousand miles, with a two-day stop-over at Malta. He was already gravely ill and the journey would be a physical ordeal. He must have known that this would be his last great summit, a farewell appearance on the stage of history. His doctors had already told him that he might not have more than three months to live, which made him even more determined; he wanted his way in this last great effort.

In December of 1944, Dr. Robert Duncan had conducted a thorough examination of the president, the results of which Roosevelt refused to see. The president had always been stubborn about his health, even though he was now dieting and had reduced his cigarette smoking. He had spent less time in the White House and more at Hyde Park or at Warm Springs with Lucy Mercer Rutherford.[9] Letters to Churchill were often drafted and signed on his behalf by his staff.[10] He remained abreast of major issues, but was too sick to entertain new ideas or to fully understand the implications of the constantly changing progress of the war. He husbanded his energy and periods of alertness for the shaping of universal, grandiose policy.

Roosevelt's physical state compared badly with Churchill, who, even at 70, was able to travel thousands of miles, or with Stalin, who often appeared phlegmatic but was supremely alert. Roosevelt's health constituted an undeniable disadvantage. He had little time for reflection, for thorough examination of issues, for following ongoing events or dealing with details. His illness accentuated his working habits.

Others saw the effects on Roosevelt and were concerned. William D. Hassett, his confidential secretary, reflected with foreboding in his diary as Roosevelt left for Yalta on January 22:

> Can think of only one thing as the President sets out on this momentous journey. Having achieved every political ambition a human being could aspire to, there remains only his place in history. That will be determined by the service which he renders to all mankind. . . . Stalin remains an enigma; Churchill has brains, guts, courage, and a determination to preserve the British Empire. At seventy, as at every stage of his colorful career, he has everything except vision. And F. D. R., outside of his military and naval advisers, is leaning on some pretty weak reeds. But who am I to ponder the imponderable? God give the President strength, courage and heavenly wisdom.[11]

In Malta, on the way to Yalta, conferring with Churchill, Roosevelt did his best to stay away from discussions of affairs of state. He was killing time, saving his strength. In his diary, Lord Moran, Churchill's physician, looking at Roosevelt with a doctor's eye, could see that Roosevelt needed the rest.

The president appears to be a very sick man. He has all the symp-
toms of hardening of the arteries of the brain, in an advanced
stage. . . . I give him only a few months to live . . . the Americans
here cannot bring themselves to believe that he is finished . . .
Roosevelt had heart failure eight months ago. There are, of course,
degrees of congestive failure, but Roosevelt had enlargement of his
liver and was puffy. A post-mortem would have shown congestive-
ness of his organs. He was irascible and became very irritable if he
had to concentrate his mind for long. If anything was brought up
that wanted thinking out he would change the subject. He was, too,
sleeping badly. Winston is puzzled and distressed. The President no
longer seems to the Prime Minister to take an intelligent interest in
the war; often he does not seem even to read the papers the Prime
Minister gives him.[12]

Physically, Roosevelt was gravely ill, but his health did not change
his approach to Stalin. It is possible that Roosevelt might have been
more insistent in his courtship of Stalin had he been in good health.

Yalta was chosen as the place for the conference by Roosevelt.
Hopkins writes, "As early as the middle of September, 1944, the
President was contemplating a second conference with Stalin and
Churchill."[13] The president was searching for "ideas about places"
for the conference; Hopkins told FDR that "there was not a chance of
getting Stalin out of Russia at this time" and suggested the Crimea as
a possible site. After the 1944 elections, Hopkins saw Andrei Gromyko, who told him that Stalin was prepared for the conference but
could not leave the Soviet Union because he was preoccupied with
the war. In the following weeks, Hopkins' Crimea suggestion surfaced
and Stalin agreed that Yalta was "a desirable place."

Most of the president's advisers were opposed to a conference in
Russia; but Roosevelt was determined, Stalin agreed, and Churchill
acquiesced.[14] Those attending the conference had vivid memories.
Churchill is expansive in his memoirs. The British delegation had
been assigned to a very large villa five miles away from the center of
the city. It had been built for Prince Vorontzov, a one-time ambassador to the court of St. James, by a nineteenth-century British
architect, and evacuated only ten months earlier by the Germans. The
surrounding buildings still bore the marks of the occupation and the

area had not been completely cleared of mines. Food was brought in from Moscow. "The setting of our abode," wrote Churchill, "was very impressive. Behind the villa, half Gothic and half Moorish style, rose the mountains, covered in snow, culminating in the highest peak in the Crimea."[15]

Roosevelt was quartered in the Livadia Palace, where most of the conference took place. The palace had once been used by the Tsars, and it sported a first floor of fifty rooms that had been used by Tsar Nicholas and his son Alexi and now served as Roosevelt's quarters. Sir Alexander Cadogan, the permanent under secretary of the British Foreign Office, Eden, and Hopkins had to drive eighty miles from Sati on the Black Sea to the Palace. Cadogan remembers the food as excellent, served up by Royal marines and "innumerable waiters." Cadogan was impressed by Stalin. "He looks well, rather grayer, and seemed in very good form," he wrote. "I must say, I think Uncle Joe much the most impressive of all the three men."[16]

Stalin did not say a word for the first hour of the first day, February 8. "The President flapped about and the Prime Minister boomed, but Joe just sat taking it all in and being rather amused." Cadogan thought Stalin to have "a very good sense of humor and a rather quick temper."[17] Averell Harriman remembers having to drive for five hours to get to the conference, traveling through a sparsely populated countryside, full of wrecked cars and charred tanks all in "crazy disarray." Once, the ailing president traveled along the same road and remarked to Stalin with a certain bitterness the following day, "I'm more blood thirsty than a year ago." According to Harriman, the president's health was so precarious that he left his bed only once a day for the full-dress meetings.[18] Harriman was concerned about Roosevelt's health. "In better health, Roosevelt might have held out longer, but I can't believe that it would have made a great difference." Hopkins was also ailing during the conference and was prohibited by Admiral Dr. Ross McIntire from eating at the big dinners.

The president had quite a large entourage that included Hopkins, Stettinius, Leahy, Harriman, Freeman, Mathews, and Bohlen, as well as James Byrnes, Alger Hiss, Ed Flynn, Mrs. Anna Boettiger, and Wilder Foote among the civilians, and military men like Marshall,

King, and General Deane, General Laurence Kuder, and General Andreas McFarland, secretary of the U.S. Joint Chiefs. By contrast, Stalin had a small entourage that included Molotov, Vyshinsky and his deputy Maisky, Gromyko, Feder Gousev, and a translator, Vladimir Pavlov. The military was represented by Admiral Nikolay Kuznetsov, Air Marshall Sergei Khudyakov and General Alexey Antonov, first deputy of the Soviet army, not very senior Soviet army generals.

Roosevelt and Stalin presented startling contrasts in appearance and demeanor. Stalin made a grand entrance at the Livadia Palace, looking confident. Dressed in a plain woolen tunic, a short man, his left arm hanging stiffly at his side, Stalin looked over the gathering at length. His speech was methodical and uninspiring, but still impressive. He struck some observers as sinister with his pockmarked complexion, graying hair, drooping mustache, and slightly oriental appearance. He had come to Yalta as a winner, with his armies defeating the Germans in crushing battles. Roosevelt's entrance was also stunning, but his appearance was very different.

> Once more all eyes turned toward the entrance. President Roosevelt had arrived in a wheel chair. The heavy boat cloak he wore over his shoulders helped to cover his legs, but his arms were free to manipulate his distinctive long cigarette holder and to wave at the spectators. Though he sat upright, he looked very fragile, and it was obvious that he was not in good health. He was undeniably pleased with himself, and rightly so, for regardless of his own poor health and his heavy world-wide war commitments, it was his, and only his, persistence and determination that had finally brought about this conference—a conference to settle the final and postwar policies of World War II, and one that would affect the affairs of the entire world.[19]

The Issues at Yalta

For the most part, the three Allied war leaders and their staffs agreed on the Yalta agenda. The key issues were Poland, liberated Europe, the Far East, the United Nations, and Germany. The differences were of priority. In the immediate aftermath of Yalta, the Allies thought that something had been achieved, that, as Clemens argues, each of the leaders had compromised at some point and that the result was satisfactory for all. It seemed that way to Roosevelt, and even the seasoned Cadogan wrote in his diaries, "I think that the conference was successful."[20] Lord Moran's view was different. "Poland was a Cossack outpost of Russia," he wrote in a February 13 entry in his diary.[21] Much of the conference was taken up with military matters concerning the logistics of the final assault on Nazi Germany. Roosevelt was eager to get the European war concluded without any fissures appearing in the alliance so that he could negotiate Stalin's help in the war against Japan.

But Poland was at the center of the conference. Roosevelt was noncommittal on Poland, deferring the detailed bargaining over the issue to Churchill, always being careful not to challenge or confront Stalin. Stalin's position on Poland, presented in great detail, was not negotiable.[22] Refuting Western arguments on the Curzon Line, Lublin, and the London Poles, he stated his case with vigor. He could appear to be accommodating and stated that the Poles should decide on their own government—meaning that the Lublin Poles would be free to establish a government at the very least sympathetic to the Soviet Union, preferably controlled by the Soviet Union.

His presentation captivated Roosevelt so that for once he followed up and suggested a commitment from Stalin: "It goes without saying," he wrote to Stalin, "that any interim government which could be formed as a result of our conference with the Poles here would be pledged to the holding of free elections in Poland at the earliest possible date."[23] Stalin was not going to make such concessions, and the issue was referred to a Foreign Ministers forum, where it died.

The differences over Poland had not changed since Teheran. The United States and Great Britain recognized the London Polish government with which Stalin had broken relations, preferring the Lublin Poles. The British recognized the Curzon Line as one boundary, but not the Oder-Neisse as the second. The Americans refused to commit themselves on the issue of boundaries, with Roosevelt preferring to emphasize the importance of the nature of the Polish government over the question of territory. The president was annoyed with what he viewed as the reactionaries among the London Poles, just as he had had difficulty dealing with what he called the "anti-democratic" de Gaulle.

Just as he had done at Teheran, Stalin pursued his policy that the future of Poland was linked to that of the Soviet Union. He insisted on the borders of the Curzon Line on the east and the Oder-Neisse on the west. The government in Poland would be "democratic," which to him meant the Communist-dominated Lublin government, under Soviet hegemony. The continuing presence of the London Poles presented Stalin's principal obstacle to the achievement of his goals, and part of his strategy at Yalta was to attempt to delegitimize them. British support of the London Poles was lukewarm at best, and with the death of Sikorski, who had both moral authority and pragmatic vision, their situation worsened. Roosevelt was susceptible to Stalin's propaganda about the London Poles, whom he continually referred to as "reactionaries."

Roosevelt, in any case, always shunted the Polish problem to Churchill and the British, since the London Poles resided in Britain. In Churchill, the Poles had a more eloquent spokesman for their cause and a more clear-headed diplomat at their side; but he, too, undercut the Polish bargaining position by readily accepting the Curzon Line as Poland's eastern border. The London Poles were adamant about boundaries and territory and refused to accept that boundary. The Lublin Poles, not surprisingly, accepted the Curzon Line. The fact that the majority of Poles in Poland as well as in America still supported London was irrelevant to Stalin. More and more, American and British support of London and opposition to Lublin seemed halfhearted. "The Anglo-American opposition to Stalin's Lublin Committee rested on a tenuous base, since both the President and the Prime Minister only minimally (if at all) supported the alternative Polish government in London."[24]

The tenuous support for London was a bridge to a tacit support of a coalition government, provided that it included a Lublin minority. This was a step away from the London Poles and an admission, however vague, of Soviet claims. The compromise on Poland was gradually made, begun at Teheran and legitimized at Yalta. Western concessions to Stalin were cumulative until they amounted to an overwhelming whole that could not be dismantled. Just as Roosevelt's and Churchill's positions changed, so did public opinion in the United States, which gradually shifted from a pro-London stance toward Lublin.

The real betrayal came on the issue of elections to the Polish government. On February 8, the fifth plenary session was held at Livadia Palace, to discuss Poland, as well as the "world security organization," the United Nations. All the parties present, including Stalin and Molotov, agreed to call for "free" Polish elections. The president, as moderator, said, "We were all agreed on the necessity of free elections." Stalin, responding to Churchill, who had spoken on behalf of the London Poles, said with some humor that "they may not be geniuses but they were the legitimate government of Poland." He compared the Polish provisional government with de Gaulle's. "Neither had been elected . . . why should we be so different with regards to the Polish government."[25] He even suggested that the provisional government was quite popular with the Polish people, according to the minutes of Chip Bohlen.

The president, weary of the detailed wrangling, deferred the matter to a foreign ministers meeting that would eventually be held in Moscow and would include Harriman, Archibald Clark Kerr, and Molotov. It was decided to invite Boleslaw Beirut and Wincenty Witos and two others from the Lublin provisional government and Mikolajczyk and Wladyslaw Grabski from London to undertake the formation of a provisional government of national unity that would pledge itself to hold free elections. Secretary of State Stettinius, in his statement, pledged a "fully representative Polish National Provisional Government,"[26] which would hold free elections. So at Yalta, it was the Stettinius "formula," probably coauthored by Assistant Secretary of State Alger Hiss, which prevailed. The pledge or promise of free elections would come back to haunt the Americans. The word *guarantee* was the key, along with the vague date of "very soon" for the elections. The concessions were serious and were wrung from a Roosevelt who wanted to protect his interest in the world organization.[27]

What the formula meant was American and Allied acceptance of the expansion of the Lublin government, which would become the base of the new Polish government. The sixth plenary meeting on February 9 demonstrated that the Allies had given up any provisional government in which the London Poles would have a strong voice. What they were dealing with now was a provisional government overshadowed by the Lublin Poles.

Roosevelt wanted the provisional government to be called "the government now operating in Poland,"[28] preparing an explanation for the millions of American-Polish voters at home. Stalin pushed a little harder. He asked Roosevelt and Churchill if they were now ready to abandon the London Poles, once a new government had been established.[29] The compromise was the result.

At no point did either Churchill or Roosevelt seriously challenge Stalin. Stalin made it difficult by seeming to accept the sovereignty and independence of Poland while maneuvering to undermine both. He had conceded to a few London Poles for the provisional government, which would nevertheless be dominated by the Lublin Poles. "This sought to create the impression that any government would meet the high standards of political freedom."[30]

At the February 9 meeting, Molotov insisted that the Allied ambassadors be denied the right to observe the elections and that only "anti-Fascist" parties could participate.[31] Other than that, the language which emerged from the tripartite meeting of ministers was vague, sprinkled with words like *feel* and *consider*. Nothing of detail had actually been settled, not even a formal decision about the Curzon or Oder-Neisse lines, which the Soviets quite literally would transfer to their client government in Warsaw after the peace treaties had been signed and the elections had been rigged.

Kennan has argued that there was no leverage to use on Stalin, that the Allies should not have accepted a share in the responsibilities of the protocols, that they "should have separated themselves from the Russian proposals for Poland."[32] They should not have acknowledged the Soviet program for Poland's boundaries and regime. The Polish question for Stalin was always more than a territorial question; it always centered on the type of regime that Poland would have, and he pursued that end with great focus at Yalta.[33] Churchill and Roosevelt made the mistake of seeking to resolve the boundary dispute. Kennan felt that a Finland solution—a Poland friendly to the Soviets, even pro-Soviet—might have worked, but Roosevelt and Churchill never even considered such a solution.[34]

Roosevelt's issue at Yalta was the United Nations. In December, when the issue was being discussed before the conference, a disagreement arose over the composition of the Security Council and the veto. A compromise had been reached on December 5 that the president wanted Churchill and Stalin to adopt at Yalta. Public opinion polls had shown that almost 80 percent of the country was in favor of U.S. participation and membership in the UN, and Roosevelt knew he would not repeat Wilson's tragedy in failing to get the Senate to join the League of Nations. At Yalta, Roosevelt assured the creation and continued existence of the United Nations, and settled the voting dispute.

Yalta was not as important as Teheran, but it gained such notoriety because of what happened after the conference—the collapse of the Alliance, the breaking of agreements. "Yalta," writes Mastny, "was certainly not a glorious occasion for Western statesmanship, but neither was it in any tangible way 'Stalin's greatest victory.' If it stands out as a landmark, this is because of the precipitous breakdown that soon followed, a shock to all of its participants."[35] After Yalta, Poland was Stalin's to blackmail, in much the manner he attempted to blackmail de Gaulle and failed; he succeeded with Benes, whose "eager subservience" to Stalin was unrivaled by his "condescending benevolence."[36] Benes had offered Czechoslovakia political arrangements that would become the model to be used for Poland. It would be a coalition government of "anti-Fascists" (Communists) and "non-Fascists" (Western parties). At Yalta, neither Stalin nor Molotov explained those terms—except that all London-based liberation movements were "uncritically pro Soviet."[37] Benes' wartime mediation and talk with Stalin, writes Mastny, was "a devastating document [the record of his talk] of shoddy statesmanship."[38] Pushed by Churchill, Stalin had referred to the declaration of liberated nations, which provided for free elections but never mentioned democratic elections. For Stalin, free elections meant exactly the sort that Lenin had invented and he himself had perfected.

Clemens and the other revisionist historians are correct when they say that Yalta was a bargaining conference—Stalin got Poland for the United Nations, as well as concessions in the Far East that were a bonus he had not planned on. Roosevelt got his way on the Security Council, and Churchill managed to bargain well with Stalin on the issue of France remaining a major and balancing power in Europe. Stalin did not get his way on excessive reparations on Germany; the Alliance, on the surface, remained intact.

What was wrong about Yalta was not the negotiations or the bargaining, but the weakness of the Western Allies in their bargaining. They lacked two things that Stalin had—they were not tough bargainers, and they did not pay attention to crucial details. Roosevelt made it apparent from the start that he was not wedded at any point to Poland and that he would not fight for its future. On February 6, Roosevelt and Churchill made a proposal that Polish-American representatives and Lublin members be brought to Yalta to agree on the formation of a new constitutional government to replace Stalin's demand for an enlarged Lublin government. "It would have been a skillful maneuver if adequately executed; however, its authors failed to anticipate Stalin's elaborate obstruction."[39] When Stalin was not using the United Nations issue to get his way on Poland, then he distracted Churchill by bargaining about territory. Stalin mastered the details involved in the Polish question, and neither Churchill nor Roosevelt pinned him down on the definition of free elections or the time table for such elections. Stalin's insinuation that his treatment of Poland was not any different from what the British had been doing elsewhere was a fraud. In Yugoslavia, it was Tito, rather than Churchill, who had been causing trouble.[40]

The incorrigibly optimistic Roosevelt seems to have anticipated—intuitively rather than rationally—that the Russians would somehow allow free elections, whereupon the eastern Europeans would somehow elect pro-Soviet governments, so that in the end everybody would be happy. Churchill was not given to such cheap optimism, but he knew that for most of his countrymen a break with Russia on the eve of common victory was unthinkable.[41]

The Roosevelt Dream: The United Nations at Yalta

History may remember Yalta best for what happened regarding Poland, but for Roosevelt the purpose of the trip was to give shape to his dream of the United Nations. He would succeed where Wilson had failed and secure his place in history. As far back as the Atlantic Charter, Roosevelt had been searching for a lofty but practical concept of international behavior and rule of law that would justify the war.

The four Allies would assume responsibility for world security, but Roosevelt thought the United Nations should deal with health, education, economics, and agriculture. The details were left to the State Department. The United Nations structure, its rules of procedure and organization, can be said to be a State Department creation. Though dear to Roosevelt's heart, the United Nations was not a priority for the British, who were unimpressed with the idea of global cooperation. Churchill expected the world organization to be an association consisting in the main of the four Allies, including China. He saw it primarily as an Anglo-American cooperative organization.

Germany and its future represented a tug of war between Stalin and Churchill at Yalta; the United Nations was a jousting bout between Roosevelt and Stalin, for it was on this issue that Roosevelt expended most of his waning energy. Thus such issues as the permanent membership in the Security Council and the veto power were important issues for the Americans. The American proposal called for four permanent members, with each maintaining veto power.

The Soviets rejected the veto, instead proposing unanimity on all issues among the four great powers. They also sought to pack the organization with sixteen Soviet republics. Having failed to reach an agreement earlier in the summer of 1944 at Dumbarton Oaks, where delegates of the United States, Great Britain, the Soviet Union, and China were discussing plans for a postwar arrangement to maintain permanent peace, Roosevelt was determined to reach an agreement on the structure and mechanism of the world organization at Yalta. He insisted that the world organization would not merely be a great powers council, but would become a system of collective security. Stalin had in mind an organization European in orientation in which the Soviet Union would be allowed to play a central role.

The decision on permanent membership was one of the issues to be resolved at Yalta. The president used all of his dwindling powers of persuasion to convince Stalin. Roosevelt warned his allies at Yalta that the United States would not be the policeman of the world. It was obvious to Stalin and Churchill that Roosevelt would have to be given his world organization, if the working partnership were to continue.

Churchill was willing to support the plan. Stalin stalled for time, and Roosevelt, sensing Stalin's hesitation, offered to compromise on Poland. As the Soviet delegates were still working on proposals for Poland, the Soviets became accommodating on the role of the four powers in the Security Council. The procedural question of unanimity or veto was still unresolved.

Harriman believed that the Soviets were concerned about the organization's potential to interfere with Soviet expansion.[42] Stalin also objected to the role of nonpermanent members in the Security Council, since it was not in his interests to enhance the influence of small powers. Roosevelt was not decided on the degree of influence small powers should have, except that all members would have one vote. The central mission of the United Nations charter was to make small states more equal. So anxious was Roosevelt to gain Stalin's support that at first he did not object to the idea of representation for the sixteen Soviet republics. Under the prodding of Stettinius, he agreed that the Ukraine, Belorussia, and the Soviet Union would constitute a three-state member vote. Stalin behaved as if he had made a major concession in order to gain acceptance of the Lublin government. If it was so easy to agree on the membership of the Security Council, why should things be difficult on the issue of the Lublin Poles? The president agreed with Molotov that his formula on the nature of the Polish government showed "signs of progress."

Churchill now put in his bid, claiming, perhaps not entirely seri-

ously, that if Russia was to have three votes, the five British domin-
ions should be equal to the Soviet republics in power. Neither the
Soviet nor the British multivote proposal was adopted, and Roosevelt
ridiculed the Soviet proposals in private to James Byrnes. More
importantly, it was obvious that the exercise of power would lie with
the great powers in the Security Council, not the membership of the
general assembly.

Of all the issues discussed at Yalta, none raised the hopes of
President Roosevelt and other American officials so high as the
agreement on the United Nations. On no other issue were the results
so illusory. Because of the inability to secure agreement at the Dumbarton Oaks Conference, members of the U.S. delegation went to
Yalta skeptical of their chances to gain Soviet cooperation, the latter a
necessary precondition to any successful international organization.
When the Soviets accepted the entire American package, Roosevelt
and Stettinius were ecstatic, hailing this acceptance as proof in itself
of the success of the summit.

The important question for the historian is: What was achieved?
Stalin desired an international organization as a vehicle for preserving Anglo-American-Soviet hegemony. For the Soviets, this meant a
sphere of influence in Eastern and Central Europe which the British
and Americans, acting through the organization, would help guarantee.

That Stalin had no interest in establishing a body that would limit
Soviet sovereignty or freedom of action goes without saying. He
understood that neither the voting formula nor any other provision of
the U.S. proposals at Yalta posed any threat whatsoever to the great
powers that might themselves threaten international order. Roosevelt
also understood this, but he had a great capacity to persuade both the
American people and himself. He wanted an accord that would look
good to the world and would begin the process of cooperation. He
then convinced himself that the new organization, once launched,
would have an organic quality, allowing it to grow into an instrument
for lasting peace.

Chapter 9

Roosevelt and the Balance of Power in Europe

Britain and Imperialism

Franklin Delano Roosevelt did not subscribe to a policy of preserving the balance of power in Europe, but his actions affected that balance. As a politician, he was removed from European affairs. The Depression and the establishment of the New Deal had preoccupied him, and by the time he turned his attention to Europe, the continent's political landscape was already marked by Hitler's aggressive intervention in Eastern and Central Europe.

Roosevelt was not quite so indifferent to Europe as millions of his fellow Americans had become since the brief U.S. intervention in 1917–1918, when FDR had served as assistant secretary of the Navy. Domestic considerations and the experience of the previous war made Roosevelt cautious about Europe. He had just tested the limits of his power in his unsuccessful attempt to pack the Supreme Court, and the isolationists in Congress were beginning to demonstrate their political influence. Roosevelt hesitated to mobilize, sensing that the American people would not be receptive, and he became even more careful in dealing with the isolationist senators.

But the European conflict was politically timely for Roosevelt. By 1937, the New Deal was running out of steam, and Roosevelt turned to the crisis in Europe as a way of mobilizing public support. To do this, he had to educate the nation. The early influences of Teddy Roosevelt, Admiral Alfred T. Mahan, and Henry Cabot Lodge were important to FDR's approach to the war, as were the tenets of liberal imperialism.

Professor Willard Range contends that by the 1941 Atlantic Conference, Roosevelt had become "a confirmed anti imperialist."[1] Roosevelt shared this attitude with other leading New Dealers, but his was a truly anti-imperialist rather than anti-British stance.

A division of spheres of influence in World War II mattered less to Roosevelt than did achieving final victory over Nazi Germany. Winston Churchill, in his multi-volume *The Second World War,* portrays the Anglo-American alliance as an epic. "Throughout *The Second World War* Anglo-American relations generally appeared in a roseate hue, with little evidence of suspicion or controversy."[2] This view has been revised since, with the relationship now being described in terms such as "ambiguous partnership" or "allies of a kind."[3] The camaraderie between Roosevelt and Churchill was real, but it was Roosevelt and Stalin who shaped the postwar world, not Roosevelt and Churchill.

The story of Lend-Lease has been exaggerated; in both the British and Soviet cases, the program consisted of short-term projects forged for the purpose of winning the war. It did not evolve into a permanent policy precisely because there was no real postwar policy. Only after the war did President Truman and his advisers design one of America's most successful and enduring foreign and security policies.

Roosevelt's policies unintentionally but logically created a postwar power vacuum in Europe that Stalin filled, until he was challenged by the containment policy Kennan and others inspired Truman to adopt. That policy offered the political and military grand strategy that had been absent during the war.

Anti-imperialism was an American tradition. Americans were instinctively hostile to imperialism, which meant mainly British imperialism, although it was also directed against other colonial powers like Spain, France, Germany, and the Netherlands. American anti-British imperialism was a consequence of, among other things, American naval and maritime competition with the British navy. Anglo-American naval policies in the 1920s were characterized by the great British naval historian Captain Stephen Roskill as "the period of Anglo-American antagonism," with cooperation coming only after 1937.

> The events leading to the British-American alliance of World War II, in which an unprecedented degree of military, economic and political coordination was for a time achieved, have resulted in a tendency by historians to underplay, if not actually ignore, the serious differences of opinion and the rivalry in many areas which arose between nations during the inter-war period.[4]

Isolationists and progressives railed against Great Britain because Britain symbolized the essence of imperialism. In a harsh 1942 *Life Magazine* editorial, Russell Davenport cautioned that "Americans were not fighting to hold the British Empire together. We don't like to put the matter so bluntly."[5]

The American hostility to Great Britain's naval supremacy was fueled by America's own political mythology and symbols. Americans talked about access to markets and economic expansion without ever mentioning imperialism. The most outspoken anti-imperialist was Henry Wallace, Roosevelt's second- and third-term vice-president. A recognized authority on corn, Wallace advocated agrarian radicalism. His Wilsonian idealism was based on a profound ignorance of the world, hidden by his pretense at an expertise acquired through extensive travels. His Anglophobia was intense and led him to champion the American alliance with Stalin.

Wallace was not the only anti-British voice in Washington. Hostility toward British imperialism ranged across the political spectrum, the administration, and the governmental bureaucracy that ran the New Deal, showing its worst face in the popular suspicion that Great Britain was misappropriating Lend-Lease funds.

The American public did not think much of Great Britain's contributions to the war effort. Public opinion polls in 1942 showed that Americans thought the Soviets and the United States were bearing the major brunt of fighting the war. Only 7 percent thought that Great

Britain was doing enough, and that percentage dropped later in the year.[6] In 1943, a bipartisan consensus among New Dealers such as Ickes, Wallace, Hopkins, A. A. Berle, and Republicans like Vandenberg, Taft, Burton Wheeler, and Hamilton Fish suggested that Great Britain should divest itself of its imperial assets at the war's conclusion.[7]

Economic cooperation between Britain and the U.S. also proved to be difficult. American economic and financial preeminence was becoming increasingly evident as the rivalry deepened, and the rising economic tensions between the countries gave the State Department, which had played only a marginal role in political and strategic matters relating to the conduct of the war, a chance to regain some of its lost influence. Secretary of State Hull finally had a means to pursue his own goal of liberal internationalism, free trade, and domination of the dollar. American well-being was linked with the spreading of a free and prosperous democracy, and Hull now concentrated on implementing a global economic structure.[8]

Hull pressured the British to agree to a design for world international financial cooperative arrangements. The war had pulled America out of the Depression and fueled its economic capabilities, but Great Britain had suffered constant bombardment, seeing four million homes destroyed and its merchant marines decimated. An Englishman who lived through the period put it in vivid, personal terms. "When you in America hear a plane overhead, you look into the sky. You are thrilled. An airplane flying is a symbol of progress to you. When we in England hear a plane overhead, we don't look up. We look for the nearest air raid shelter."[9]

Great Britain's options were to join the American program of multilateralism and hope to profit from an expanding world, strive for bilateralism, or recreate the sterling bloc, for which the role of the Empire was crucial. The Republican, anti-imperialist, anti-British sentiment among leading U.S. opinion-makers and legislators caused concerns among British officials.[10]

A. A. Berle, a prominent New Dealer, corporate lawyer, and legal scholar was assistant secretary of state for Latin America at the time, and would become a nemesis to Great Britain because of his considerable influence in the Treasury Department and with the president.[11] "Berle thought," wrote Jordan Schwarz, his biographer, "that America 'had not quite adjusted itself to the fact that the British empire was dead, that the U.S. was supposed to inherit that empire.'"[12] This, after all, was meant to be the era that ended imperialism and ushered in Luce's "American Century," Wallace's "People's Century," and Willkie's "One World." Roosevelt certainly shared these sentiments. He was careful not to say publicly what he felt about the British Empire, but he never ceased to malign it privately and work toward bringing about its end.[13]

None of the Anglophobic New Dealers realized that by hastening the end of the empire they were assuring that Great Britain would emerge from the war as a weak nation, reduced to a minor role in European politics. They failed to see how they were threatening the balance of power in Europe. In a 1943 article in the *Saturday Evening Post,* presidential adviser Forrest Davis noted that Roosevelt, Welles, Hull, and Berle had publicly stressed "the excellence of this (Pan-American) American Model."[14] General Patrick Hurley, secretary of war in the Hoover administration, a self-made Texas millionaire, and one of the president's advisers and surrogate diplomats as an envoy to the Middle East, London, and China, wrote:

> The economy of colonial imperialism is decadent, obsolete, and has failed as an economic system. . . . British leaders have themselves pointed out that the colonial imperialism of Britain, France and the Netherlands are all bankrupt. Every one of them relies on the productive capacity and the material power of the United States as the deciding factor of whether they fail or continue to exist. This is aside from the moral question, which is roughly this: Does the ambition, the greed, or the dire necessity of one nation ever justify the transgression of the rights of weaker nations?[15]

This Texas oil man, sent by Roosevelt to handle U.S.-Iranian relations, was hostile to a Great Britain that had previously dominated the Iranian oil industry. Hurley was enraged when he found that Lend-Lease money was used on British Arab oil interests. In his report to

Roosevelt, he wrote that he believed "Great Britain was attempting to foster imperialism in the area through distribution of Lend-Lease supplies, and in his view, this should be stopped."[16]

Roosevelt admired Hurley.

> Roosevelt's admiration for Hurley could be boundless. While at the Cairo Conference he commented that men like Pat Hurley are invaluable. Why? Because they're loyal. I can give him assignments that I'd never give a man in the State Department, because I can depend on him, the President told his son Elliott. "That Pat Hurley . . ." father went on ruminatively. "He did a good job. In politics, he's the man. You know, Elliott," he said, throwing off a quilt and preparing to get up, "men like Pat Hurley are invaluable. Why? Because they're loyal. I can give him assignments that I'd never give a man in the State Department, because I can depend on him. You know what I mean?"[17]

In describing his relationship with Hurley, the president once said, "Only two persons know how Pat and I get along, the other person is Pat himself."[18]

Hurley complained that "Americans are not getting credit for their part in the war effort in the Middle East," and once demanded taking away Lend-Lease vehicle plates from the British and selling them to Arab countries.[19] He shared Roosevelt's mistrust of the State Department professionals. "They (the career diplomats) should be working for Winston," he told Elliott Roosevelt.[20]

Another indication of the shift away from Great Britain was the September, 1943, appointment of James Landis to be U.S. minister and director of American economic operations in the Middle East. The son of missionaries and a member of Roosevelt's social class, Landis was a professor of law at Harvard. But his appointment signaled a dramatic shift away from his pro-British predecessor. "Landis' appointment marked what now must be seen as the opening shot in a new round of competition between British and American commercial interests in the region."[21]

Did the president's anti-British emissaries act independently or did Roosevelt initiate their actions? Records showing what the president thought are scarce. He was strong and domineering, and it is hard to believe that envoys used to circumvent the State Department would make their own policies. By deduction, then, we may reasonably assume that their anti-imperialism reflected the president's.

The envoys' goal was to win the war and help the American economic empire grow. But being hostile to British and French imperialism meant weakening England and France and reducing the status of both as major European powers in the postwar world. The president did not see the effects of his policy in terms of the balance of power, as was especially clear when it came to the French.

France: Total Calamity

The popular conception persists that France and the United States were allies during World War II. But the full story is not so much one of a strong alliance, but of fierce antagonism. It would be hard to imagine two men who treated each other with more hostility than de Gaulle and Roosevelt. Roosevelt tried to out-maneuver de Gaulle as he pursued a relationship, not with the Free French, but with Vichy France. France had been traumatized by the defeat of 1940, which destroyed the Third Republic and led to the collaborationist Vichy government. That government became America's tacit partner and was never accorded the treatment reserved for an enemy state.

The Americans and British viewed the French through different prisms. Churchill saw Vichy as the collaborationist regime that had betrayed England and joined with Hitler. Vichy leader Marshall Pétain sought support from America, while Free French leader Charles de Gaulle looked to England. Roosevelt was not hostile to France, but he sometimes spoke of the desirability of reducing French power by stripping France of its colonies, though he never took concrete steps in that direction. De Gaulle described Roosevelt's attitude as being that of a "disappointed Francophile."[22] In spite of his Vichy-oriented policy and his personal hostility toward de Gaulle, Roosevelt helped France to restore its prestige and rebuild its armies. Even before the

North African campaign, Roosevelt had decided to rearm French forces in Africa.

Yet the story of American-French relations during the war is one of failure, a story from which Roosevelt and his principal advisers, especially his ambassador to Vichy, Admiral William D. Leahy, emerge with few laurels. Almost to the end, the administration supported Vichy and snubbed de Gaulle, creating havoc for the Allied liberation policy after 1944.

The alliance with the enigmatic Charles de Gaulle was difficult, and Roosevelt preferred other Frenchmen. Roosevelt's goal was to pressure Vichy to keep French naval power and what was left of France out of Nazi hands while strengthening Marshall Pétain against Hitler. His chief fear was that the collapse of France would lay the groundwork for a greater reich, prefigured by the Franco-German industrial cartel negotiated by Vichy in 1941.

The United States sanctioned Vichy's colonial rule on the theory that French African, Middle Eastern, and Southeast Asian colonies were to be "free" from Nazi domination. The support may have had some merit in 1940, when Britain was alone and an American presence in France benefited England, but it made little sense later on.

Vichy sought American legitimacy and to a surprising degree received it. Admiral Leahy was sent as ambassador to France, replacing the popular Wilsonian William Bullitt. Leahy, a Pacific-oriented officer who could not speak French and knew little about French politics or history, was chief of naval operations in the late 1930s. His long ties with the president dated back to 1913, when Roosevelt was an inexperienced assistant secretary of the navy. As was true of Hopkins and Hurley, Leahy's principal qualification was his loyalty to the president. "Neither politics, nor diplomacy nor France herself had ever been a consuming interest of Leahy. His presence in Vichy is best viewed as a mission from one court to another, a reversal to an earlier mode of diplomacy."[23] To another historian, Robert Paxton, Vichy was the old guard and the new order, and in those terms Leahy may have been the proper emissary to the court of the octogenarian Marshall Henry Philippe Pétain.

Unlike Leahy, Otto Abetz, the Nazi gauleiter in occupied France, had encyclopedic knowledge of France and was married to a French woman. He befriended Frenchmen outside the Vichy circle, artfully played on French Third Republic antagonisms, even though officially he dealt only with the Vichyites. Leahy hated his post, and he was eager to return to the U.S. and receive an active duty post.

Leahy cultivated Pétain, a fellow old soldier, and defended Vichy to the end. He felt close to the old marshall, although this did not prevent him from observing that his presence had little effect on Vichy loyalties. "According to him, the German influence at Vichy was decisive and American influence negligible."[24]

Leahy also shared the president's active dislike of de Gaulle. De Gaulle was reared a devout Roman Catholic, and was part of a group of Republican generals who loved the monarchy but aspired for France to be a republic. This still goes back to nineteenth-century "Republican generals." During World War I de Gaulle served as a junior officer under Pétain and became a national hero. Between the wars he foresaw the role of tank and armored warfare, just as the German general staff had done in the same period.

Roosevelt would at times needle Churchill about colonialism, but with de Gaulle it was a sore point the president never failed to prod. His intervention on behalf of Lebanese independence provides a case in point. De Gaulle promised independence to Syria and Lebanon once the British and Free French forces freed the countries, but when the Lebanese government demanded that he fulfill his promise in November, 1943, de Gaulle refused, suspending the Lebanese constitution and imprisoning Lebanese leaders. Roosevelt supported the Lebanese claims. The Free French leadership was itself divided, with support going to both de Gaulle and General Henri Giraud. Giraud proclaimed himself head of a committee for the liberation of North Africa, with de Gaulle as his military chief. Forced to choose between the two generals, Roosevelt chose Giraud.

Roosevelt saw de Gaulle as a destabilizing factor in North Africa, creating civil strife and raising the specter of a dictatorship after the end of the war. De Gaulle was planning to take over Dakar, the capital of French North Africa, and Roosevelt strongly warned Churchill that this was endangering the next sequence of Allied operations in the

Mediterranean. To remedy the confusion over who dominated French North Africa in 1943, Roosevelt engineered a brief reconciliation between Giraud and de Gaulle at Casablanca in January, 1943, but the truce did not hold.

There followed the disastrous meeting between de Gaulle and Roosevelt at Casablanca. Roosevelt challenged de Gaulle, refusing to recognize his leadership because he had not been elected. De Gaulle replied that Joan of Arc, who saved France, had not been elected either. Soon Roosevelt and his intimates were joking that de Gaulle was Joan of Arc one day, Napoleon and Clemenceau the next. In spite of Churchill's support for de Gaulle, Roosevelt's antagonism toward the Frenchman hardened into vindictiveness. De Gaulle temporarily accepted Giraud's leadership of the French committee of national liberation, but demanded domination over Vichy armies in North Africa, a very delicate issue.

The president's Vichy and anti-Gaullist policy had been unpopular at home with American opinion-makers such as Walter Lippmann, William Shirer, and Dorothy Thompson. To overcome administration attitudes, de Gaulle sent a delegation of people untainted by the politics of the Third Republic to carry his message to the United States. In 1942, Lend-Lease was granted directly to the Free French. Sumner Welles, the under secretary of state and Hull's rival, supported the Free French, tempering his support only by calling for more democratic representation. The Darlan affair exemplifies Roosevelt's Vichy policy. François Darlan, a Vichy naval officer and vice-president of the Vichy council, was eager to replace Pétain at the head of the Vichy government. Although he was the most pro-German of all the collaborationists, Roosevelt and Leahy tried to deal with him in North Africa, even though Churchill saw Darlan as a menace and wrote Roosevelt that dealing with him "is dealing with Germany."[25] The president wanted Darlan's military cooperation to assure the American invasion into North Africa. Darlan was to command French troops from Algeria who would join the Americans on the ground. Aware of the Darlan-de Gaulle struggle over leadership of the French troops, Roosevelt sided with the Vichy admiral.

Roosevelt also directed General Eisenhower not to deal with civilian French personnel, but to make decisions only on the basis of military concerns. There were three issues to be addressed concerning the future of France: the first two were who would lead France's postwar government and who would administer its colonies; the third issue had to do with Hopkins' suggestion of a possible civil war in France. "The Germans are easier to handle than would be the French under the chaotic conditions that could be expected in France."[26] Churchill worried about civil war between the Communists and de Gaulle's supporters in the Resistance, while Roosevelt feared civil war between Vichy and Free France, an unlikely possibility in 1944. Leahy thought that the discredited collaborationist government still had enough power to mobilize a struggle against the Free French.

William Hassett, Roosevelt's confidential secretary, wrote on June 23, 1944, that the president was concerned that de Gaulle, as head of the Free Committee of National Liberation (FCNL), had already appointed prefects and subalterns in the liberated area of Normandy. "He said more territory must be liberated before the problem of civil administration, which involves the question of recognition of de Gaulle's Committee as a provisional government, would be considered in Washington."[27] The president was inclined toward a military occupation, not a civil one. De Gaulle defied him every step of the way, and began winning his struggle against the Communists in the Resistance. (The emergence of the Communist party in France after 1941 as a highly effective resistance force meant that Stalin enjoyed considerable support there.) Yet, the president seemingly remained unaware of what was actually happening. He could have used de Gaulle as a political counterweight to Stalin when de Gaulle appointed a civilian government for France that successfully preempted the Communist party's plan to infiltrate local and provisional governments during the liberation process.[28]

At the Teheran conference, on the afternoon of November 28, 1943, Roosevelt and Stalin met in the Soviet quarter for a discussion without formal agenda concerning Stalin's view of the FCNL and de Gaulle. Stalin said he did not know the general, but that "frankly, in his opinion he was very unreal in his political activities."[29] He said that de Gaulle, however, was the "soul of sympathetic France while a physical France under Pétain was helping our common enemy, Germany." De Gaulle's "movement had no communication with the physical France."[30] "De Gaulle acts as though he were the head of a great state, whereas, in fact, it (FCNL) actually commands little power." The president agreed. In fact, "no Frenchman over 40 . . . should be allowed to return to position in the future." When the president related Churchill's opinion that France "would be very quickly reconstructed as a strong nation," he added that he did not share that view and that it "would take years of hard labor before that happened."[31]

Indochina, like Lebanon, provides another example of FDR's defiance of the Free French. In this instance America supported the Communist-dominated nationalist Vietminh led by Ho Chi Minh operating against the French on May 9, 1945, "an event of calamitous consequences."[32] The French mission in Washington had asked for help from the Combined Chiefs to support beleaguered French columns in Indochina, but the Chiefs did not act on that request. In Paris, on March 13, 1945, de Gaulle summoned U.S. Ambassador Jefferson Caffery, saying he could not understand America's French policy.

> In a cold fury, he turned on Caffery: "What are you driving at? Do you want us to become, for example, one of the federated states under the Russian aegis? The Russians are advancing apace as you well know. When Germany falls they will be upon us. If the public here comes to realize that you are against us in Indochina, there will be a terrific disappointment and nobody knows to what this will lead. We do not want to become Communist; we do not want to fall into the Russian orbit, but I hope that you do not push us into it."[33]

Churchill now took a hand in matters. He wrote Field Marshal Sir Henry Miatland Wilson asking him to tell Roosevelt and George Marshall that "it will look very bad in history if we were to let the French force in Indochina be cut to pieces by the Japanese through shortage of ammunition, if there is anything we can do to save them."[34] "In the United States, the French could not even get credit for their belated [*sic*] struggle."[35] Marshall ordered the American commander of the Chinese air task force, the former Flying Tigers, General Claire Chennault, to help the French.

To circumvent Churchill, the British and American generals and the president used an agreement between Lord Mountbatten, supreme commander of the South-East Asia Command (SEAC), and Chiang Kai-Shek as an excuse not to help. The reason was presumably a gentleman's agreement whereby Indochina, a Chinese sphere of influence, was open territory only for Allied military operations. Thus, the Americans were "in no position" to violate Chiang's "territory." The president delayed the decision to assist the French, leaving it to the commanders to decide.[36] Chennault never came with help—and de Gaulle was furious. "It seems clear now that your Government does not want to help our troops in Indo-China."[37] Churchill, the self-appointed trustee of the French and British empires, clashed with the president on the future of China in a way that he had not done on the future of Europe.

The Indochina collision was a mirror image of the China policy, but it was also, in the words of revisionist historian Walter Le Feber, "a case study of how supposed idealism, in this instance anti-colonialism, can blend perfectly with American interest."[38] Lurking behind the Wilsonian idealism was a greater commitment to Theodore Roosevelt's vision of the U.S. and Asia. Indicting the French empire in Indochina and the British Empire in the Far East was the perfect blend of Wilsonian zealotry and American expansionism.

In 1945, the political scene in France and in Indochina changed, pressed by the emergence of aggressive Communist forces. As Le Feber has written, "In a matter of months, de Gaulle, Communists and economic development replaced Giraud, Chiang and colonial independence as fundamentals of the President's strategy."[39] Roosevelt's Vichy policy and his anti-colonialist policies proved short-sighted in terms of postwar realities.

It would be a mistake to reduce the U.S.-Free French relations to nothing more than a de Gaulle-Roosevelt personal rivalry. It is significant that the president was agreeing with Stalin that France should have no role in the postwar order, with the president dismissing

France as "null." Jean Lacouture, de Gaulle's biographer, writes that "FDR's thesis in those days [1940–1942] was that 'there was no France,' and that the country was Re Nullius (these expressions are to be found in many of his conversations) until the French people spoke by means of an election."[40]

> Franklin Roosevelt, contemplating a France "that did not exist," in order to further his strategic aims, his prejudices and his impulses, decided to bring it into "existence" at least on the diplomatic level, and to show the world and the French citizens that he, the most powerful man on earth and the certain victor, legitimated only those Frenchmen who were not fighting and the rulers who shook hands with Adolph Hitler two or three times a year.[41]

FDR wanted General de Gaulle out-maneuvered, and his plan was to make the liberation of France one of military occupation, and to dominate the future politics of France in a manner similar to the German case, by means of American-supervised democratic elections. In this Roosevelt failed. To the end, he believed that "General de Gaulle seems to want to force himself upon the French nation by making use of the allied armies."[42]

Germany and Hitler: Just Another European State?

Most appeasers of the 1930s did not read Hitler's *Mein Kampf* or did not take it seriously. Roosevelt lacked any understanding of Hitler and of ideological mass movements. Roosevelt, the master politician, was the first American president to handle mass communication effectively. But he was indifferent to the uses of mass movements elsewhere. Roosevelt and Chamberlain saw Hitler as another European dictator, if a particularly vulgar one. Roosevelt objected to Hitler in the way liberals objected to such dictators as Mussolini, Primo de Rivera, Salazar, Pilsudski, Metaxas. Roosevelt did not concern himself with Nazi doctrine, social ideas, the concentration camps, or the steady persecution of Germany's Jews. Roosevelt did not fear Hitler, and this led him to underestimate him, a failing he shared with Chamberlain and the rest of the European statesmen of the time.

In 1938, Roosevelt had Welles try to organize an international conference to resolve Hitler's claims. If Latin American dictators, with whom Roosevelt was familiar, could be handled by a combination of financial promises and threats, why not Hitler or Mussolini? The appeasers, with their distorted sense of political realism, did not realize that Hitler's ideological commitments were nonnegotiable. Hitler's vision of war and conquest and the destruction of whole races was impossible for men like Chamberlain or Roosevelt to envision or understand.

Roosevelt's almost casual attitude toward Hitler in the 1930s came full circle during the war years. But FDR's unconditional surrender policy also suffered from the same misunderstanding of context and details. Identifying Germany with Hitler, Roosevelt was unwilling to strike a deal with it, unlike Churchill, who was motivated by realpolitik and practical considerations of the future.

The debate over unconditional surrender and the Morgenthau plan illustrates Roosevelt's method of operation. Some supported maximal punishment of Germany that included its dismemberment, deindustrialization, and demilitarization. The deindustrialization of Germany and turning it into an agricultural nation was the essence of the Morgenthau plan. The debate among the Americans continued from the Teheran conference to the second Quebec conference to the Yalta conference. "Franklin Roosevelt's administrative style made for uncertainty and competition within the American government, and the jealousy which characterized relations between the War and State Departments finds no better illustration than in planning for Germany."[43]

The Morgenthau plan intended to destroy Germany as a state and an industrial power for years to come. The War Department plan concerned itself with how to administer an occupied Germany. The State Department opposed deindustrialization on the grounds that America's prosperity and security would depend on a strong Europe and Germany would be crucial for that. Another option was a complete occupation by the Anglo-American Allies before the Soviets reached Germany.[44]

There was no final decision, although it appeared after the Quebec conference that Morgenthau's plan, which had been leaked to the *New York Times* and the *Wall Street Journal* before the 1944 elections, had won out. Kimball raises the question of whether Roosevelt was motivated by a commitment to Morgenthau's plan or whether he favored dismemberment as a way to satisfy Russian demands for physical security. The State Department professionals, who were largely anti-Soviet, were concerned about a "pastoralized" Germany that would facilitate Soviet expansion, fearing the Soviet Union would replace Germany as the major Central European state.[45] Roosevelt's procrastination and refusal to choose between Morgenthau's plan and those who opposed it allowed events to take their course.

In the end, Roosevelt's hesitation doomed the Morgenthau plan. Roosevelt refused to deal with details concerning the future of Germany, Poland, and the European balance of power. The outcome was, in the words of one historian, "a classic example of the Roosevelt style: a vague consensus achieved by virtually ignoring arguments which did not appeal to him."[46] The division of Germany stemmed from his moralistic anti-German stance after four years of war. It was not based on American interests or even on cooperation with the USSR.

Yet, the president, the Congress, and the American people were not prepared to play power politics, to participate in spheres of influence, or act out the policy of the Four Policemen. The Four Policemen, made up by implication of the United States, Great Britain, the USSR, and China, meant a division of the world into spheres of influence under the hegemony of the four great powers "which would make all the more important decisions and wield police powers."[47] Grand as the theory sounded, there was nothing in the actions of FDR or his close advisors and surrogates that would indicate that the United States was prepared and willing to assume its postwar responsibilities, certainly not in the European theater. There was nothing in the summits at Casablanca, Yalta, and even Potsdam that foreshadowed American participation in spheres of influence. The State Department had made studies and proposals, but they did not have the ear of the White House.

There was no evidence that the United States was willing to stay militarily in force in Europe and to help arrange the new postwar order. Partitions of the world meant the pursuit of "imperial" policies. At best, the great arbiter FDR was willing to preside over reconciling nations' conflicts, but not to policing the world, and certainly not Europe. The task of a hegemonic power was permanent military and political involvement in international power politics, a world the likes of which Roosevelt, Hopkins, and the rest of the surrogates eschewed. Woods, to my mind, is charitable when he writes that "Hemmed in by congressional chauvinism, isolationist opinion and popular, romantic notions of internationalism, Roosevelt fell back on a policy of personal diplomacy and appeasement of the Soviet Union."[48]

Roosevelt appeased the Soviet Union by postwar restrictions on Lend-Lease and public attacks on British imperialism, which were popular with Stalin as well as with the American public. Already at Yalta, the die had been cast in the direction of appeasement of the Soviet Union as a postwar policy, leaving a desperate Churchill to unsuccessfully negotiate with Stalin on his own. By relegating to the Soviet Union the eastern part of Germany, the president in fact tacitly accepted the Russian claims of hegemony over Eastern Europe. What started in Teheran with the abandonment of Poland ended with the partition of Germany. Appeasing Stalin was the price the U.S. paid for staying out of European power politics.

Until 1938, Roosevelt had been a closet isolationist. By 1945, he had come full circle. With the threat of nazism eliminated, he returned to his previous inclinations. The rhetorics of world community, collective security, and the like were reminiscent of Roosevelt's 1937 speech urging the "Quarantine of the Aggressor"; that is, a speech that was inspiring, eloquent, romantic, but without any real practical consequence. Faced with the Churchill-Eden plan of a European federation designed to protect weaker, smaller states against aggression (this time in the form of Stalin), Roosevelt turned his back on his old ally. His internationalism was only rhetorical, not practical. The president's postwar policy amounted to appeasing the Soviets and keeping Great Britain at arm's length.

FDR's internationalism was a mixture of Wilsonian collective security ideas and a pragmatic world New Deal under the most strenuous circumstances. Hitler's unprecedented aggression finally awakened the president to the uncompromising Nazi destruction of the European system and the enslavement of it to some form of an international SS state. Stalin unfortunately did not evoke the same reaction from the president. Stalin was just another European statesman, another imperialist; unlike Hitler, he was harmless. We know of no reference by the president or his advisors to Stalin's atrocities and purges. In fact in two cases of the great purge trials, FDR swallowed Ambassador Davies' shameless defense of Stalin. In the case of the Katyn Polish officers massacre, FDR's first instincts had been to accept the Nazi discovery of Stalin's activities as a Goebbelsian propaganda ploy to thwart the Allies.

All that Roosevelt wanted was to keep the U.S. out of European power politics and to delegate authority instead to a surrogate international order—the United Nations. FDR supposedly never resolved in his own mind whether he was more committed to ridding Europe of its old ills, *i.e.,* imperialism, than he was to maintaining collective security. At least collective security would have meant an end to the balance of power which was, in FDR's view, the conceptual tool of Old World European imperialists. Collective security was FDR's global New Deal, wherein Stalin's Russia—not old Britain and France—became the U.S.'s senior partner.

Chapter 10

President Roosevelt as a Diplomatic Failure

Franklin Roosevelt's political grandeur in the twentieth century stands almost purely on the basis of his leadership, first during the Great Depression and later, and more importantly, during World War II. There is no question that FDR was a great war leader, not in terms of substance, detail, or strategy, but by the sheer force of his personality and magnetism. He was a great generalist, not a great general; and he could describe and lead the American war effort with dramatic and rhetorical power.

His virtues—the ability to lead with passion, to be unencumbered by and indeed to ignore detail, his belief in his own vision, and his ability to project supreme optimism—were virtues that made him a great leader. But those qualities were also flaws that produced a diplomatic failure of huge proportions, because they were flaws that produced an unreasoning blindness and an unwillingness to deal with reality in his pursuit of Wilsonian goals. As George Kennan has written:

> The truth is—there is no avoiding it—that Franklin Roosevelt, for all his charm and for all his skill as a political leader, was, when it came to foreign policy, a very superficial man, ignorant, dilettantish, with

a severely limited intellectual horizon. One has only to glance at the list of ideas he had in the thirties and then during the war for solving his various problems of external policy. . . . The prewar schemes for consultative pacts and disarmament agreements, summit conferences and quarantines were as unrealistic as were the concepts of unconditional surrender, the "four policemen" and the Morgenthau plan for Germany by which his war-time policy was informed. Either these schemes were cynically designed to appeal to a series of opinionated and unenlightened domestic lobbies, without serious regard to their external effect, or they bore witness to a very poor understanding of international affairs on the part of their author.[1]

Confined to a wheelchair by his crippling illness, FDR nevertheless projected the image of an activist, a pragmatist, an optimist, which rewarded him with huge popularity. By 1940, FDR was already beginning to shed the isolationism of his administration and gearing up for an unprecedented fourth term. It was obvious that he loved the office he held and that the American people responded wholeheartedly to his dynamism, the ebullient spirit he projected. He was talkative, charismatic, a man totally at one with his place in the world. He was seen as a master of electoral politics; and to the nation, he was seen as Mr. Recovery, even though that image was largely a matter of style over substance, since all of the administration's whirlwind programs had not managed to pull the country out of the Depression. It took the war to do that, but FDR had overcome the worst effects of the Depression and, more importantly, had given the people a measure of hope, a belief that the worst was over.

His record, his personality, and his popularity made him the perfect war president. He was the Commander in Chief in deed and perception. He was "the administration," which made his job of leading the nation through the war that much easier. Getting into the war was another matter, and Pearl Harbor made that hotly debated issue a moot one. With the Japanese attack, FDR no longer needed to seek congressional support—there was no question that he would get it.

Before that, Roosevelt had wrestled with his own doubt and, more difficult, with the strong isolationist forces in Congress. He had hedged before, first by inclination, then by political necessity, at becoming a direct belligerent, but there was no question where his sympathies lay. Slowly, and with considerable political maneuvering, he managed to move Congress and public opinion toward the idea that the question was no longer whether the country would enter the war, but when.

Certainly, by the time of Pearl Harbor, there was no question of the United States being neutral. FDR and the United States were merely postponing what was inevitable. Lend-Lease and assistance to Great Britain, measures of everything short of war, were hardly the acts of a neutral country. Yet FDR refused to rush into the war, indeed probably lacked the support to do so.

Instead, he kept friends and foe alike guessing. FDR had become a tacit belligerent by supporting Britain's struggle for survival against Nazi Germany. He knew that a Nazi-occupied England was a disaster for the United States, a dagger aimed at America. The Atlantic would become a Nazi ocean. He would not allow that to happen. The question was when, where, and how the United States would eventually enter the war, when it would commit its potential economic might, and whether the effort would be limited or total.

Hitler, for one, had no idea, and he got no help from his intelligence services. No one really knew, because the president himself was not sure. His style—reacting to events by procrastinating, bluffing, resorting to blustering rhetoric and warnings—short-circuited any intelligent analysis or interpretation of the president's plans beyond immediate events. FDR's habit of consulting with many and listening to few if any prevented Axis intelligence services from gauging American intentions. His free-lance style circumvented normal bureaucratic channels, his unpredictable behavior offered no guide or clues. He was inconsistent, aloof, armed with an impenetrable charm and an entertaining manner—the tilted, jaunty cigarette-holder, the sparkling eyes, the exaggerated bravado.

Most of his rivals, in short, found it difficult to understand him, to find some consistent theme that would let them anticipate future action. Hitler was a Eurocentrist who was profoundly ignorant of the United States, and he misinterpreted Roosevelt's gentlemanly posture and easygoing style as signs of a lack of hardness and fiber.

FDR was not a military strategist, but then he never pretended to be one. In this, he differed markedly from Churchill, Hitler, and Stalin, each of whom embodied and symbolized the great war leader for his country. Hitler directly guided and interfered with every detail, following his vaunted intuition, overriding his generals, proclaiming his military genius with disastrous results. Stalin, too, had total control over his country's military operations. Even Churchill liked to think of himself as a brilliant strategist, and he drove his generals to fits of distraction with his meddling.

FDR was wise enough to leave the actual running of the war to his generals and military advisors, especially Generals Marshall and Eisenhower. He trusted them completely, and relied heavily on Marshall. The generals had few if any political axes to grind. They were able, competent, sometimes brilliant, and, more importantly, they understood the president's distaste for detail, sparing him the complex operational plans of their campaigns.

Kent Roberts Greenfield, chief historian of the Department of the Army, wrote in *American Strategy* that of eight crucial American strategic decisions in World War II, Roosevelt, after being consulted, adopted and supported the decisions of his chiefs. At times, he bowed to martially oriented Churchill's advice, overriding his military advisors, as in the decision to make Europe the theater priority over Asia (a decision that miffed the admirals, not to mention General Douglas MacArthur) and in the decision on timing for the opening of the Second Front. Unlike Churchill, Roosevelt had no military experience; he did not pretend to understand the nuances of military strategy, in spite of his experience as a former assistant secretary of the navy during World War I.

True, his affections rested with the Navy, but never to the point that he displayed favoritism for one service arm over another. He would not meddle, because he was, after all, the Commander in Chief and he, along with Churchill, ran the war. He was by no means a grand strategist, for that would require an immersion in detail, which he loathed. He conducted the American war effort with a personal, noninstitutional, and domineering style. He was Mr. America at war. The qualities that made him a great war leader had nothing to do with military thinking; rather it was his determination, his personality, his authoritarian behavior, and his projection of absolute confidence that made him, along with Churchill and Stalin, a great war leader.

But just as FDR was a great war leader, so he was also a great failure as a diplomat. He helped win the war, but he lost the peace. This is not a resurrection of the old warhorse charge that Roosevelt was duped by the Communists. Rather my argument is that he was deceived by his own vision. This was a tragic failure, especially for a president who had led and conducted his country in its greatest foreign war.

The example of Lincoln, to whom FDR is sometimes compared, is instructive. Lincoln was a great war leader—even something of a grand strategist and a supreme military chief—but he also succeeded as a diplomat. Lincoln's stated goal in fighting the Civil War was not to free the slaves but to preserve the Union, which he did. Preparing for and waging a war is only half the task of a war leader.

What was Roosevelt's goal? What was his postwar policy? His war goals were crusading in nature, to fight a holy war to defeat the totalitarian Axis nations, in particular the evils of nazism and fascism. In this, he and the Alliance he forged and sometimes led, succeeded. But his vision for a postwar world was idealistic, Wilsonian, totally at odds with reality. He would help create a new international order, presided over in an equal partnership by the two emerging super-powers, the United States and the Soviet Union, and buttressed by the newly created world organization, the United Nations.

FDR's wartime diplomacy, geared to his vision of the postwar world, was fueled by what could almost be called a desperate desire to fulfill the dream that the Soviets would be America's postwar partner. This required an amazing ignorance, a willingness to ignore past and present facts, and a complete misunderstanding of the Soviet system and of Stalin. FDR was right that the United States and the Soviet Union would be the postwar superpowers, but he was absolutely and disastrously wrong about the nature of their future relationship.

FDR's diplomacy and postwar vision were wrong from the outset, based on an unworkable premise that poisoned any number of political-military decisions throughout the war. FDR was wrong because he never understood or wanted to understand; he never inquired into the nature and structure of the Soviet political system, as did, for instance, George Kennan, the brilliant young State Department officer who lost all of his illusions about the nature of Soviet conduct early in the game.

When Hitler invaded the Soviet Union and the USSR became the West's ally, a good deal of clumsy propaganda-shuffling was required. Because the Nazis had invaded Mother Russia and the USSR was now allied to the Western democracies, the USSR became a "democracy," at least a Socialist one, fighting alongside the United States against the criminal, totalitarian Nazis. A wholesale propaganda campaign was launched to persuade the public of Russia's and Stalin's democratic nature. It may be that FDR convinced himself more than he did anyone else. He could not conceive of the fact that Stalin, the USSR, international communism, and the Communist party were not what he said they were—that is, at heart democratic and benign future partners of America. Thus, Soviet occupation and manipulation of Eastern European countries become "territorial adjustments."

Stalin had no dreamy ideas for the future. He was ruthlessly pragmatic and consistent and steadfast in his goals throughout the course of the war. Before, during, and after the turning point battle of Stalingrad, Stalin was consistent in his world outlook and stance. He was a Communist, a totalitarian, a despot who meant to gain as much territory as he could for his nation, certainly the lands he had secured in the Nazi-Soviet Pact. He had no intentions whatsoever of becoming a partner to America, or anyone else, after the war. He was shrewd enough, however, to understand FDR's weaknesses and play to them.

If one judges success by achieving stated war aims, FDR was a total and abject failure, and FDR had only himself to blame for his failure. For the most part he chose advisors who would tell him what he wanted to hear. Those with bad news, warnings, or forebodings and misgivings about the Soviets were cut off from the president or were ignored.

It is clear that Hopkins shared and echoed FDR's feelings, that Davies was a venal, grasping proselytizer for the Soviets, and that Harriman did not wake up to the Soviet danger until very late in the game, circa 1944. Cordell Hull shared FDR's free trade and internationalist visions. These were the men FDR listened to, if he listened to anybody.

The younger State Department professionals, many of them educated in the ways of the Soviet Union, like Bohlen, Henderson, and Kennan, could make no difference. The rabidly anti-Bolshevik and experienced Bullitt, who had once been mesmerized by the Leninist vision back in the 1920s, saw the reality of Stalin's state as the first U.S. Ambassador to the USSR in the 1930s and had been sounding the alarm ever since. During the war, he was all but persona non grata at the White House.

To achieve his postwar goal, FDR made continued concessions to pacify Stalin. The argument that the president and his men were concerned about a possible Stalin-Hitler rapprochement rings hollow today, based as it was on the fact of a few low-level contacts between Germans and Russians. Keeping Stalin in the war was not sufficient reason to make the kind of territorial concessions the Western powers ended up making.

FDR's behavior and attitudes at Teheran and Yalta, and the attitudes of his surrogate diplomats that reflected his, led to his diplomatic failure. The world he envisioned and so desperately wanted to create never materialized, and, more importantly, never had a chance of materializing, because it rested on a false premise, buttressed by willful ignorance. FDR did not have a glimmer that the pursuit of his vision, and the concessions he made to it, would result, not in a partnership with Stalin and the USSR, but rather in its opposite, in the onset of the Cold War that would last almost half a century.

Since the president was his own diplomat, secretary of state, and national security chief, he alone bears full and direct responsibility for America's diplomatic failure in the Second World War. The great war leader failed to win the peace.

Appendix 1

Characteristics of Wendell Willkie

Declassified December 12, 1989
Classified September 3, 1942

To: THE CHAIRMAN OF THE STATE DEFENSE COMMITTEE

    COMRADE *STALIN I.V.*

THE PEOPLE'S COMMISSAR OF FOREIGN AFFAIRS

    COMRADE *MOLOTOV V.M.*

Herewith I enclose a detailed *characteristics of Wendell Willkie.* I direct your attention to Willkie's demagogic statement of August 23, which he made to the papers before his departure from the United States. Willkie deliberately demonstrates his anti-Fascist moods, as he is of German extraction and is afraid to be accused of insufficient American patriotism. All of his pro-Soviet statements are evidently of a selective nature, as he hopes to win presidential election in 1944, using the tide of sympathy for the Soviet Union.

Deputy People's Commissar of Foreign Affairs

S. Lozovsky

Forward to: Stalin, Molotov, Mikoyan, Voroshilov, Beria, Kaganovich, Vyshinsky, Sobolev, Lozovsky, Umansky.

Classified September 2, 1942

Wendell Willkie

Willkie was born on February 18, 1892, in Elwood (Indiana), a small, typical midwestern town. His grandmother and grandfather were of German extraction. During the election campaign Willkie used to say that his father's and mother's parents left Germany in order "to breathe the free air of America." Willkie's father was a lawyer who once worked as a school principal. Willkie's mother was a schoolteacher.

Having finished school in Elwood, Willkie entered the University of Indiana in Bloomington. During summer vacations, he and other students did odd jobs in different parts of the country. Willkie worked at a metallurgical shop, helped with harvesting in Dakota, and also served as a cook.

In his 1940 speeches to the electorate, during his presidential campaign, Willkie tried to prove that he, coming from a modest American family, had broken through to the position he had at that time. "Same as you, I have gone along a thorny path," Willkie told the electorate in Iowa, speaking at one of his numerous campaign meetings.

But as the *New Republic* magazine wrote in its special issue devoted to Willkie, "His real path was nearly as thorny as that of Roosevelt. Willkie was brought up in a family that was able to give education to all the children and to help them settle down in life."

Right after his graduation from the university, Willkie showed an interest in teaching. In 1913 he started to teach in a secondary school in Coffeyville (Kansas) where he taught history and oratory, and coached basketball. But very soon teaching disillusioned him, and a year later he left for Puerto Rico, where he worked as a laboratory hand at one of the sugar refineries. After learning by experience that his father's occupation was much better, Willkie returned to his native Indiana. He received a degree in law and joined his father's solicitor's firm in Elwood.

During the First World War Willkie served in the army. He stayed in

Europe with the American expeditionary forces. Upon his return from Europe with the rank of captain, Willkie began to practice law with the Firestone Tire Co. in Akron, Ohio. Having worked for some months with this firm, he jumped at the opportunity to become a co-owner of a solicitor's firm in the same town.

During the following years, working with this firm, Willkie became well known in that town. A talented orator and solicitor, he delivered speeches on cases connected with the promotion of democratic freedoms, and that experience has assisted him a lot in his career. A play for democracy, the presentation of himself as one of the people's own, a liberal who cherished American constitutional freedoms and was ready to promote them—all of this was characteristic of Willkie and his subsequent political career. For example, being the worst enemy of the Communist party, Willkie as a lawyer did not think twice about pleading the case of Schneider, secretary of the Communist party of California, in the U.S. Supreme Court after California's legal bodies had delivered a judgment the preceding year about deportation of Schneider as an "undesirable foreigner."

With his abilities and vigor Willkie managed to attract the attention of the heads of some companies that owned public-use enterprises. In 1926 Irvin S. Cobb, one of the heads of Penn-Ohio and Commonwealth Power, said, "Do not let this young man get away."

Willkie started to function on the national level in 1927–1928, and in 1929 he was invited to New York to join as a junior partner the law firm Weadock and Weadock, which was affiliated with the board of the big electric company Commonwealth and Southern Corporation, an associate of the Dupont banking-house [and its legal counsel]. In 1933, when the question arose about a head for this company (Commonwealth and Southern Corporation), Willkie was the choice. He served as head of this company from 1933 to 1940 and left it in connection with his preparations for the presidential election campaign.

As chairman of the board of directors for Commonwealth and Southern Corporation, Willkie received annually not less than 75 thousand dollars. Taking into consideration the fact that he was simultaneously the director of some smaller companies that were members of Commonwealth and Southern Corporation (he was the director of Consumers Power Co., Central Illinois Light Co., Trustee Edison Electric Institute, Ohio Edison Co., Southern Indiana Gas and Electric Co.), then one can say with certainty that Willkie earned not less than 100–125 thousand dollars a year.

Willkie's life story does not remind one of those of Edison or Ford. He never was a wage-worker. Willkie enjoyed the reputation of an orator and liberal who was hired by the heads of the public-use enterprises of Akron for the purpose of defending their interests.

During his election campaign Willkie said practically nothing about his attitude toward the workers' organizations, except for a few remarks in some of his speeches. But as the head of the biggest electric company, Willkie demonstrated his position on this question. Commonwealth and Southern Corporation, a company with capital exceeding 1 billion dollars, was combating the workers' organizations. This circumstance to a great extent created problems for his associates in conducting the election campaign in his favor.

According to the information of the Committee of Civil Liberties [Willkie's struggle against TVA?] once headed by La Follette, seven out of ten subsidiary enterprises of Commonwealth and Southern Corporation used the services of out-and-out spies who were known as thugs of trade union organizations. For the period from 1934 up to 1936, one of Willkie's companies, Georgia Power Co. [in conflict with FDR's TVA], spent 31 thousand dollars on spies [it employed Pinkerton's detectives] who at the same time served the Alabama Power Co. Another of Willkie's firms, Central Illinois Light, purchased bombs, pistols with teargas bullets, and grenades from a military firm. Three of Willkie's firms, namely Consumers Power of Michigan, Ohio Edison Power, and Pennsylvania Edison Power, used the services of a secret service agency called Corporation Auxiliary Co. La Follette's committee had no opportunity to disclose the amount of money spent by Willkie on the dispersal of the workers' organizations, and thus, naturally, the picture is incomplete.

Willkie's companies waged a struggle against workers, members of trade unions, members of the Congress of Industrial Trade Unions. No stone was left unturned; there were even terrorist acts. Willkie fought against the state electric company that was set up upon Roosevelt's initiative in keeping with his New Deal program. Roosevelt intended to limit Willkie's monopoly through the organization of this company.

In the opinion of the *New Republic,* representing the views of the American liberal intellectuals, which covered Willkie in detail during his presidential campaign of 1940, Willkie is an ardent exponent of big capital and an opponent of any state interference into business undertakings. First of all, Willkie believes that public control, allegedly conducted in the interests of consumers, workers, and farmers, in fact does not represent the interests of the people but rather addresses the politicians' craving for power. What we should be afraid of, Willkie says, is not big business, but an ambitious government. Deep depression and deprivations were caused not so much by the industrialists' and financiers' activity, but by the government's interference into business life. Willkie holds that the essence of freedom lies in free enterprise and that striving for profit forms the basis of civilization. In Willkie's opinion, "people and business life are inseparable," and "promotion of the freedom of people against the omnipresent control of the government—this is today's liberalism."

New York Times, which came out against the candidacy of Roosevelt for a third term, wrote that "Willkie enjoys the confidence of business circles and is an industrialist himself." The biggest and most influential financiers and industrial barons—such as Dupont, Rockefeller, Vanderbilt, Whitney, Thomas Lamont (one of the main partners of Morgan); Davison, Morgan's company solicitor; Mooney, vice-chairman of General Motors (and the holder of Hitler's Iron Cross); and others—supported Willkie's candidacy.

But despite the fact that Willkie is closely connected with all of the Wall Street circle, this circumstance does not prevent him from demagogically playing the role of the supporter of democratic rights. In his speech to the convention of the Democratic party, Willkie said that "the democratic forces are facing the most radical test at the moment and we, Republicans and Americans, should promote the principles of the USA, which is the stronghold of democracy in the whole world. I am going to conduct a decisive campaign in order to achieve the unity of America, the unity of farmers, workers, and all classes for the promotion of freedom."

Willkie's position on the question of assistance to Great Britain is characterized best of all by his words: "We should go on with our assistance to Great Britain which is our best line of defense and our only remaining friend. We should render assistance to Great Britain within the limits of reason and efficiency, determined by impartial experts" (from his speech in San Francisco on September 21, 1940).

In one of his campaign speeches Willkie gave the following reasons for American assistance to Great Britain. He said,

> We should admit that the loss of the British Navy would consider-ably weaken our defense. If the British Navy were destroyed or captured then Germany would dominate in the Atlantic Ocean and would have control over the majority of vessels and shipbuilding enterprises of Europe. That would be a real disaster for us. We would find ourselves unprotected against the attacks from the Atlantic. Our defense would be weakened unless we managed to build the Navy and Aviation. Our foreign trade would be affected seriously as well. This kind of trade is absolutely necessary for our prosperity, but if we had to trade with Europe under conditions of present-day German trade policy, probably we would also have to change our methods in favor of some totalitarian forms. Anyone who likes democracy should take this perspective into consideration.
> (from a speech in Indiana on August 17, 1940)

Some words about the history of the struggle that flared up be-tween the Republicans and the Democrats during the last presiden-tial campaign in 1940 enable us to comprehend better the stand adopted by Willkie and his associates on the question of the U.S. domestic and foreign policies.

In the election platform adopted by the convention of the Republi-can party in Philadelphia, the Republicans assured their electorate that they were against the involvement of the country in the war in Europe; that they stood for the Monroe Doctrine regarding support to Great Britain "within the international law" and "without damage to the national defense." Like the Democrats, the Republicans de-manded promotion of the Monroe Doctrine. Sharply attacking the Democrats for having done too little toward the arming of the country, the Republicans came out for an increase of the military budget.

Thus there were no divergences in principle on the question of foreign policy between the Republicans and the Democrats. The matter of internal policy was a more complicated one. The Republicans had to thoroughly disguise their reactionary essence as they could not but see that broad layers of the electorate gave their votes to Roosevelt as the fighter for their interests.

The Republicans did not promise anything concrete to the voters on the question of the internal political problems in their election platform. Though they had abandoned direct attacks on Roosevelt, still the Republicans and their candidate Willkie accused the president of a dictatorial style, promised to preserve democracy, and "to make the U.S. powerful," all the while demanding great sacrifices from the people.

In his election speeches Willkie hinted at possible increases in taxation in connection with the war, at decreases in wages, and at introduction of compulsory military service. With the purpose of obtaining workers' votes, Willkie demagogically stated that he was for collective bargaining, for assistance to the unemployed, for the regulation of wages and working hours, for improvement of the farmers' position.

There was no unanimity in the ranks of the Republican party during the presidential election campaign of 1940. As early as then, two camps could be singled out. On the one hand, there was a powerful group uniting around Willkie and his interventionist policy, in principle aimed at the support of Roosevelt's foreign policy, unlimited assistance to the countries fighting against aggression. At that time Willkie's group broke away radically from isolationism. On the other hand, there was a group composed of such pillars of isolationism as Herbert Hoover, Senators Taft, Vandenberg, Ney, Brooks, Burton, and members of Congress Hamilton Fish, George Tinkham, and others. This group (Hoover/Taft) accused Roosevelt of inactivity in the sphere of U.S. military preparedness (while they themselves always voted in Congress against allocations for military purposes and defensive installations). They spoke against any kind of assistance to Great Britain and other countries fighting against Hitler's aggression, recommended acting as a go-between for Great Britain and Germany, and appeasement of the aggressor countries.

During the whole period after the termination of the presidential campaign up to the assault on Pearl Harbor, Willkie and his associates (Senators Austin, Lodge, Desverine [no senator, but a Willkie aide]) were trying to prove to the Hooverites the banality of the isolationism that led the party toward destruction. In their turn, the Hooverites accused Willkie of letting the Republicans down, claiming that he might as well consider himself a Democrat instead of a Republican.

In summer, 1941, the contradictions between these two groups were so great that the press started to speak about a possible split in the Republican party and the formation of a new party of Republicans under the leadership of Willkie. This became most noticeable after all the right-wing reactionary Republicans (Hoover, Landon, Taft, Brooks, Dewey, Fish, Tinkham) united around the Fascist committee of Lindberg-Wood, America First, and unleashed dirty pro-Fascist propaganda against Roosevelt and his foreign policy course.

This traitorous activity of the Hooverites, in union with such undisguised Fascists as Lindberg, Wood, radio-priest Cofflin, a black-shirt Belly, and others, did not stop after Hitler's hordes invaded the USSR. It would be correct to say that America First escalated its frenzied activity right after Hitler's Germany aimed its aggression against the USSR.

Basing themselves on mighty press coverage (*Chicago Tribune, New York Daily News,* Scripps-Howard press), the right-wing reactionaries—Republicans with the support of reactionary Democrats like Senators Reynolds, Clark, Miller—counted on sowing discord between the U.S. and the USSR, on achieving an end to combat actions between the Germans and the British, on appeasing Japan at the expense of China and the USSR, etc. The old bugaboo of Red Threat to Europe and the whole world in case of the victory of Bolshevik Russia was brought out on the stage again.

The conflicts between Willkie and the Hoover/Taft groups have not been overcome yet. They resurfaced at the meeting of the national committee of the Republican party that took place on April 10, 1942, while the political resolution was being endorsed. Two resolutions had been submitted to the national committee: one by Willkie and the other by Senator Taft of Ohio.

Willkie's draft resolution on this question demanded unconditional continuation of the war, regardless of its cost, until "the U.S. and the

Allies gain the complete victory over Germany, Italy, Japan and their Allies." Willkie stated, "We cannot agree to peace with the above mentioned nations except as a result of victory and we, on all conditions, until the final victory is gained, will reject any propositions however convincing these propositions may be." Willkie spoke in favor of the U.S. "undertaking both at present and future everything that might be expedient in relation to international pledges in the present-day world."

Willkie's opponents in the Republican party, the Hoover/Taft associates, promised in their draft resolution to unconditionally support the president in the course of conducting the war until complete victory was gained, but the resolution did not come out against acceptance of peaceful proposals by the enemy, nor did it approve of the U.S. adopting international pledges.

Sharp conflict flared up around these two drafts, but on the whole Willkie's resolution was passed in a slightly amended form. All of the American press regarded the resolution of the Republican party's national committee as a complete defeat for the isolationist elements, since Willkie's victory demanded that the party resolutely express its stand against the policy of appeasement or compromise.

In his interview with American press representatives, Willkie himself stated that the passing of the resolution testified to the Republican party's denial of the isolationist stand and that in its resolution the national committee of the party had "declined any appeasement policy and expressed the desire of the American people to continue the war ruthlessly, unconditionally, up to the complete victory over any enemy."

Willkie's article published in *Fortune* magazine during the days of the Soviet-Finnish conflict is characteristic of his position in relation to the USSR. In this article he wrote: "We resolutely sympathize with the Finns in their struggle against the USSR. If Finland rebuffs the attack of the USSR, then universal peace and economic order will be more safeguarded. But if the USSR defeats Finland, then universal peace and economic order will be jeopardized. We'd like to assist Finland to the extent we can without participating in the war." [This by the darling of the Progressives!]

After June 22, 1941, Willkie adopted a resolute line of assisting us in the struggle against Hitler's Germany. In his salutary telegram to the meeting devoted to our demand for opening the Second Front, which took place on July 22 of this year, Willkie wrote: "I hoped to be with you this evening, but as it is impossible, I'd like you to know that, in my opinion, you behave perfectly." And further: "You are letting the Russians know that we, the Americans, admire their courage, resoluteness and heroism and do not want their victims to die in vain. You are letting the fearless defenders of this country know that we, the Americans, are going to prove our words with deeds."

And finally it is worthwhile to mention Willkie's statement made to the New York TASS correspondent in connection with his forthcoming visit to the Soviet Union. Willkie declared that "this visit will lead to the establishment of more complete mutual understanding between the Soviet and the American peoples. Russia and the U.S. should act together not only at present, but in the future too. As a result of this trip I'd like to have an opportunity to present the viewpoints of the Russians to the U.S. and also to inform Russia about the U.S. point of view. I am looking forward to meeting Mister Stalin and intend to learn as much as possible about Russia. I have long looked forward to it and am very grateful to the government for granting me permission to make this trip."

In Willkie's opinion the Red Army's courageous resistance is one of the most outstanding phenomena in history. Willkie spoke with enthusiasm about the "combat spirit of the Russian people who are conducting the war under the great leadership."

Willkie is still enjoying great prestige and influence in the Republican party. But he regularly encounters opposition on the part of his rivals who are seeking to grab the leadership in the Republican party. In particular, some elements confront Willkie who were against his support of Roosevelt's foreign policy before the events at Pearl Harbor. The conflicts inside the Republican party have especially revealed themselves at the meeting of the Republican organization in the state of New York which took place some days before (the Congress was convened for the nomination of a candidate for the governor of the state and also for the elaboration of the party program). At present the party apparatus of the state is under the control of

[Thomas] Dewey, the former attorney-general of the state of New York, who failed to secure the nomination for the presidency in 1940.

The resolution submitted by Willkie's supporters was radically changed by the executive committee of the Republican party of the state of New York. This resolution proposed that the Republican convention approve the resolution that contained well-wishing to Willkie's mission to the USSR and the Middle East and also expressed a high estimation of Willkie's leadership. But the final text of the resolution approved by the committee did contain well-wishing toward Willkie's mission, but expressed no "high estimation" of his leadership of the party. The *New York Times* wrote in connection with this that "the original draft had caused sharp debates because Willkie was against Dewey and, besides, Willkie is not favored by the party organization of the state of New York because of his support for Roosevelt's foreign policy" (TASS, August 24, 1942).

Willkie's last speech broadcast over the radio to the whole country on August 21, this year, is characteristic of his stand on the current conduct of the war against the Axis states. In this speech Willkie said: "If we are going to defeat our enemies, then we should be prepared to fight and die for our cause. Many of us believe that real war is only the war of guns, aircraft, and production and that we will be able to win in the war only by surpassing the production level of the Axis powers. Following this path alone, we shall not win the war, unless there is strong and unshakable dedication to our cause behind the production of armaments, aircraft, and tanks" (*Izvestia,* August 22, 1942).

Head of the American Department
    Zarubin

September 3, 1942

Appendix 2

U.S. Policies

Declassified December 25, 1989
Classified June 2, 1943

USSR

PEOPLE'S COMMISSARIAT OF FOREIGN AFFAIRS

To: THE PEOPLE'S COMMISSAR OF FOREIGN AFFAIRS

    COMRADE V. M. MOLOTOV

    Herewith I enclose a memorandum on the United States requested by you. Possibly I have gone beyond the topic outlined by you, but I hope you will not object to it.

    As I do not know to whom I should forward copies, I have made four copies, one of which I forward to Comrade Stalin and two to you. I want you to deal with any further duplication and distribution of copies to such members of the Politbureau and the leadership of the People's Commissariat of Foreign Affairs as you find appropriate.

M. M. Litvinov

Declassified, December 25, 1989
Top Secret, June 2, 1943

The U.S. Policy

As for the policy of the U.S., it is certainly necessary to distinguish its war policy and politics, which determine its diplomatic aims. Right now, of course, we are concerned primarily with the war policy, and I'll start with it.

War Policy of the U.S.

We have very few opportunities to follow the war policy of the U.S., because there are no permanent contacts between the U.S. and the USSR, no source for consultations or at least information like the Anglo-American commissions or the Pacific Council, and because of the special secrecy of everything connected with the military sphere. Furthermore, the strategic plans of the Allies are mainly elaborated and changed in London, not in Washington.

The main problem, the essence of which is whether they should attach paramount importance to the struggle against the European members of the Axis or against Japan, could be regarded as resolved in favor of the first option. In the press, and even in the Congress, there have been many articles and speeches expressing the point of view of the isolationists, who prefer to concentrate the military efforts of the U.S. on the struggle against Japan. However, this is so absurd from the military point of view that there will hardly be many proponents of this stance in the War and Navy departments.

The president, the State Department, and the secretaries of War and Navy are decisively against this position. Paying a certain tribute to the proponents of isolationism and yielding to pressure from China and Australia, Roosevelt has had to send a lot of naval and air forces to the theaters of war in the Pacific, detaching considerable means of transport for this purpose. The most important strategic task of the

U.S. is the struggle against Hitler, especially since this is the point of view of British strategists.

The Second Front

As far as the struggle against Hitler is concerned, during the first months of my stay in Washington, when I had frequent contacts with Roosevelt, I got the impression that he was completely convinced of the necessity to open the Second Front as soon as possible and, certainly, in Western Europe. However, his military advisers seemed to be gradually dissuading him from that conviction, or maybe it was mainly Churchill. According to the available information, Churchill had pointed out the difficulty and even danger of landing in Western Europe and insisted on participation by a considerable number of American troops in that landing. He stipulated that condition, being well aware of its impracticality because of the lack of the means of transport for delivering the considerable American army with the necessary accoutrements to Europe. The plan of landing in North Africa is Roosevelt's, but it is very unlikely that he was prompted to that plan by the same Churchill who had lost any hope of defeating Rommel with British forces only. Moreover, Churchill's plan was to bury the idea of landing in the West for a long time. I can say for sure, regarding the war policy, Roosevelt is being towed by Churchill.

Strategic plans elaborated in Casablanca are known to us. I have every reason to think that lately American, and probably British, ruling circles have begun to doubt the expediency and sufficiency—maybe even the feasibility—of those plans. [Vice-President] Wallace openly told me about the coming review of them. Maybe he referred to Churchill's forthcoming visit to Washington, and that is why, I believe, this review will be the subject of meetings between Roosevelt and Churchill in Washington. However, I am very much concerned about the arrival of Field Marshall Sir Archibald Wavell [Supreme Commander, South-West Pacific, formerly Supreme Commander North-African Campaign, 1941–1942], along with Churchill. I fear that once again the question about activation of war operations in the Pacific

Ocean will be raised. On the way here one American general told me that the trip of Wavell would be just a camouflage meant for deceiving Hitler. But I greatly doubt it. Abandoning decisions made in Casablanca does not mean landing somewhere else. I assume that the refusal to land until slightly later, along with intensification of the bombing of Germany and Italy, is in hopes of forcing the latter to capitulate.

The British and Americans will probably refer to the difficulties of transporting British North-African armies to the English Isles. These armies are considered the most efficient and the only ones having combat experience. I am inclined to think that there can be no hope of opening the Second Front even in the South, to say nothing of the West of Europe, without very strong pressure on our part.

After drawing a distinction between the political aims and the strategic plans of Britain and America, we must also bear in mind a certain interaction between them. There is no doubt that the military plans of both countries are based on the goal of maximum exhaustion of the Soviet Union in order to diminish its role in the solution of postwar problems. Opening of the Second Front at the desirable point could be accelerated should the British and Americans apprehend catastrophic consequences resulting from our single combat against Hitler. Our successes at Stalingrad and in the Caucasus, as well as some of our own statements, leave no room for such apprehensions. They will wait for the development of combat actions at the Russian front. However, I cannot shake off the thought that if we wish, we can greatly influence the strategic plans of the Allies.

The U.S. Political Aims

Going on to the question of the political aims of the U.S., I should remind you that during the interim era between World War I and World War II U.S. political aims were far from clear and distinct, especially where European affairs were concerned, though American policy with respect to the Western hemisphere and the adjacent islands was more or less definite. There could be arguments about whether more or less independence should be granted to Cuba, the Philippines, Puerto Rico, but all American political orientations concur about the necessity to defend and strengthen the Monroe Doctrine, to prevent any interference into Latin American affairs, to oust European influence and competition from there, and to institute control by the U.S. over the Western hemisphere.

Japanese expansion into China caused some concern in America, and the American administration even began talks with Japan in connection with that. As for European affairs, all presidents, beginning with Wilson and including Roosevelt, were actually executing a policy of isolationism. It goes without saying that Roosevelt personally stands for the broadest participation of the U.S. in the solution of all world problems; he used to make fine gestures seeking a Platonic intimacy with the League of Nations, sermonizing and making diplomatic maneuvers for peace. He even took part in the conference at Brussels on the occasion of Japan's attack on China; however, he abstained from any formal acts, commitments, or binding agreements. Passing the Neutrality Act, and maintaining its strict observance even during the Spanish Civil War, was the most concrete manifestation of American isolationism, which nullified all the gestures Roosevelt had made in favor of European peace. That policy showed the limits of American isolationism.

Isolationism

It is a mistake to think that isolationism relies only on the nonindustrial midwestern states of America. There are many industrialists and financiers among those who side with the isolationists. They proceed from the idea that the U.S., with its rich mineral and vegetation resources, can exist happily as a secluded nation—carrying on foreign trade with other countries, maintaining high customs-tariffs, and avoiding interference into the affairs of the other continents from which the U.S. is guarded and protected by two oceans. The extreme isolationists go so far as to say that they are ready to acknowledge Japan's complete freedom to pursue expansion into Asia, considering

China unable to overcome its backwardness alone and anticipating that Japan will set up an order under which the U.S. could more readily deal with China than is now the case. Those who are more moderate don't go that far: they feel somewhat apprehensive about Japanese expansion, but they are ready to give up Europe as entirely lost, leaving it to its own destiny. Isolationism, along with Anglo- and Sovietphobia in foreign policy, is usually combined with extreme conservatism, reaction, and anti-Semitism in domestic policy. American isolationists, as well as the reactionaries of Great Britain and other countries, are ready to regard nazism as the only counterforce against communism; thus a struggle against nazism is not necessary. They also enjoy observing Hitler's struggle against Britain. Isolationism was a powerful instrument in the struggle against Roosevelt, too, and consequently against his domestic policy of concessions to the labor movement and reduction of the profits of big business and banking. The absence of a working-class party in the U.S., organizational weaknesses in liberal-radical circles, a new economic welfare era following the Depression of 1929–32, and the ensuing political indifference of the masses—all of these factors created a favorable base for isolationism and everything related to it. Taking into account those circumstances, Roosevelt made serious concessions to isolationism in his foreign policy over an extended period.

Deviation from Isolationism

Hitler's aggression against small and medium-sized European countries, from within which many American people had originated, the defeat of France and the existence of a direct threat to Great Britain, as well as the growing significance of aviation that reduced oceanic distances to nothing caused Roosevelt to begin a gradual and careful deviation from isolationist positions. This change in policy ultimately found expression in revocation of the Neutrality Act, in allowing Great Britain to have military vessels in exchange for U.S. use of its naval bases, and then in passage of the Lend-Lease Act.

The Japanese attack on Pearl Harbor and the declaration of war on

America by Germany and Italy completely untied the president's hands. There is no doubt that since there was no opportunity for Roosevelt and his followers to join the war of their own initiative, they were glad to support these causes and thereby become involved. Suffice it to recall the corresponding remarks made by Harriman in the Kremlin during the autumn of 1941. It is likewise interesting to note that when the president informed me by telephone about the Japanese assault several hours after my arrival in Washington and while I was having lunch with [Ambassador] Davies, the latter received that information with the words "Thank God." Isolationists who were there still grumbling that the U.S. could have avoided the war but for the policy of Roosevelt had to accept the facts and stop espousing the stance of noninterference and passiveness.

What are the aims being pursued by the U.S. in this war? It is difficult to answer this question because of the disorder that exists in the ruling circles and in both political parties. Neither the Republican nor Democratic party has a single clear program on international policy. The Republican party, which mainly consists of isolationists, also includes such leaders as Willkie, who actually supports Roosevelt's foreign policy. On the other hand, there are many isolationists in the Democratic party, too. Roughly speaking, we have to subdivide American politicians into isolationists and anti-isolationists, and both of them have different gradations.

Political Aspirations of Isolationists and Nationalists

There is no doubt that the extreme isolationists, though they don't express it openly, dream about the earliest cessation of the war not only in Europe, but in the Pacific basin, by means of a compromise peace at the expense of the British Empire and the Soviet Union. These isolationists become bolder and more open as the war becomes more protracted and there is no evident preponderance of one or another belligerent. Lately it has been rumored that the Soviet Union has already shown its inability to overcome Hitler's army, that Britain and the U.S. have shown their inability to deliver a crushing blow to

Japan, and that since the war seems a drawn game it is high time peace negotiations were begun. More moderate isolationists support cessation of the war in Europe, or at least an end to American participation in it, while supporting continuation of the struggle against Japan. This position is usually accompanied by attacks on both Great Britain and the USSR or on the USSR alone.

Some American nationalists do not object to the continuation of the war, but demand that the advantageous positions of the U.S. be guaranteed in response to American assistance to other members of the United Nations with U.S. air and naval forces, as well as with its military industry provided via Lend-Lease. First of all, they want to guarantee U.S. supremacy in the air and sea ways and to assure U.S. receipt of the corresponding bases. At the same time, they would not mind enriching themselves at the expense of the British Empire, which in their opinion is destined for elimination or reduction. These American nationalists are hardly interested in such problems as the postwar destiny of Germany, France, or other European countries. Disguising their own genuine aspirations, they frequently wear the cloak of the Atlantic Charter and other great international ethical principles, using them as basis for their attacks on Great Britain and the Soviet Union. This camouflage tactic is similar to the methods used by radical intellectuals who shout about a fair peace and justice for all nations, including Germany. However, neither isolationists nor semi-isolationists nor nationalists have put forward any comprehensive and concrete programs for the postwar order.

Intermediate and Intellectual Circles

Intermediate and intellectual circles, which to some extent support the isolationists' hypocritical 100 percent defense of the Atlantic Charter and ignore all attacks on Great Britain and the Soviet Union, nevertheless side with anti-isolationists and Roosevelt in their efforts to bring the war to a victorious end and to secure the unconditional capitulation of the Axis countries. Various concrete programs for a postwar order are elaborated and popularized in this environment.

The most comprehensive concrete plan for the territorial reorganization of the world is a plan of Kalbertson, the famous theoretician of the card game known as "bridge." Amongst those circles, the future of Germany is the most controversial issue—particularly whether it should be divided and rendered harmless by remolding or other measures, whether it should be controlled by the removal of the top leaders of nazism, or whether all German people should be regarded as the culprits of the war and be punished as such.

Anti-isolationist Camp

Within the anti-isolationist camp the argument is certainly set by the governmental circles and people surrounding Roosevelt. Their aims are to bring the war to a victorious end; to eliminate nazism and fascism, at least in their present-day form; and to participate generally in solutions to postwar problems and subsequent international life. Beyond these broad goals, a considerable divergence exists regarding particular questions.

The State Department

We cannot even speak about a single opinion on all problems in a governmental body like the State Department. Nominally, the policy of the State Department is determined by Secretary of State [Cordell] Hull. However, because of his age and his personal relationship with Roosevelt on the one hand and with his various assistants on the other, Hull is not the sole master in his department. In order to understand this, it is necessary to bear in mind that among Hull's assistants are such people as Wallace, Berle, and Breckinridge Long; these are people who personally have a lot of money, maybe tens of millions, and are absolutely independent of their careers. By contributing substantially to the party fund during presidential election campaigns, they insure their influence on the president. But this cannot be said about Hull, who is connected with the president only by the ties of party and ideology. Hull is at odds with some of his assistants; and there is also controversy among the assistants themselves, one with another. Each of them is trying to exert influence and pressure on the president in favor of his own theory or concept. This explains why those surrounding Roosevelt can induce a person like Berle who, in the opinion of all people, is pursuing his own line in the State Department and maintaining contact with the most reactionary elements of European political emigration.

By the way, I should point out that other departments are also headed by people who are absolutely independent of their official careers—for example, the Secretary of Commerce Jesse Johns, who is one of the most prominent millionaires; Stimson, the Republican Secretary of War; Knox, Secretary of the Navy and another Republican (owner of the *Chicago Daily News*), and such prominent industrialists as Nelson, Stettinius, Rockefeller, etc.

There is a certain unanimity among those who are very close to Roosevelt, i.e., Harry Hopkins; Morgenthau (though he is also a well-to-do person); Frankfurter, a member of the Supreme Court; Rosenman, a judge from New York; Vice-President Wallace; Ickes, Secretary of the Interior; Joseph Davies (another absolutely independent and rich man), etc. These people completely support the plan of Roosevelt, because of either shared ideas or personal devotion to and admiration of the man himself. However, some of them influence the president sometimes. On the other hand, the president cooperates closely with such persons as Admiral Leahy and certain generals who maintain an outlook different from his.

The Policy of Roosevelt

We have to acknowledge that American foreign policy is determined by Roosevelt, though from time to time it undergoes changes within the executive bodies. Roosevelt relies on the progressive members of the industrial and financial bourgeoisie, searching for markets outside the U.S. and the Western hemisphere for implementation of his policy. Holding a bourgeois-radical world outlook, Roosevelt gains support from within the intermediate and intellectual strata of the bourgeoisie and the most progressive level of the working class. He is ambitious and strives to make his name a part of history by playing an important role in international affairs. He is a staunch anti-Nazi and anti-Fascist, and he personally hates Hitler and Mussolini. That is why there is no doubt that while the U.S. depends on Roosevelt and while he is still at his post, his country won't drop out of the war before the complete defeat of the Axis countries. He hardly thinks of carrying out the war or completing it unselfishly; rather he hopes to get as much benefit from it for his country as is possible. As I've already reported, he plans to secure those benefits mainly at the expense of the British Empire. In that regard he used to count on cooperation with us, but since there was no response on our part he has considerably softened his anti-British attitude. He had supposed that it would be easier to come to an agreement with us than with Great Britain on the solution of certain postwar problems, and I am inclined to attribute his persistent suggestions for a meeting with Comrade Stalin to this intended agreement. His first outlines for the settlement of postwar problems were expressed in this last year's conversation with me and in consultations with Eden, as has been reported by me and Comrade Maisky. Certainly, he has no final solutions for all problems, and he is still under the influence of the persons in command of the State Department.

Let me remind you briefly that he spoke of disarmament and of the division of Germany, the annexation of Eastern Prussia to Poland, [the expected] deprivation of France, Belgium, Holland, and Britain of their colonial possessions, granting independence to some of those colonial territories after a certain period of time and putting some of them under international trusteeship. He also spoke of the directorship of four powers, which should have a final say in international affairs, etc. It is beyond all question that later on he will be accessible to our influence and to the influence of Britain and especially of Latin American countries, since the State Department lends an attentive ear to their opinion.

U.S. and Great Britain

I can learn little about Anglo-American relations besides the news from the press. The State Department doesn't consider it necessary to share all information from that area with me, but regularly reminds me that we have opposed a triple agreement [of sharing intelligence]. Maybe the British are less secretive as allies. It is known that there were many disagreements between London and Washington—first in connection with Vichy, then the agreement with Darlan and the occupation of San Pierre and Michelon islands.

There were also cases of misunderstanding associated with Lend-Lease deliveries. We believe that the fewer contacts we have with the Americans, the more closely they unite with the British; during the last year and a half relations between them have considerably and obviously improved. This improvement was certainly encouraged by the frequent meetings of Churchill with the president, regular visits to Washington by British government representatives and people from various British establishments, and by the trips of American representatives to London. Now we can observe a certain change in the previously somewhat hostile public opinion toward the British as a result of broad British agitation and propaganda.

U.S. and China

American diplomacy spares no effort in strengthening friendly relations with China and, in particular, in coaxing Chiang Kai-Shek. This policy is mainly determined by serious apprehensions that China will possibly drop out of the war and conclude a separate treaty with Japan. These apprehensions are supported by rumors at times circulated by the Chinese themselves. The wife of Wellington Koo, Chinese ambassador to London, recently appeared in New York with direct threats of the separate peace treaty. Although she is not taken seriously, and is even divorced from her husband, I can hardly believe that she dared to make such a statement without permission from above. The visit and successful speeches of the wife of Chiang Kai-Shek substantially consolidated the position of China. Soong, who permanently resides in Washington as Minister of Foreign Affairs, enjoys American sympathy and exerts steady influence on the president through personal contacts and by means of the Pacific Council.

The countries represented in that council are certainly conducting a common policy for the president aimed at enforcement of the Pacific fronts. With representatives in Vichy and in North Africa for a long time, it became possible to accomplish the landing in Morocco and Algeria and to conclude an agreement with Darlan. Likewise Hull is naive to believe that he will manage to keep Franco from fighting on the side of Hitler, wheedling him skillfully and excluding Spain from the objects of naval blockade. Liberal-radical elements severely criticize the State Department policy relating to Vichy, Darlan, and Franco. As for these problems, it goes without saying that the leading role here is played by the State Department, which influences the president by taking advantage of his lack of time to study such problems attentively.

Some American gifts are granted to Turkey, though the State Department has no illusions about enticing Turkey onto the side of the United Nations. However, considerations for Turkey will be quite sufficient if it maintains benevolent neutrality.

The U.S. pays little attention to the stateless governments represented in Washington, though it is possible to discern a greater cordiality in those relations: there is a most favorable attitude toward the very reactionary governments [e.g., Poland], and the least sympathy is rendered to the government of Benes [considered an ally of Stalin]. Along with that the State Department, in the person of Berle, maintains permanent contacts with the reactionary representatives of emigrant communities of those countries [such as Poland and the Baltic States].

Roosevelt and the USSR

In comparison with 1933, when I first met Roosevelt, his attitude toward the USSR has obviously changed for the worse. The unsettled problem of debts is now being ignored. It was the hostile agitation of

Bullitt that influenced the president, especially regarding some aspects of our foreign policy. However, Roosevelt is more friendly to us than any other prominent American, and it is quite obvious that he wishes to cooperate with us. Right now he is undoubtedly discontented with the fact that one of his requests of us is not being fulfilled and with our unwillingness to discuss current and postwar political problems or to establish permanent contact with him. Nevertheless, this discontent is unlikely to be evident during deliveries accomplished according to Lend-Lease. I know for sure that he was actively promoting our requests in the executive bodies.

The U.S. is not at all interested in the economic or foreign political aspects of the Baltic regions' problems or in the frontier issue between them and Poland. Taking into consideration the forthcoming presidential election campaign, Roosevelt cannot be indifferent to the votes of those who come from the Baltic States and Poland or of American Catholics; for that reason he is not likely to support our requirements openly. There are not so many people in America who come from Finland, but for a number of years Finland has enjoyed U.S. sympathy. Finland adroitly used its reputation as the only country alleged to have paid its World War I debts to the U.S. But in fact Finland had no war debt and now is paying only for the postwar deliveries; however, American public opinion is still erroneous on this problem. Finland's obstinate disregard for America's urging it to drop out of the war and conclude a separate agreement with us has certainly reduced the popularity of Finland and American interest in it.

In the postwar settlement of our argument with the bordering states, Roosevelt won't support their claims if he finds himself facing a fait accompli. Considering American public opinion, Roosevelt will try to present his decisions in a manner that corresponds with the ideas of "international justice" and the Atlantic Charter.

The U.S. Policy in Cases of Change of the President

I've reported on the U.S. policy under Roosevelt. But the change of the president that can take place next year will create alterations in that policy. With the president's dependence on the Senate it is difficult to say whether even Roosevelt will manage to execute his policy, or whether Wilson's destiny will befall him. There is guesswork about that in America. Some prominent politicians and industrialists, being free-tongued in my presence, debated on this theme but failed to come to any conclusion about the possibility of a return to isolationism. It is even more difficult to answer this question if there is a change in the presidency. The closest friends of Roosevelt, such as Hopkins and Davies, are very optimistic; they have no doubt that Roosevelt will be reelected for the fourth time. As I've already reported, Vice-President Wallace is more realistic about the situation, and he anticipates Roosevelt's defeat. I believe that Wallace himself has even less chance of being elected.

Summary

1. Under the Roosevelt presidency, the U.S. dropping out of the war is impossible. In the event of a protracted war without apparent chances for victory, the Senate may yield to the propaganda of the isolationists and try to cause a serious crisis by refusing credit. However, a premature cessation of the war is possible and could occur if an isolationist or semi-isolationist were elected as president.

2. There is no hope for the immediate opening of the Second Front in Western Europe without serious pressure from us. Even an Anglo-American offensive from the North-African bases is unlikely. If no meeting is planned between Comrade Stalin and Roosevelt soon, then pressure should be exerted in a specific form.

3. If we virtually settle the problem of our western borders ourselves, there will be no major counteraction on the part of the U.S. However, since we'll need U.S. assistance for that, American public opinion will be influential.

4. The U.S. ruling circles are discontented with the USSR mainly because of a lack of contact with us and our restraint in discussing postwar problems. The discontent in American public opinion is determined by similar prejudices and by ignorance regarding our country.

5. Lack of Soviet-American contact consolidates Anglo-American relations and increases our isolationism.

Conclusions

If we are aware of the role and significance of the U.S. in the war against our common enemies, and especially after the war, by the end of which it will be less exhausted and weak, more mighty in the industrial and financial spheres, and if we wish to eliminate existing misunderstandings and to prepare conditions for mutual cooperation, then the following measures and arrangements suggest themselves:

1. To create a body for permanent military-political contact with the president and the War Department in Washington. At one time Roosevelt suggested creating a common commission of Allies, but we had to turn down this suggestion because it implied not only European and African, but Pacific theaters of war. Nevertheless, in my opinion there is no reason to avoid participation in an Anglo-American commission for discussion of the military-political items springing out of our common struggle against the Axis countries of Europe. That doesn't mean we must discuss the strategic plan of our war against Germany. Even the Pacific Council does not discuss such problems. Nevertheless, its members from time to time receive at least useful information on the course of combat actions and on some political problems, and they can express their recommendations and demands. It will be sufficient to have one ambassador and one general, if possible—one admiral, in the proposed commission. Creation of such a commission: (1) will permit us to influence in due time the strategic plans of the U.S. and Great Britain, (2) will give us useful information, (3) will put an end to complaints and discontents in public opinion and the ruling sections who say that we are the only country among the United Nations that evades contact with the others in our pursuit of secret aims.

2. To initiate discussion of postwar problems in the press and public debate.

3. To place our ambassador in a position where he can speak frequently in front of the American public, explaining our general policy, or certain aspects of it, at present and in the future.

4. To discuss, with London and Washington simultaneously, the emerging political problems, as they are connected with Anglo-Soviet relations.

5. To strengthen the information department of the embassy with a number of people who can speak English fluently. If there are no such people, then we should send one or several serious officials, with sufficient erudition in politics, who will be able to write speeches, articles, and answers to inquiries that can later be translated into English. It is necessary to permit the embassy to admit some reliable Americans to work as translators and editors.

6. To send regular representatives of science and the arts for public presentation in the U.S. The most advisable is the visit of the Red Army Band and Dance Company. It can be brought here by one of our Pacific oceanliners.

(M. M. Litvinov)

4 copies typed
Nr1 for Stalin
Nr2 and 3 for Molotov
Nr4 to the file

Distributed to comrades:
    Voroshilov
    Mikoyan
    Beria
    Malenkov
    Vyshinsky
    Dekanozov
    Lozovsky
    Korneychuck

Appendix 3

USSR Foreign Affairs

Declassified December 25, 1989
Classified May 5, 1943

Telegram from Soviet Ambassador to the United States to People's Commissariat of Foreign Affairs of the USSR

May 5, 1943

The president invited me to visit him to inform me about Davies' mission. This mission seems to be restricted to the purpose of passing to Stalin a sealed letter dealing once again with arrangements for the summit. The president explained to me that he was ready to go to Chukotkato for this meeting, and he believes he will be provided a cruiser or fighter of ours to spend the night aboard if there is no dwelling on the shore. According to the estimates, Stalin will need only a day and a half to get there and as much time to return. Roosevelt especially emphasized that he was willing to hold the meeting without Churchill, without State Department representatives or any military officials, with Hopkins' presence only. The time for the meeting as suggested by the president is late July. It seems that Davies is not going to discuss any other questions. He asked me to support his proposal.

On his own initiative the president touched upon the question of Soviet-Polish relations [emphasis added], and said that according to him neither the United States nor Britain should take responsibility for protecting Polish interests in the Soviet Union. He would prefer to suggest that a nonofficial committee be set up in London with the participation of Maisky, Sikorski, and Eden or Winnant. This committee, which would not function as a permanent body, could debate the disputable questions emerging in the relations between us and Poland.

M. Litvinov

Declassified December 25, 1989
Classified May 7, 1943

Telegram from Soviet Ambassador to the United States to People's Commissariat of Foreign Affairs of the USSR

May 7, 1943

During my farewell visit [Cordell] Hull as usual spoke on general topics related to the need for Soviet-American cooperation. When he mentioned the lack of mutual understanding between the two countries I reminded him of the memorandum I had given to Welles, which emphasized the impediments to data about the Soviet Union being disseminated in the United States. I tried hard on many occasions, and without success, to get information from Hull about American views on concrete postwar problems, and I deliberately referred to the existence of a special body within the State Department to study these issues. During my conversation with Hull, this committee was in session in the adjoining room; and I had noted the presence there of Secretary of Labor [Dorothy] Perkins and of Chairman of the American Federation of Labor, [Philip] Green. Hull voiced his opinion only on the necessity for ceasing military activities and immediately proceeding to punish the parties guilty of war, though he promised to discuss the rest of the issues confidentially upon my return.

Sumner Welles turned out to be, as I had expected, less reserved. In most instances he confirmed what Mr. Eden had told me and Mr. Maisky. The Great Council, as he conceives it, should be comprised of eleven members; besides the four whose unanimous decision should be a precondition for every resolution of the council, there should be two representatives from Europe, two from the western hemisphere (with the exception of Canada), and one representative from the Far East, Africa, and the British Empire. Welles was saying to Eden that he was in agreement with the president on every issue mentioned here, with the exception of the question of France, which, as Welles sees it, should be returned to the status of a great power. The East European Federation Welles conceives as without Poland and comprising Austria, Czechoslovakia, and Hungary. Welles attaches prime importance to the preliminary agreement among the four powers on the transitional period, and there should be an agreement among them on maximum and minimum levels of armamentation. The federation of countries he conceives is based not on a political but on an economic foundation, in the sense of customs and currency union. First of all, he says, a complete agreement or cooperation between the United States and the Soviet Union is needed; without this he cannot imagine any other agreement. In this respect he places considerable hope on the meeting between Stalin and Roosevelt. He promised to transmit to me in the future all sorts of confidential information that I may require, as far as American views on postwar problems are concerned.

I reminded him about his declaration during our last meeting on the rupture with Finland to be announced in two days' time, and I asked him to explain the change of attitude on this problem. He said that the president had decided, after our rupture with Poland, that he should not disturb public opinion by immediately announcing our subsequent rupture with Finland, a motivation quite clear to me even without his explanation.[1]

M. Litvinov

Declassified December 25, 1989
Classified June 11, 1943

Telegram from Chargé d'Affaires of the USSR to the United States to People's Commissariat of Foreign Affairs of the USSR

June 11, 1943

Mr. Halifax [the British Ambassador to the U.S.], whom I saw this morning, was very reserved in his considerations about the Second Front. He spoke in general terms and rather vaguely about Britain as

well as the United States, speaking now in favor of offensive operations to be conducted by the British and the Americans in the region
of the Mediterranean, which would distract a certain amount of
German forces from the Eastern front. However, he did not mention
any definite objects against which those operations would be held. He
voiced the opinion that the German aviation is now on the defensive
and will remain so in the future. The dominant role in the air belongs
and will belong to the Allies. He emphasized the importance of this
dominance by all means possible, as well as the importance of British
air forces bombing German cities and military installations. Halifax
expressed his confidence that Stalin is comprehensively informed
about what the British and the Americans can possibly do this year
and about what they are unable to do. Halifax remarked that Mr.
Welles, during a recent conversation, had expressed the idea that the
U.S. government intends to initiate a number of conferences like the
recently terminated one on food; conferences on metals, rubber, and
certain other types of strategic materials, and also on civil aviation,
will be held separately. However, Halifax said, Britain did not receive
official invitations to any of the suggested conferences. The conference to create the Aid and Recovery Administration, according to the
data he possesses, is to be convened this July. This supposition was
expressed by [Assistant Secretary of State Dean] Acheson, Hull's
deputy, with whom I dined on June 9. The final date, however, is not
established, since the opinions of all of the United Nations on the
draft of the agreement is not yet known. Halifax expressed his satisfaction with the results of the work done at the food conference. He
said that the British delegation to the food conference was glad to
enjoy cooperation with the Soviet delegation. This is a positive indication, noted Halifax, especially in regard to our future cooperation. It is
beyond any doubt, he added, that the future of the world will depend
upon the cooperation of three countries: Britain, the United States,
and the USSR. He did not mention China.

A. Gromyko

Declassified December 25, 1989
Classified July 2, 1942

Telegram from Chargé d'Affaires of the USSR to the United States to People's Commissariat of Foreign Affairs of the USSR

July 2, 1943

The chairman of the Committee on Foreign Affairs of the U.S. House of Representatives, Solomon Bloom, with whom I had a talk, told me that the Congress in general is positively disposed toward the Soviet Union (some time ago, when inviting me to a concert devoted to Rachmaninov, Bloom had expressed his willingness to visit me and have a talk). There are only a few members of Congress who either have not yet determined their attitudes toward us or are treating us with mistrust. The Congressmen are in dismay now, Bloom said, about why the promised Second Front has not yet been opened. Bloom himself is of the same opinion. He believes that conditions are very favorable now for inaugurating the Second Front. Speaking about the attitudes of the public in general toward the Soviet Union, Bloom remarked that the southern states and the states of the middle west in the Mississippi River Valley are the most reserved. Those are the states with traditionally strong isolationist attitudes. However, Bloom believes the populations of these states also treat the Germans, Italians, and Japanese with reservation. Bloom spoke at length about the fact that the United States and the Soviet Union cannot have any differences on territorial issues. Both countries have all the prerequisites for cooperation, not only during the war but also upon its termination. He stated that the Committee on Foreign Affairs, which he heads, is not interested in either Polish or Baltic territorial questions. The respective Senate committee is also not interested in these issues. "In general," he said, "this is a question which relates to you Russians, only. Only you have the right to and must resolve it." Bloom does not support the opinion that Japan is the U.S.'s principal adversary. He believes that the main enemy is Germany, and to defeat Japan one should first of all gain victory in the war against Germany. Bloom spoke at length about the common nature of the interests of

Britain, the United States, and the Soviet Union, about the roles of these countries in the postwar world, about the necessity for consolidating U.S. cooperation with the Soviet Union, and so on. Bloom hinted that he would not like for the State Department to learn about the nature of our conversation. He definitely is inimical to the latter.

A. Gromyko

Declassified December 25, 1989
Classified July 12, 1943

Telegram from People's Commissar of Foreign Affairs of the USSR to Chargé d'Affaires of the USSR to the United States

July 12, 1943

Pay a visit to Hull and communicate to him the following:

First: Molotov has gotten acquainted with your information about the French question, and he asks that the following be transmitted to you: Of course, the Americans know better who precisely among the figures of the French Committee of National Liberations deserves more attention and may accord better assistance in conducting the present Anglo-American military activities in Italy. Generally speaking, on the French question we hope we will find grounds for mutual understanding.

Second: The German offensive is of a very serious nature and is undertaken by strong forces, with an unprecedented number of armored troops and planes involved. Beginning on July 5, unceasing and violent battles to the south of Orel and to the north of Belgorod have gone on. It is too early to judge the possible developments of this new and extensive German offensive. Telegraph immediately the results of conversation with Hull.

V. Molotov

Declassified December 25, 1989
Classified July 13, 1943

Telegram from Chargé d'Affaires of the USSR to the United States to People's Commissariat of Foreign Affairs of the USSR

July 13, 1943

Today I paid a visit to Hull. I passed on to him both of your messages. Hull expressed his satisfaction in connection with the opinion you formulated on the French question. He says he is thankful for your understanding of the problem and for the spirit of your response. He repeated once again that General Eisenhower, Supreme Commander, European Theater, as well as the British generals, cannot allow the political struggle to develop in their rear in Africa; this could inflict damage to the conduct of military operations in the Mediterranean.

While listening to my statement on the second question Hull was making notes. He remarked that, as he had pointed out before, opinions were unclear about prospects for development of the German offensive according to different people he spoke to. The morning after our conversation, when we touched upon this issue, Hull had read the information about the battles in the Eastern front and was persuaded that they were of serious character. He was very glad he had gotten the official and exact picture of the situation in the Eastern front. He will meet with the president today and will transmit to him the information received from me. Hull expressed his satisfaction regarding the fact that the Germans have not enjoyed any success during the last day or two in the Belgorod direction. Hull himself mentioned the situation in Sicily; he confirmed what he had told me yesterday that according to the data he received today the operations on the island go on successfully and with few losses for the Allies. In response to my question about when he thought they could possibly defeat Italy, Hull told me the following. They are planning to do away with Sicily in ten to fourteen days. He cannot give his word for it, but based on the assessment of the military situation in Sicily they believe it will be possible to occupy the island within this period of time. Then, Hull said, they are going to move northward into continental Italy. Hull did not say precisely whether this forward movement would mean landing operations. After Sicily's seizure Italy will be subjected to intensified bombings. Great hopes are associated with the possibility for ending the operation of Italian industries by this destruction of the power plants. Under such conditions, according to Hull, Italy will not be able to resist for a long period of time. Hull displayed exceptional courtesy, especially during our last three meetings. Almost on every occasion he has invited me to call on him at any time with any questions and so on.

A. Gromyko

Declassified December 25, 1989
Classified probably July 14–15, 1943

Telegram from Chargé d'Affaires of the USSR to the United States to People's Commissariat of Foreign Affairs of the USSR

[undated]

1. Hopkins, whom I saw today, told me that the answer to our proposal on the Third Protocol would be given in the nearest future and that this answer would be generally positive. He did not make his statement any more precise, for the final decision in our proposals is not yet formulated. General Burns [head of Lend-Lease USSR], at the negotiations with Belyaev, expressed the opinion that the Protocol would have one clause added, directing the convoys again to our northern ports if the situation in the North Atlantic and the North Sea allows it.

2. Hopkins asked my opinion about the present stage of Soviet-American relations. I responded in general terms and said that the relations in my view are quite good, but they could be even better. Hopkins agreed with me.

Although Hopkins believes that even after the war there could be some difficulties of different kinds in relations between the U.S. and the Soviet Union, the cooperation of the two countries is indispensable and quite possible. After the war, Hopkins said, the Soviet Union will need American goods to fulfill the five-year plans to the same extent that it had needed American equipment to fulfill similar plans in the past. I remarked that everything Hopkins said constitutes a kind of economic basis for the cooperation, but that our cooperation should not be concentrated on commerce only. It should have a wider basis, including political cooperation in the interests of maintaining the peace. Hopkins agreed to this, saying that in his view this type of cooperation is also possible.

Hopkins spoke about the reactionary American press like *New York Daily News* that goes on attacking the Soviet Union. There are also some anti-Soviet people in Congress. Unfortunately the reactionary press and reactionary members of Congress both exert a certain influence upon public opinion in the country. In assessing this phenomenon one should always take into consideration the specific components of the country. In the U.S., there are numerous national minorities—Poles, Lithuanians, and others. They always have their representatives in Congress who voice their opinions, in particular, regarding the Soviet Union.

3. Hopkins thinks the best way to resolve all principal issues that are of interest for both countries would be a personal meeting of both heads of government. Hopkins is sure that at such a personal meeting *Roosevelt would surprise Stalin by how far he, Roosevelt, is ready to go to acknowledge our rights, in particular, on territorial issues* [emphasis added]. Hopkins said that Roosevelt possesses certain elaborate plans on territorial questions, as well as on a number of other problems, which he would like to present at the meeting with Stalin.

4. Undoubtedly, as Hopkins stated, at this meeting Roosevelt would ask about the attitude of the Soviet government toward Japan, after Germany's defeat. The policy of the Soviet Union in relation to Japan is already determined: Japan does not touch the Soviet Union, while the latter leaves Japan intact. It is hard to envisage any changes of this policy before the defeat of Germany. But at the meeting with Stalin, Roosevelt may well ask the above-mentioned question.

5. Hopkins is optimistic in relation to military developments in Sicily. The questions proceed smoothly. Still he expects to overcome the German and Italian resistance on the island. One needs about three weeks. Hopkins and Hull stated, during the conversation of July 13, that the British and the Americans are relying heavily upon the results

of the intensified bombings to which Italy will be subjected in the nearest future, and especially after the complete occupation of Sicily. About four hundred planes took part in today's air raid on Rome.

6. Hopkins expects friendly relations to be maintained between our two countries, and he thinks that it is of considerable importance who is the American Ambassador in Moscow. In his view Standley is not the kind of person who is up to the mark with the requirements of the time. However, Hopkins referred to Standley's old age only, though by the character of his remarks it was clear he meant not only Standley's age but his political and business qualities. I asked him, among other things, whether the information that had appeared some time ago in the American press that Standley is going to retire is well grounded. Hopkins responded that he had no information about such an intention of Standley. But his answer, however, was not persuasive in its tone.

A. Gromyko

Declassified December 25, 1989
Classified July 30, 1943

Telegram from Chargé d'Affaires of the USSR to the United States to People's Commissariat of Foreign Affairs of the USSR

July 30, 1943

General Watson, whom I visited at his request in the White House, informed me that the president wished to see me. Roosevelt began by saying that he, of course, had been waiting and was waiting for Stalin's response to Davies' message. He understands that since Stalin is on the front he is very busy. Roosevelt will be glad to receive an answer upon Stalin's return from the front to Moscow on August 7 or 8. Roosevelt informed me that today or tomorrow he leaves Washington, "to go fishing" for approximately a week. He requested that I communicate to Stalin that "he will terminate his work in Washington on August 24," adding that Stalin will understand what this means. I took it as a figurative expression which is known to you and did not consider it polite to ask for explanations. Until August 24, he will be engaged in two very serious matters. Roosevelt would gladly communicate with Stalin on the telephone (through the interpreter) the way he does with Churchill, but the distance does not allow this. Roosevelt hinted that a personal meeting with Stalin would be the best way to exchange views.

He himself started the conversation about Italy. He began by making reference to a certain complicated quality in the situation there. According to the data available the Germans are bringing troops into northern Italy and dispersing them along the river Roe where they supposedly plan to set up the defense line. From the tone of Roosevelt's information one could see he is rather anxious about this move by the Germans. I asked Roosevelt how soon, according to his estimations, Italy would be brought out of the war and whether he took seriously the Italians' declaration that they would continue their struggle. Roosevelt responded that the Italians, in his view, would capitulate as soon as Sicily was completely occupied by the Anglo-American troops. As soon as they see that the Allies are ready to move onto continental Italy, Roosevelt said, they will not withstand the attack and will give up.

The complete occupation of Sicily, in his view, will take about two more weeks for the German troops stationed there under considerable resistance. As far as Italian declarations about continuing to fight are concerned, Roosevelt does not take them seriously. The Italian people, he knows pretty well, do not wish to go on with the war. The army may also refuse to fight against the Allies.

Roosevelt attaches great importance to the fact that the population of Sicily met the Anglo-American troops with enthusiasm. To attract the population over to their side, the Anglo-American authorities in Sicily possess the required stock of foodstuffs and other resources which are being distributed among the population immediately after the occupation of this or that region. In his view, dissemination of information about the Allies according assistance to the population of Sicily will promote growing popularity of the Allies among the Italians.

Roosevelt believes that capitulation of Italy would create a convenient bridgehead for the Allies to conduct Anglo-American air raids against southern Germany and Austria. Having bases in the north of Italy, the aviation could strike German centers also from the south.

Roosevelt informed me that he had sent a telegram to Churchill expressing his opinion about inviting the Soviet government to resolve the questions emerging, and due to emerge, in connection with the situation in Italy. I asked him whether he had received any answer from Churchill, and Roosevelt responded that he had not yet received any answer for he had only sent the telegram on the previous night. I estimate that there is a preliminary agreement between Roosevelt and Churchill on this account, for otherwise Roosevelt would never have told me about it. Anyhow, the fact that he has now told the Soviet government about it testifies that he evidently does not expect to receive any objections from Churchill. Of course, Roosevelt also wishes to show us that the initiative on this issue belongs to him, not to Churchill. Roosevelt asked me how Litvinov was, and I responded by saying that Litvinov is doing very well.

General Watson, whom I bumped into when leaving Roosevelt's office, said that he also planned "to go fishing" with Roosevelt, but that I could communicate with him (Watson) any time through the White House in case I had any questions to ask him or the president.

A. Gromyko

Declassified December 25, 1989
Classified August 24, 1943

Telegram from Soviet Ambassador to the United States to People's Commissariat of Foreign Affairs of the USSR

August 24, 1943

During the last two days the reaction to Litvinov's release from the duties of the ambassador and to my nomination is the same as in the first two days. The only difference is that now it is more "frequent than in the first two days that the question is posed whether this shuffle of diplomats means the Soviet government intends to make a certain sharp turn in its foreign policy." It is emphasized that this decision coincides with the conference of Roosevelt and Churchill in Quebec.

A. Gromyko

Appendix 4

Soviet-American Relations

Declassified December 25, 1989
Classified July 14, 1944

It is known that before June 22, 1941, when Germany attacked the Soviet Union, relations between the United States and the USSR were far from perfect. Moreover, between the end of 1939 and the middle of 1941, relations were rather tense. At that time the causes for the dampening of relations between our two countries were well known, and there is no need to explain them in this report.

Deterioration in Soviet-American relations was first of all expressed in reduction of Soviet-American trade. The U.S. official circles were putting various obstacles in our way regarding the purchase of American equipment. Then the so-called "moral embargo," which was aimed mainly at the Soviet Union, was put in place. A system of licensing for the most important items of export meant governmental control over exporting industrial equipment and other important commodities from the United States. This measure was in fact directed against the Soviet Union. Talks between the State Department and the Soviet Ambassador to Washington, which lasted for the first six months of 1941 and were dedicated to the problems of trade, produced no appreciable positive results. The situation was growing worse and worse.

Fascist Germany's attack on the Soviet Union caused a drastic change of attitude toward the USSR among the U.S.'s ruling circles. During the first days of the war the State Department, expressing the point of view of the American administration, declared its intention to render assistance until the end to the Soviet Union as a victim of aggression. This change of attitude found its expression in cancellation of the previously existing obstacles in the sphere of trade between the two countries. In particular, the above-mentioned "moral embargo" was lifted. Since that period the U.S. administration has occupied a position of rendering definite economic assistance to the Soviet Union by supplying armaments, industrial equipment, and other strategic materials.

It is necessary to point out, however, that in spite of the considerable improvement in relations between our two countries and in spite of the statement of the U.S. administration about its wish to render assistance to the Soviet Union, at the beginning of the war opportunities for getting substantial material aid from the U.S. were very limited. Initially, opportunity was limited regarding armaments and ammunition. To a certain extent this could be explained by the poor development of the military industry in the U.S., which was just emerging from the restrictions imposed by various state officials of the U.S. on the means of delivery of armaments and equipment to the Soviet Union.

Among the general public and in official U.S. circles, an opinion was dominant that the Soviet Union would be defeated several months after the beginning of the Soviet-German war. Such an idea was expressed quite openly by some officials. One could frequently hear the opinion that by supplying the Soviet Union, the U.S. would be helping Fascist Germany, since the latter might seize armaments and materials left after the German victory over the USSR.

Thus, on the one hand, there was a favorable political situation for the USSR, but, on the other hand, during the first month of the war actual U.S. economic aid was insignificant. Mainly this was so because nobody believed in the likelihood of serious resistance by the USSR to German aggression. Assistance to the USSR during that period was regarded by the U.S. as a palliative that would be unable to considerably improve the situation of the Soviet Union.

Everything said above about the mental attitude in official quarters can also be said about the sentiments in broad sections of the U.S. public. The public's sympathy was on the side of the Soviet Union. However, the overwhelming majority of the population expected the prompt German victory over the USSR.

Considerable difficulty in attaining economic assistance from the U.S. during the first period of the war was attached to the need for finding ways to finance our purchases. In 1941 some armaments and other materials in the U.S. were purchased through the sale of gold to the United States. The situation changed for the better at the end of 1941, and it had changed drastically by the middle of 1942 after the U.S.-USSR agreement on American deliveries to the Soviet Union was signed on June 11, 1942, as a result of the visit to Washington by V. M. Molotov, People's Commissar of Foreign Affairs. That agreement made delivery of armaments and materials from the U.S. to the USSR official on the basis of the Lend-Lease Act. These deliveries are officially registered annually, for a 1-year term, by the signing of so-called protocol agreements on deliveries by the USSR and the United States (with the participation of Great Britain and Canada) according to which the above-mentioned governments assume certain responsibilities.

Analyzing the period under review—that is, since June, 1941—we can reach conclusions concerning Soviet-American relations as they have been since the beginning of the Soviet-German war. On the basis of this analysis we can conclude that Roosevelt and his administration have occupied and still occupy a firm position aimed at maintaining friendly relations and cooperation with the Soviet Union. Soviet-American relations are now determined mainly by the common objective of both countries to defeat Hitler's Germany. As president, Roosevelt is actively supported by his cabinet as far as his attitude and policy toward the Soviet Union are concerned. The most active proponents of Roosevelt's policy within the cabinet are: Hull, Ickes, and Morgenthau. Biddle, the attorney-general, is the only one who keeps aloof. The latter is known as an anti-Soviet, though he has never openly objected to Roosevelt's policy regarding the USSR. It is necessary to mention Hopkins, Vice-President Wallace, Stettinius,

[Donald] Nelson, as well as some other prominent and influential members of the cabinet who actively support the president.

The policy of cooperation with the Soviet Union, carried out by the administration of Roosevelt, became more and more evident along with the successes of the Red Army in its war against Germany. Roosevelt and his team gradually were convinced of the economic and military might of the Soviet Union as a power. This manifestation of the might of the country and the Red Army became the main reason for the altered attitudes of Roosevelt's administration and of influential circles outside the government toward the Soviet Union as they concluded that it was necessary to cooperate with the USSR.

Convinced of the USSR and Red Army might, the U.S. administration concluded that economic assistance to the Soviet Union would be profitable for the U.S., too, because both countries were waging a common struggle against Germany. The USSR's successes in war showed how efficiently armaments and other materials supplied to the Soviet Union were being used in the struggle against Germany. Roosevelt's administration understands quite well that while rendering assistance to the Soviet Union, it is acting in its own interests, because that aid accelerates the utter defeat of Germany and reduces the American sacrifices in that war.

The past period of the war has proved that Roosevelt's policy regarding the USSR was supported by the overwhelming majority of members of the two leading political parties of the U.S.—Democratic and Republican. During the last three years Roosevelt had to discuss in Congress a number of important laws, directly or indirectly connected with U.S. economic aid to its Allies, including the Soviet Union. Although during those discussions there were some anti-Soviet votes (in the Congress, in particular), nevertheless the majority of both the House and the Senate always supported the president. There were instances, during discussions of some important laws relating to U.S. foreign policy, when some anti-Soviet statements were made by certain groups and individuals (mainly Republicans). In particular, those statements were frequently made by the representatives of states with a large percentage of Polish population. However, those statements failed to influence the U.S. administration, though their influence was rather significant in the Congress.

Now all in all, the Congress supports Roosevelt and his policy with respect to the Soviet Union. Not only the behavior of the Senate and House of Representatives' members during discussions of various laws relating to American foreign policy, but also the opinions expressed in personal expressions by the leaders of various political groupings of the Congress prove the correctness of my conclusion. Almost all of them, without exception, underline the need to maintain friendly relations with the Soviet Union—not only during the war, but also after it. Similar views were frequently expressed during my conversations with Senator [Tom] Connolly, chairman of the Senate's Foreign Affairs Committee, [Sol] Bloom, chairman of the Foreign Affairs Committee of the House of Representatives, Vice-President Wallace, and the Democratic majority leader—more than two dozen representatives in the Congress. The latter use every occasion and every possibility for anti-Soviet attacks.

The reactionary anti-Soviet American press, such as the newspapers of Hearst, McCormick, do serious damage to Soviet-American relations. Unfortunately, this press is rather influential. Its influence is especially strong in such cities as New York, Chicago, Washington, San Francisco, Detroit, and some other large centers of the country. As an anti-Roosevelt press, it cannot exert serious influence on the administration of Roosevelt and his attitude to the USSR. However, it does damage as it sows doubts and suspicion concerning the Soviet Union. It negatively influences the molding of sentiments in the general public of the country. These sentiments find their expression in the Congress and thereby create some difficulty for Roosevelt.

The U.S. Catholic Church also negatively influences Soviet-American relations. The Catholic Church is the most important political factor in the country. The following data can give you an idea about its influence and authority: there are 23 million Catholics in the U.S., 18,970 churches. As for the numbers, Catholics are second only to Protestants in this respect. However, the influence of the U.S. Catholic Church is stronger than that of the Protestant one. The problem is that the Catholic Church since old times has considered it to be its right to deal not only with religion, but also with politics. It has close connections with the Pope. The latter has his nuncio (apostolic delegate)—Amleto Tzyconiani—to whom 21 archbishops are subordinated, 2 of whom are cardinals (members of the Vatican Council), and archbishops of certain important areas of the country, in particular: Cardinal O'Connely, Archbishop of Boston; Cardinal Doherty, Archbishop of Philadelphia. There are others who work in important centers of the country: Stritig [?], Archbishop of Chicago; Mooney, Archbishop of Detroit; Spellman, Archbishop of New York; Mittey, Archbishop of San Francisco; Curley, Archbishop of Washington; Volly, Archbishop of Newark, etc. There are 129 bishops who are subordinated to archbishops. Accordingly, 36,970 Catholic priests are subordinated to the bishops.

The U.S. Catholic Church has a vast network of schools, colleges, seminaries, and other organizations, through which it exerts its influence. All in all, it has 9 thousand parish schools, seminaries, colleges, academies, and parishes, wherein about 2 million people study. Besides that the Church has 183 old people's homes and 726 hospitals. The Church also has its own press. It publishes more than 150 Catholic newspapers and magazines. Editors and journalists are trained by special faculties of some American universities.

Right from the establishment of diplomatic relations between the U.S. and the USSR, the Catholic Church was more than once an instigator of various anti-Soviet campaigns. Lately, Roman Catholics have concentrated their attention on Polish problems. They support the emigrant Polish government in London while the Catholic Church is actively propagating against the USSR and Poland in the U.S. As always, Catholics often use religious phrases and cock-and-bull stories about the lack of religious liberty in the USSR as a cover for their attitude towards the Soviet Union. However, recently those arguments have become less convincing for the general public. And Catholics frequently confine themselves to purely political aspects of the mentioned problems.

An article about the Vatican, recently published in *Izvestia* newspaper, caused a new wave of anti-Soviet slander on the part of the U.S. Catholic clergymen. Nevertheless, the article has played a certain positive role in attracting the attention of the American public to the activities of the Vatican and the Pope as accomplices of fascism.

The U.S. Catholic Church is actively supported by the large Polish minority in the United States. There are about five million Poles in the country who mainly hold anti-Soviet positions and support the Polish emigrant government. The Poles have numerous organizations, societies, and press (about fifty newspapers) in the U.S. The Polish government always generously financed Polish organizations and the Polish press, and it is still doing this now. Millions of dollars are spent on this. The Polish government is spending money from a special presidential fund, allocated for anti-German propaganda in Poland and on anti-Soviet propaganda. About two months ago Morgenthau told me about a suspicion that the Polish emigrant government had spent ten million dollars, received from the above-mentioned presidential fund some time before, on anti-Soviet propaganda. Later I received information proving that the Poles were actually spending that sum of money on anti-Soviet propaganda in the U.S. The official Polish information center in New York is especially active in this propagandist work. The work of the center, as well as all activities of Polish organizations in the U.S., is directed by the emigrant government through its official representatives in the U.S. and, in particular, through the Polish embassy in Washington.

Roosevelt, whose position on the Polish issue is mainly favorable for the Soviet Union, nevertheless takes into consideration the influence and behavior of the Polish minority. That is to a great extent connected with political factors, *i.e.,* the pre-election campaign. Roosevelt is trying to keep the votes of American Poles during the next election. Roosevelt and his friends believe that a million and a half Polish voters will seriously affect the results of election.

As was mentioned above, Roosevelt and his administration stand on the position of support for the Soviet Union and friendly relations and cooperation with it. But this doesn't mean the absence of doubts, with regard to the future, among official and business circles of the U.S. For example, these circles are concerned with the destiny of some European countries, including the Balkan countries, in relation to the victories of the Red Army in the war against Germany and the growing influence of the Soviet Union in Europe and in European affairs. Generally, they view the growing influence of the Soviet Union in Poland, Germany, Finland, the Balkan States, and some other countries of Europe as inevitable. However, they are worried about possible social upheavals that might occur in European countries as a result of the USSR's growing influence in Europe in the course of the war.

Such a concern is frequently expressed in various forms. It will continue to be expressed with each new success of the Soviet Union in the war against Germany. But right now, when the main attention of the Allies is concentrated on the waging of war against Germany, the understanding of the common interests of both countries in this war stifles this alarm to a certain extent.

The established relations between the U.S. and the USSR will to a considerable degree determine the destiny of future relations between the two countries, particularly in the postwar period. The last period of U.S.-USSR relations since the attack of Fascist Germany against the Soviet Union, and the common objectives of both countries brought to light in the course of the war, showed that existing relations were on quite solid ground. The decade since the restoration of diplomatic relations between the U.S. and the USSR has provided a sufficient material basis for drawing a conclusion about the great influence of both countries on international events. In the course of the war the U.S. became the virtual ally of the USSR's struggle against Germany, whose struggle for world supremacy could not help setting such a big world power as the U.S. against it. There are grounds for believing that after the present-day European war is over the United States will be interested in economic and political cooperation with the Soviet Union. Below I'll detail the reasons for such an interest in cooperation with the USSR. To a considerable degree that cooperation could determine world-scale relations, their content and character. Of course, any international organization created after the war to safeguard peace and security would not be efficient without the coordinated actions of the U.S. and the USSR.

There are grounds for belief in drastic changes in the mental attitude of the ruling classes and the broad public of the country since the moment when America joined the war. Although isolationist attitudes had from time to time been manifested, there is no doubt that in the process of the war isolationism was radically undermined.

Important shifts took place in the frame of mind of the leaders of the Republican party which had been the main bearer of isolationist attitudes. Now the Republican party majority is on the verge of understanding that the United States won't be able to return to its previous positions or to conduct isolationist policy as it did before the war. The Republican party is gradually coming to the conclusion that cooperation with other countries, primarily such major countries of the world as the USSR and the British Empire, is in the best interests of the U.S.

The Democrats hold an even more definite position. With certain exceptions, during the war they supported the foreign policy of Roosevelt utterly; and they continue to support this policy, because it is aimed at cooperation with the Allies and active involvement of the U.S. in European and international affairs.

There is no need to say that the overwhelming majority of the population of the country, especially the working class, completely supports Roosevelt's foreign policy. But this doesn't preclude the possibility of occasional outbursts of isolationism. Isolationist policy has deep rooted over a very long historical period. Among a certain segment of the Republican leaders there are still persons and groups (Hoover, Landon, Taft), unfortunately still influential in the party, who try to pull the Republican party back to its previous positions of isolationism in the sphere of foreign policy. In view of that fact, it's quite possible that conflict on the degree and the form of cooperation with other countries may occur in the political circles of the U.S. (and, first of all, in the Congress). Such a fight cannot help affecting Soviet-American relations. Roosevelt, Hull, and the U.S. administration are absolutely sure of their ability to overcome isolationist trends in the Congress. Hull expressed such an idea in one of our conversations on the eve of my departure from Washington to Moscow. Speaking about an international organization for security, Hull expressed his confidence that the administration would manage to guide the Congress and that the latter would approve the president's policy of active participation in the international organization.

This means we'll have even more hope for successfully overcoming isolationism if Roosevelt is reelected for the fourth term, which is

almost certain. His reelection will be of great positive political significance not only from the point of view of future U.S. foreign policy and
the extent of U.S. cooperation with other countries, but also for the
future of Soviet-American relations.

Correspondingly, election of a Republican representative to the
presidential post would be a very strong blow to Soviet-American
relations. In that case the isolationists will once again hold up their
heads, various large and small anti-Soviet groups in the country will
become even more active. Election of Dewey would mean the advent
to power of people known as desperate anti-Soviets, and this would
mean their taking posts in the cabinet and in the state machinery.
The press and influential circles of the Republican party, supporting
Dewey, are already seriously discussing a would-be composition of
the cabinet in case Dewey is elected. The names mentioned in those
circles as possible members of the cabinet speak for themselves. For
instance, Hoover is proposed as the secretary of state; he is a friend of
Dewey and an inveterate enemy of the Soviet Union. General Mac-
Arthur is intended for the war minister. Aldrich, chairman of Chase
National Bank, an extreme reactionary who is personally hostile to us,
is proposed as secretary of the treasury. John Lewis, president of the
miners' association and a person with anti-Roosevelt views, is proposed as secretary of labor. No less reactionary persons are named as
candidates to other posts in the cabinet. Such a team of a Republican
president would be a telling blow to Soviet-American relations.

However, taking into account the possibility of Republican power in
1948, for example, it is nevertheless feasible to determine probable
trends in the U.S. ruling classes' attitudes toward the USSR, irre-
spective of the president's personality—whoever he may be—a Republican or a Democrat. We believe that the USSR and the U.S. will
manage to find common issues for the solution of a number of
problems emerging in the future and of interest to both countries.

I. The United States, as well as the Soviet Union, is interested in
the defeat of Germany and its subsequent economic and military
weakening. Roosevelt, his administration, and the ruling circles are
carrying out quite a definite policy in this respect. Furthermore, the
industrial and financial bourgeoisie of the U.S. is not interested in

having such a serious economic competitor as Germany after the end of the European war. However, right now it is difficult to say how far the administration and the ruling circles will go in that direction.

II. After the war is over the United States will be interested in safeguarding the peace, at least for a certain period of time. In the course of this war it has substantially increased its political and economic influence in many countries and made its international position stronger. The strengthening of the U.S. in this regard has been expressed in the following ways:

(1) In the course of the war the U.S. has consolidated its positions in Latin America, making them even stronger than before the war by reducing Britain's influence there; and, of course, Germany was ousted from Latin America at the beginning of the war.

(2) Canada became even more dependent upon U.S. economic influence than before the war.

(3) The U.S. has consolidated its positions in the Mediterranean Sea and in Africa, and it holds a number of key strategic positions among French possessions.

(4) American influence in the Middle and Near East and in China has increased in comparison with the prewar period.

(5) Correlation of the naval forces of the U.S. and Britain has changed in favor of the U.S. during the war. The same can be said about the mercantile marines.

(6) The U.S. has taken a number of the most important naval bases from Great Britain. Taking advantage of the difficult situation of Britain, especially in 1940, the U.S. got a number of British naval bases in exchange for fifty torpedo-boats which Britain badly needed at that moment.

(7) In the course of the war the economic and, to a certain extent, political dependence of Great Britain on the U.S. has increased. Supply of armaments, food, and other materials to Britain is used and surely will continue to be used by Americans as a lever of political pressure in future.

(8) During the war the U.S. considerably extended the production apparatus of industry, especially individual branches of it (engineering, chemical industry, aircraft industry, ship-building, etc.). During

the years of war American industry has progressed technologically. In view of that, American business circles anticipate that, despite a high subsistence minimum [wage] in the country, other countries won't be able to compete with U.S. industry, and the U.S. will maintain advantages in this respect over other countries.

Certainly, the United States will be interested in taking maximum advantage of every wartime achievement during the time of peace. There will be one common feature in the U.S. position after World War I and after this war is over. World War I also brought with it a number of benefits—primarily economic ones. The only difference will be in the amount of benefits, which will be much higher after this war. That is why there is reason to believe that the U.S. will be interested in the maintenance of peace, at least, for a certain period of time. In light of all this, the readiness of the U.S. to take an active part in a peace- and security-keeping organization becomes clear.

III. The U.S. will sympathize with the countries of Western Europe, especially Germany, and will assist them in establishing bourgeois-democratic political regimes. The president, as well as other top officials, has made such statements more than once.

Speaking about the possible attitude of the U.S. toward the forms of state-political systems in the postwar West European countries, it is necessary to bear in mind an important circumstance: should it come to establishing a pro-Soviet regime in one or another country, the U.S. ruling classes might not refrain from setting up a Fascist dictatorship in such a country. Anyhow, we cannot ignore the historical lesson of Spain (1936–39). We should also take into consideration the policy conducted by the U.S. administration toward Spain under Franco and the reality of the U.S. getting along with a semi-Fascist regime in Brazil.

Nevertheless, laying aside the possibility of Socialist revolutions in some European countries, then the idea of the U.S. becoming an opponent of Fascist forms of government for a certain period would seem to be quite logical.

IV. Economic interests in both the U.S. and the USSR can become a solid base for postwar relations and cooperation between the two countries. It goes without saying that the Soviet Union will need considerable equipment from the U.S., purchases that will be necessary for the restoration of war-ravaged areas and for further development of Socialist industry in the future. But the U.S. will also be interested in further development of trade with the Soviet Union. American business circles and the administration have shown great interest in the development of trade with the Soviet Union after the war. Often I've heard statements about the necessity for further development of trade with the USSR, made by official representatives of the administration and by representatives of American business. The striving of industrial firms to develop trade with the USSR can be accounted for their extremely high interest in the commodity markets for their industrial equipment.

The moment the U.S. joined the war, the total volume of American industrial output doubled. Business and official circles expect that during the early postwar period the U.S. may find itself in a difficult situation regarding the sale of industrial equipment. It is thought that conversion of the economy from wartime to peaceful purposes will take an indefinite period, at least two to three years; the majority of people in the U.S. believe that the industrial output that is particularly related to the war against Japan will last for two years after the end of the war in Europe. However, in spite of that, it is expected that after the end of the European war, there will be excessive commodities and the U.S. will need external markets for their sale.

In conversations with officials and businessmen of the U.S., I've heard the opinion that after the war the United States will need a market for various kinds of industrial equipment. It was also pointed out that U.S. industry will need to import some types of raw materials from the USSR. Speaking about the import of raw materials from the USSR, people usually name manganese, chrome ore, platinum, and some other raw materials. American companies and firms set their hopes on development of the Soviet-American trade. Thus, mutual interest in the development of trade makes us believe that the postwar Soviet-American relations will have a proper economic base.

Development of our postwar trade with the U.S. demands a solution to the problem of its financing. It is already clear that more or less sizable trade between the two countries can be accomplished only if the Soviet Union gets credit. The U.S. administration and corresponding bodies such as the Treasury, Administration for Foreign Aid, and State Department were entrusted with studying the issue of granting credit to the Soviet Union. And the suggestions made by the U.S. administration in the form of the draft agreement, supplementary to the agreement of June 11, 1942, delivered through me, resulted from that study. The agreement suggested by the U.S. administration is to be a document providing for transition from the Lend-Lease Act to new forms of commercial relations between the two countries, the financial basis of which will be credit granted to the Soviet Union through governmental channels.

Roosevelt's administration considers that credit can be granted to the Soviet Union through the so-called Export-Import Bank, i.e., a governmental channel. They expect that the amount of credit may make up several billion dollars. During my conversations with various officials, a sum of five to six, or even more, billion dollars was mentioned. In common opinion, a presumable term of credit will be twenty to twenty-five years, with an annual interest rate of from 2 to 2.5 percent. The above-mentioned solution to the credit problem, which the administration of Roosevelt plans to implement, is very likely to be the most appropriate for us.

Later on Roosevelt may come across some difficulties regarding the method of assigning credit to the Soviet Union. American banks, as well as Republican opponents of Roosevelt, are blaming him and his administration for tackling problems that have always depended on the competence of private banks and firms. A similar point of view has already been expressed once—in connection with a well-known plan by Roosevelt to grant credit to other countries through governmental channels. However, Roosevelt hopes to overcome resistance among the U.S. financial circles in this respect and to put his plan for financing commerce with the Soviet Union and several other countries into practice.

Receiving substantial credit from private U.S. banks before the war's end is hardly probable. These banks won't run the risk of serious financial deals with the Soviet Union or any other country until the end of the war. That's the opinion prevailing in bankers' circles.

Private banks will initiate a serious deal only after a peace conference when the war in Europe is over and the political situation of the world is more certain.

In order to defend their interests properly, key banks of the U.S. are going to send their representatives to the peace conference. General opinion is that the delegation will be headed by a representative of the most influential and major bank in the country, i.e., the Chase Manhattan Bank. There is already an understanding on this issue among banks. Right now it's difficult to say whether private banks will run the risk of serious deals with the USSR. It is advisable for us to maintain contacts with some of them, just to make certain of the future. In particular, it might be well to contact the firm of Morgan (Thomas Lamont) and probably Chase Manhattan Bank.

V. Perhaps, after the war, we will get American technological assistance, which Soviet industry will need. Such assistance for chemical research, radio industry, and perhaps for ship-building would allow us to use the progressive experience accumulated by American industry during the war. Industrial firms might agree to make such deals. Until the end of the war with Japan, the U.S. administration is apparently going to restrict the rights of firms in this respect, using the excuse of a need for secrecy in technological achievements during wartime.

VI. Exchange of information on scientific and technological successes in the sphere of agriculture would be quite possible and advantageous. The U.S. displays and will continue to display its interest in agricultural achievements in our northern areas, and in areas other than cotton-growing, for example. To an even greater degree, it would be useful for the USSR to profit from the great experience accumulated by the U.S. in cattle-breeding, seed-farming, and selection. What is most astonishing about the U.S. is not only its large scale of scientific research, work, and experiments in those spheres, but also its quickness in putting those agricultural achievements into practice. There are many things in this area that we could adopt from the U.S. Very frequently we ignore the fact that 20 percent of the American population (farmers) produces not only a sufficient amount of agricultural products for the entire population of the country, but also a lot of products to be exported. This fact is worth being thoroughly analyzed in order to make use of all of the technological achievements and scientific-technological experience of American agriculture.

The above-enumerated items can become a base for common lines in the policy of the U.S. and the USSR in the future, including the postwar period. However, it doesn't mean that we'll avoid difficulties in our relations with the United States.

1. As was mentioned above, the United States' policy toward Germany is aimed at its defeat and its subsequent economic weakening. However, this general aim of the American administration regarding Germany doesn't prohibit a situation during discussions of concrete problems—in particular, the problem of the amount and form of German reparations—when certain differences might emerge. The U.S. administration, on various pretexts and taking refuge in phrases about humanism, is likely to attempt to decrease Germany's reparations. In particular, a disagreement is possible between the Soviet point of view and that of the American administration on the subject of using German manpower resources for reconstruction of the Soviet Union. It is known to us that one of the major trade union organizations of the U.S.—American Federation of Labor (its leader, William Green)—has taken a position on this problem that is against the USSR. The AFL leadership is trying to justify its position with arguments and reasons of a pseudo-humanitarian type. Green has already opposed all plans for the use of forced labor of German workers by the Allies after the war.

Although the U.S. Catholic Church hasn't yet expressed its point of view openly, one can hardly doubt that its position will challenge that of the AFL. Political guidelines of the AFL leadership, the Catholic church, and a number of other organizations, institutions, groups, and certain politicians will inevitably affect the U.S. administration on this particular problem and some other issues connected with the whole German problem.

2. The Catholic Church of the U.S., the anti-Soviet reactionary press, and individual groups hostile to the USSR will continue to come out against the Soviet Union on various occasions. Such things, of course, cannot have positive consequences. I should say that such

anti-Soviet statements will be inevitable and can be explained by general ideological hostility among the U.S. ruling classes toward the USSR, which without doubt will continue in the future.

3. As was mentioned above, the U.S. administration, the Congress, and business circles of the country don't hide their anxiety about the future of some East European countries. This anxiety is in particular connected with the advance of the Red Army toward the Balkans. These circles are frightened by the perspective of social upheavals and the establishment of the Soviet system in certain countries. In particular, they are very much concerned about Yugoslavia. There is a well-known statement by the Soviet government on Rumania, made in connection with the Red Army's crossing of the Soviet-Rumanian border, a statement that to some extent has reassured them. [?] However, it failed to eliminate existing suspicions about the USSR or to relieve the U.S.'s anxiety about the destiny of the Balkan States.

4. *The so-called Baltic issues.* Roosevelt's administration believes that the problem of the Baltic States will resolve itself in the process of their liberation by the Red Army. A similar point of view was expressed during my personal contacts with officials, in particular Hopkins, who quite openly said that this was not only his personal opinion, but the president's too. Nevertheless, from time to time the anti-Soviet press and representatives of national Baltic minorities in the U.S. begin repeating their ideas on the Baltic issue all over again.

However, until the end of the war, Roosevelt won't recognize the Baltic republics as component parts of the USSR, taking into account his domestic situation and the present-day preelection campaign.

5. As is generally known, the United States is striving to increase its influence in the Middle and Near East. In the course of the war it strengthened its positions in those regions. The American administration's decision to build an oil pipeline through Saudi Arabia to Haifa [Palestine] is one means of increasing the consolidating American influence in the countries of the Middle and Near East in the future. Partly, this can be explained by the striving of the U.S. administration to consolidate its positions in the Mediterranean for strategic reasons. Certainly, the growth of American influence in the Middle East—and especially in Iran—won't agree with the interests

of the Soviet Union, which has a common border with Iran. I suppose that the United States will use both political and economic means to increase its influence in those countries. The U.S. will try to flood those countries with American commodities, American experts and advisers, etc.

6. The U.S. administration is known to have rather vast plans concerning international civil airlines. The talks of civil aviation carried on now in Washington confirm the far-reaching character of these American plans. The draft agreement on aviation, given to me by Ambassador Joseph Grew on the eve of my departure for Moscow, suggests setting up two civil airlines between the U.S. and the USSR. The first one is Washington-London-Stockholm-Moscow-Baku-Teheran, and the second one is the U.S.-Fairbanks (Alaska)-Chukotka-Vladivostok, and on to Mukden and the south of China. These plans suggest that America has proceeded on the assumption of mutual free transit of aircraft and cargo via both U.S. and USSR territories. Such plans by Americans contradict our line, according to which sections of those airlines crossing the Soviet territory should be accomplished by our means and resources alone.

Furthermore, America evidently intends to engage a number of states bordering with us, such as Iran, China, Finland, Poland, etc., into the system of civil airlines, implying free transit of American aircraft through those countries. For both strategic and political reasons, the Soviet Union is not interested in consolidation of American positions in our neighboring countries.

7. Immense growth of the Soviet Union's popularity has created a great thirst in broad segments of American society for receiving information about the USSR. People want to know the truth about our country. People are wondering about the reasons for the enormous successes of the Soviet Union in the war against Germany, which previously seemed impossible. This desire for information about the USSR is permanently growing.

On the other hand, American authorities undertake measures to limit dissemination of information about the USSR. Lately, laws and regulations were issued in the U.S. that made the functioning of our agencies, dissemination of Soviet literature, films, photo-materials, partly music, almost impossible. Authorities qualify the dissemination of information about the USSR as a propagandist activity with all of the ensuing consequences—demand for registration as a foreign agent-propagandist or an official statement of the Embassy that one or another activity (disseminating literature, for example) is being carried out on behalf of the Soviet government.

This policy of American authorities can partly be explained by the hostility of Attorney General Francis Biddle to the USSR. However, the main causes are more profound. The American administration and authorities are expecting the emergence of postwar difficulties, primarily such economic difficulties as unemployment, the discharge of women from the production sphere, the aggravation of negotiations on wages between employers and trade unions, the emergence of conflicts on social insurance and allowance, etc. Official circles believe that if such difficulties exist in the future, the American worker will be even more susceptible to information about the USSR and will manifest his inclination toward "dangerous" thoughts. In view of the above-mentioned, I believe such limitations on the part of the American administration will continue in the future.

To a certain extent this position among American authorities explains their attempt to attain greater dissemination of American propaganda in the Soviet Union. The American administration isn't satisfied with the existing situation and its propaganda.

8. As was already mentioned above, business circles and the U.S. administration are striving, and will strive in the future, to extend trade with the Soviet Union. However, the tendency of delaying the delivery of long-term use equipment to us is already quite obvious. There are also some formal obstacles to delivery of that equipment now. According to the Lend-Lease Act, the administration has a right to deliver to its Allies only those materials that can be used for war purposes in the struggle against their common enemy. But besides this formality, there is another reason—namely an unwillingness to hasten delivery of capital equipment to the Soviet Union, calculating that in case of future difficulties regarding capital equipment we'll need American deliveries to a greater degree than if we get a considerable amount of that equipment for our industry now, during the

course of the war. Certainly, no official of the U.S. ever said openly that U.S. governmental circles have a tendency to delay deliveries of capital equipment to the Soviet Union for the above-mentioned reasons. Nevertheless, we know from reliable sources that such a tendency exists within official circles.

As was mentioned above, reelection of President Roosevelt for the fourth term would be the most important positive phenomenon in politics. Judging by the political situation in the U.S., reelection of Roosevelt is certain beyond all question. However, there is a danger that even in the case of Roosevelt's reelection as president, the American Congress will have a Republican majority. This can, first of all, impede even more the actions of Roosevelt and his administration in the sphere of foreign policy because the number of opponents of Roosevelt in the Congress will inevitably grow. And secondly, this can increase the influence of those elements in the United States who are hostile or unfriendly to the Soviet Union.

However, in spite of all possible difficulties that are likely to emerge from time to time in our relations with the United States, there are certainly conditions for continuation of cooperation between our two countries in the postwar period. To a great extent, relations between the two countries will be determined within the context of established relations and those that will take shape in the course of the war.

July 14, 1944

(Gromyko)

Notes

1. Why Another Book on FDR?

1. See Gregg Walker, "Franklin D. Roosevelt as a Summit Negotiator at Teheran, 1943 and Yalta, 1945," 101–62.

2. Isaiah Berlin, *The Crooked Timber of Humanity* (New York: Knopf, 1991), 62.

3. Walker, "Roosevelt as a Negotiator," 101–62.

4. Warren Kimball, "Crisis Diplomacy, June–December 1941," in *Soviet-US Relations, 1933–1943,* ed. Gregory Sevostianov (Moscow: Progress Publishers, 1989), 66–67.

5. John Lewis Gaddis, *Strategies of Containment: The Post War American National Security Policy,* 6, 8.

6. Ibid., 3.

7. John Lewis Gaddis, "Presidential Address: The Tragedy of the Cold War," 4, 6.

8. Gaddis, *Strategies of Containment,* 3, 5.

9. Ibid., 9.

10. Ibid., 18.

11. Warren Kimball, *The Juggler: Franklin Roosevelt as Wartime States-man* (Princeton: Princeton University Press, 1991), xi, 63.

12. Ibid., 22, 31, 34, 38.

13. Ibid., 38.

14. Ibid.

15. See the bibliography for these and other standard works on Stalin.

2. The President's Style and World View

1. John M. Lewis, "Franklin Roosevelt and the United States Strategy in World War II," 134.

2. Ibid.

3. Ibid., 158–59.

4. Henry Adams, *The Letters of Henry Adams,* vol. 4.

5. Lewis, "Roosevelt and World War II," 345.

6. Ibid., 361.

7. Quoted in David F. Healy, *U.S. Expansionism: The Imperialist Urge in the 1890's,* 38.

8. Quoted in Lewis, "Roosevelt and World War II," 136.

9. See Donald Cameron Watt, *How War Came: The Immediate Origins of the Second World War, 1938–1939,* 193–96.

10. Donald Watt, "Roosevelt and Neville Chamberlain: Two Appeasers," 201–3; and David Reynolds, *The Creation of the Anglo-American Alliance, 1937–41: A Study in Competitive Co-operation,* 69–72.

11. Lewis, "Roosevelt and World War II," 135, 137.

12. Ibid., 159.

13. Ibid., 234, 235.

14. Ibid., 235.

15. Schacht report to the German Foreign Ministry quoted in Frank Friedel, *Franklin D. Roosevelt,* vol. 4, *Launching the New Deal,* 396.

16. Wayne S. Cole, *Roosevelt and the Isolationists, 1932–45,* 10–11, 298–300.

17. Ibid., 8–11.

18. Willard Range, *Franklin D. Roosevelt's World Order,* 137.

19. Watt, "Roosevelt and Chamberlain," 203.

20. Cole, *Roosevelt and the Isolationists,* 3.

21. Ibid., 7.

22. Ibid., 297.

23. C. A. MacDonald, *The United States, Britain, and Appeasement, 1936–1939,* 1.

24. Ibid.

25. Watt, "Roosevelt and Chamberlain," 185.

26. Ibid., 186–87.

27. Ibid.

28. MacDonald, *United States, Britain, and Appeasement,* 43, 48.

29. Quoted ibid., 66.

30. Ibid., 62–65, 69.

31. Reynolds, *The Creation,* 32.

32. Ibid., 33.

33. Quoted in William R. Rock, *Chamberlain and Roosevelt: British Foreign Policy and the United States, 1937–1940,* 69.

34. MacDonald, *United States, Britain, and Appeasement,* 105.

35. Ibid.

3. Roosevelt and His War Strategy

1. Maurice Matloff and Edwin Snell, *Strategic Planning for Coalition Warfare, 1941–1942,* 11–31.

2. Mark M. Lowenthal, "Roosevelt and the Coming of the War: The Search for United States Policy, 1937–1942," 433.

3. For FDR's Japanese–Far Eastern policy, see the excellent analysis by Jonathan G. Utley, *Going to War with Japan, 1937–1941* (Knoxville: University of Tennessee Press, 1985), 3–42.

4. Ibid., 181.

5. Reynolds, *The Creation,* 105.

6. Ibid., 132.

7. Letter from Churchill to FDR, 12/8/40, in Warren F. Kimball, *Churchill and Roosevelt: The Complete Correspondence,* 1:88.

8. Kimball, *Churchill and Roosevelt,* 1:101; see also Reynolds, *The Creation,* 150–68.

9. Kimball, *Churchill and Roosevelt,* 1:102.

10. Warren F. Kimball, *The Most Unsordid Act: Lend-Lease, 1939–1941,* 124.

11. Ibid., vi.

12. Ibid., 231, 240.

13. Ibid., 233.

14. The best American study is Matloff and Snell, *Strategic Planning, 1941–1942.*

15. Theodore A. Wilson, *The First Summit: Roosevelt and Churchill at Placentia Bay, 1941,* 174–76.

16. Ibid., 187, 202.

17. See Matloff and Snell, *Strategic Planning, 1941–1942,* and others.

18. Quoted in A. E. Campbell, "Franklin Roosevelt and Unconditional Surrender," 219.

19. Ibid., 231.

20. Quoted ibid., 238.

21. Author's interview with Joseph Alsop, Washington, D.C., 1986.

22. Kent Roberts Greenfield, *American Strategy in World War II: A Reconsideration,* 80–84, 50–51.

23. See the outstanding classic study by General Colin Ballard, *The Military Genius of Abraham Lincoln* (London: Oxford University Press, 1926), which argues that Lincoln had a tremendous sense of grand strategy.

24. See Kimball, *Churchill and Roosevelt,* vol. 3.

25. David E. Kaiser, "Churchill, Roosevelt, and the Limits of Power," 204.

4. Surrogate Diplomacy: Roosevelt's Informal Government

1. James H. Lazalier, "Surrogate Diplomacy: FDR's Personal Envoys, 1941–1945," 2.

2. William D. Leahy Papers, Library of Congress, Box 23.

3. See Lazalier, "Surrogate Diplomacy"; Hugh DeSantis, *The Diplomacy of Silence;* George Frost Kennan, "Comment"; William H. Standley and Arthur A. Ageton, *Admiral Ambassador to Russia.*

4. Lazalier, "Surrogate Diplomacy," 250.

5. Steven Merritt Miner, *Between Churchill and Stalin: The Soviet Union, Great Britain, and the Origins of the Grand Alliance,* 180–225; E. L. Woodward, *British Foreign Policy in the Second World War,* 2:220–80; Graham Ross, *The Foreign Office and the Kremlin: British Documents on Anglo-Soviet Relations, 1941–45,* 18–31.

6. Miner, *Between Churchill and Stalin,* 197.

7. Churchill to Eden, January 28, 1942, quoted in Miner, *Between Churchill and Stalin,* 196.

8. Woodward, *British Foreign Policy,* 2:244–45.

9. Eden quoted in Miner, *Between Churchill and Stalin,* 198.

10. For an overview of this period, see John P. Diggins, *Up from Communism: Conservative Odysseys in American Intellectual History* and *the American Left in the Twentieth Century.*

11. Quoted in Thomas R. Maddux, *Years of Estrangement: American Relations with the Soviet Union, 1933–1941,* 6.

12. Much of this information comes from the Joseph E. Davies Papers, Library of Congress; Elizabeth Kimbell MacLean, "Joseph E. Davies and Soviet-American Relations, 1941–1943"; as well as Keith David Eagles, "Ambassador Joseph E. Davies and American-Soviet Relations, 1937–1941."

13. See DeSantis, *Diplomacy of Silence.*

14. Kennan, quoted MacLean, "Davies," 75.

15. Robert Chadwell Williams, *Russian Art and American Money, 1900–1940,* 237.

16. Davies, quoted ibid., 248.

17. Ibid., 253–54.

18. Ibid., 261, 262.

19. MacLean, "Davies," 75.

20. Ibid., 76.

21. Davies Diary, 9/25/43, p. 2, Davies Papers.

22. Joseph Edward Davies, *Mission to Moscow,* 473, 474–75.

23. Quoted in MacLean, "Davies," 82, 83, 89.

24. Davies Diary, 8/4/43, Davies Papers.

25. MacLean, "Davies," 92.

26. Orville H. Bullitt, ed., *For the President, Personal and Secret; Correspondence between Franklin D. Roosevelt and William C. Bullitt,* 581, 582, 583; see also Timothy Edward O'Connor, *Diplomacy and Revolution: G. V. Chicherin and Soviet Foreign Affairs, 1918–1930.*

27. Maddux, *Years of Estrangement,* 54.

28. Robert Emmet Sherwood, *Roosevelt and Hopkins: An Intimate History.*

29. Frank J. Rider, "Harry L. Hopkins: The Ambitious Crusader," 89.

30. Ibid.

31. George T. McJimsey, *Harry Hopkins: Ally of the Poor and Defender of Democracy,* 100.

32. Oscar Cox Diary, June 23, 1941, Oscar Cox Papers, Franklin D. Roosevelt Library, Hyde Park, New York. Quoted in John D. Langer, "The Formulation of American Aid Policy toward the Soviet Union, 1940–1943: The Hopkins Shop and the Department of State," 60.

33. Langer, "The Formulation," 63.

34. George C. Herring, Jr., *Aid to Russia, 1941–1946: Strategy, Diplomacy, the Origins of the Cold War,* 35.

35. Langer, "The Formulation," 71.

36. Ibid., 72.

37. McJimsey, *Harry Hopkins,* 180–82; Winston Churchill, *The Second World War,* vol. 2., *Their Finest Hour.*

38. McJimsey, *Harry Hopkins,* 181.

39. Ibid., 180–92; quoted ibid., 185.

40. Ibid.

41. George Urban, "Was Stalin (the Terrible) Really a Great Man," 37.

42. McJimsey, *Harry Hopkins,* 180.

43. Berezhkov to author, November, 1989, Washington, D.C.

44. McJimsey, *Harry Hopkins,* 293.

45. Ibid., 293, 300.

46. Langer, "The Formulation," 1.

47. From Steinhardt to Loy Henderson, December 13, 1939, item 87, Official Letterbook, box 78, Laurence A. Steinhardt Papers, Manuscript Division, Library of Congress. Quoted in Langer, "The Formulation," 2.

48. Langer, "The Formulation," 18.

49. Unsigned, undated "Draft for the President's Signature," box 310, file "Book 5: Aid to Russia." The handwritten draft is in Burns's writing.

50. Quoted from Burns, "Recommendation," in Langer, "The Formulation," 9–102.

51. See Edward R. Stettinius, Jr., *Lend-Lease: Weapon for Victory.*

52. Raymond H. Dawson, *The Decision to Aid Russia, 1941: Foreign Policy and Domestic Politics,* 255.

53. Ibid.

54. Herring, *Aid to Russia,* 279.

55. George C. Herring, Jr., "Lend-Lease to Russia and the Origins of the Cold War, 1944–1945," 94.

56. Ibid., 95.

57. Hubert P. Van Tuyll, *Feeding the Bear: American Aid to the Soviet Union, 1941–1945,* 1–21, 32–48.

58. John D. Langer, "The 'Red General' Philip R. Faymonville and the Soviet Union, 1917–1952," 209.

59. Ibid., 211.

60. Quoted in Langer, "The Formulation," 315.

61. Quoted in Langer, "The 'Red General,'" 212.

62. Ibid.

63. Van Tuyll, *Feeding the Bear,* 10.

64. This judgment is made although Faymonville files, as of 1990, were still closed. Ibid., 10.

65. Ibid.

66. Ibid., 9.

67. Ibid., 11.

68. Richard C. Lukas, "Soviet Stalling Tactics in the Forties," 52; see also Van Tuyll, *Feeding the Bear,* 11.

69. Van Tuyll, *Feeding the Bear,* 11; Standley and Ageton, *Admiral Ambassador to Russia,* 332–33.

70. Van Tuyll, *Feeding the Bear,* 11–13.

71. Ibid., 13.

72. Herring, "Lend-Lease to Russia," 98.

73. Larry I. Bland, "W. Averell Harriman: Businessman and Diplomat, 1891–1945," iii.

74. E. J. Kahn, Jr., "Profiles: Plenipotentiary II," 38.

75. Valentin Berezhkov, Stalin's translator, to the author, July, 1989.

76. Paraphrased from Kahn, "Profiles: Plenipotentiary II," 55–57.

77. Harriette L. Chandler, "The Transition to a Cold Warrior: The Evolution of W. Averell Harriman's Polish Policy," 229.

78. Urban, "Was Stalin," 40.

79. Bland, "Harriman," 405.

80. Urban, "Was Stalin," 39.

81. Sherwood, *Roosevelt and Hopkins,* 331.

82. Langer, "The Formulation," 85.

83. Ibid., 97.

84. Standley and Ageton, *Admiral Ambassador to Russia,* 288.

85. Ellsworth Barnard, *Wendell Willkie, Fighter for Freedom,* 363–64.

86. Standley and Ageton, *Admiral Ambassador to Russia,* 292.

87. Documents declassified for author only December, 1989, from the Archives of the Soviet Foreign Office, 9/3/42. Character analysis of Wendell Willkie written by Georgy Zarubin, head of American Desk and People's Commissar of Foreign Affairs, with a covering letter by Deputy Commissar of Foreign Affairs S. A. Lozovsky for Stalin's eyes only (see note on cover signed by Molotov).

88. *Foreign Relations of the United States: Europe, 1942,* 3:640 (hereafter referred to as *FRUS* with appropriate subheading).

89. Watt, *How War Came,* 113.

90. Declassified for author only December 25, 1989.

91. Litvinov's letter to Stalin and Molotov, June 2, 1943, p. 11.

92. Ibid., 12. Emphasis added.

93. Sumner Welles memorandum, *FRUS: Soviet Union, 1943,* 522.

94. Litvinov letter to Stalin, 1.

95. Ibid., 17.

96. Document 569/USA Gromyko, Ambassador to the United States to Foreign Minister V. Molotov, July 14, 1944, Peoples Commissariat of Foreign Affairs. Declassified December 12, 1989.

97. Ibid. Emphasis added.

5. The Second Front

1. Miner, *Between Churchill and Stalin,* 1–10, 252–309.

2. Ibid., 14, 18–19.

3. See Fitzroy Maclean's eyewitness account of the purges in *Eastern Approaches.*

4. Quoted in Miner, *Between Churchill and Stalin,* 32.

5. Ibid., 38.

6. Ibid., 183.

7. Ibid., 185.

8. Ibid., 186. See also John Harvey, ed., *The War Diaries of Oliver Harvey, 1941–1945,* 72–77, 121–31.

9. General Sikorski Historical Institute, *Documents on Polish-Soviet Relations, 1939–1945* (London: Heinemann, 1967); see also Woodward, *British Foreign Policy,* 3:657–62.

10. Miner, *Between Churchill and Stalin,* 191, 195.

11. Ibid., 211. See also Francis L. Loewenheim et al., eds., *Roosevelt and*

Churchill: Their Secret Wartime Correspondence, March 7, 1942; for Churchill's letter to Roosevelt, see 186.

12. In David Carlton, *Anthony Eden: A Biography,* 260–61.

13. Ibid., 201.

14. Miner, *Between Churchill and Stalin,* 219.

15. Ibid., 212. See also Kimball, *Churchill and Roosevelt,* 1:393–94; and Mark A. Stoler, *The Politics of the Second Front: American Military Planning and Diplomacy, 1941–1943,* 3–25.

16. Roosevelt to Halifax, quoted in Miner, *Between Churchill and Stalin,* 214.

17. Stoler, *Politics of the Second Front.*

18. *History of the Second World War Grand Strategy Series,* vol. 2 by J. R. M. Butler, part 2, p. 617. See also Sir Arthur Bryant, *The Turn of the Tide: A History of the War Years Based on the Diaries of Field-Marshal Lord Alanbrooke, Chief of the Imperial General Staff.*

19. *Grand Strategy Series,* vol. 2 by Butler, part 1, pp. 617–25; and Maurice Matloff, *Strategic Planning for Coalition Warfare, 1943–1944: United States Army in World War II,* 18–43.

20. F. H. Hinsley et al., *British Intelligence in the Second World War: Its Influence on Strategy and Operations,* 2:463.

21. Quoted in Stoler, *Politics of the Second Front,* 60.

22. Bryant, *Turn of the Tide,* 22.

23. Ralph B. Levering, *American Opinion and the Russian Alliance, 1939–1945,* 65.

24. Clayton R. Koppes and Gregory D. Black, *Hollywood Goes to War: How Politics, Profits, and Propaganda Shaped World War II Movies,* 190.

25. Davies, *Mission to Moscow,* 141, 143, 153, 156.

26. Levering, *American Opinion,* 71.

27. Ibid., 74.

28. Stalin's May Day Speech, quoted in *Washington Star,* May 1, 1942. In Levering, *American Opinion,* 74.

29. Maurice Gerschon Hindus, *Hitler Cannot Conquer Russia,* 206.

30. *Time,* February 16, 1942, p. 26.

31. *Life,* March 29, 1943, p. 16.

32. Hindus, *Hitler Cannot Conquer Russia,* 8.

33. Davies, *Mission to Moscow,* 397.

34. Roy Aleksandrovich Medvedev, *Let History Judge: The Origins and Consequences of Stalinism,* 727.

35. Ibid.

36. Koppes and Black, *Hollywood Goes to War,* 191.

37. Ibid.

38. Ibid., 207.

39. Stoler, *Politics of the Second Front,* 188.

40. Litvinov to Molotov, June 2, 1943; see Appendix 2, pp. 232–33.

41. Ibid., 3.

42. Matloff, *Strategic Planning, 1943–1944,* 19.

43. See Alan Wilt, "The Significance of the Casablanca Decisions, January, 1943," 2.

44. Litvinov to Molotov, June 2, 1943.

45. John J. LeBeau, "Civil-Military Leadership in Wartime: Roosevelt, the Military and Second Front Decisions," 87.

46. Ibid., 88.

47. Robert A. Divine, *Roosevelt and World War Two,* 9; quoted in LeBeau, "Civil-Military Leadership," 92.

48. LeBeau, "Civil-Military Leadership," 93–94.

49. Stoler, *Politics of the Second Front,* 160.

50. Vojtech Mastny, "Stalin and the Prospects of a Separate Peace in World War II," 1366.

51. See letter to Stalin in *FRUS: The Conference at Washington, 1941–1942, and Casablanca, 1943,* 568.

52. Stoler, *Politics of the Second Front,* 160.

53. Quoted ibid., 90.

54. Ibid., 24.

55. The most comprehensive and readable history of Poland is Norman Davies, *God's Playground: A History of Poland;* see also R. F. Leslie, ed., *The History of Poland since 1863,* and Norman Davies, *Heart of Europe: A Short History of Poland.*

56. Davies, *God's Playground,* 1:23.

57. Leslie, ed., *History of Poland,* 218.

58. Ibid., 223–25.

59. Ibid., 224.

60. For details on this, see George H. Janczewski, "The Origin of the Lublin Government," 412–14.

61. Ibid., 415.

62. Cordell Hull, *The Memoirs of Cordell Hull,* 2:1448; quoted in Blaine David Benedict, "Roosevelt and Poland, 1943–1945: Decision Making as a Choice Value Goals," 58.

63. Ibid., 66.

64. Ibid., 67.

65. Sarah Mieklejohn Terry, *Poland's Place in Europe,* 33. See also John Coutouvidis and Jaime Reynolds, *Poland, 1939–1947,* and Jan Tomasz Gross, *Revolution from Abroad: The Soviet Conquest of Poland's Western Ukraine and Western Belorussia,* 3–70.

66. Quoted in Terry, *Poland's Place in Europe,* 37.

67. On Katyn, see J. K. Zawodny, *Death in the Forest: The Story of the Katyn Forest Massacre,* and Louis Fitzgibbon, *Katyn: A Crime without Parallel.*

68. *FRUS: Soviet Union, 1943,* 373–74.

69. Quoted in Benedict, "Roosevelt and Poland," 100.

70. Terry, *Poland's Place in Europe,* 174.

71. Benedict, "Roosevelt and Poland," 90.

72. Hull, *Memoirs,* 2:1375; quoted in Benedict, "Roosevelt and Poland," 105.

73. Keith Sainsbury, *The Turning Point: Roosevelt, Stalin, Churchill, and Chiang-Kai-Shek, 1943: The Moscow, Cairo, and Teheran Conferences,* 217–18.

74. Quoted ibid., 274.

75. *FRUS: The Conferences at Cairo and Teheran, 1943,* 381–85.

76. Sainsbury, *Turning Point,* 276.

77. Janczewski, "Lublin Government," 423.

78. *FRUS: The Conferences at Cairo and Teheran, 1943,* 594.

79. Doc. No. 239 in General Sikorski Historical Institute, *Documents on Polish-Soviet Relations, 1943–1945* (London: Heinemann, 1967), 2:416–22.

6. Stalin

1. Others have already done this, among them Robert Conquest in *The Great Terror: Stalin's Purge of the Thirties;* and Alexander Solzhenitzin in his *Gulag* chronicles.

2. Kimball, "Crisis Diplomacy," 53.

3. Adam Ulam, *Stalin: The Man and His Era,* ix.

4. Ibid., xxii.

5. A. P. Butenko, "Realnaya Drama Sovetski Istorii," 12.

6. A. Tsipko, in ibid.

7. E. E. Ambartsumov, "Osvobozhdenije ot Stalinsma."

8. O. Moroz, "Posledni Diagnoz."

9. McNeal, *Stalin,* chaps. 8, 9.

10. Boris Georgievich Bazhanov, *Bazhanov and the Damnation of Stalin,* 135–46.

11. Quoted from Dmitri Volkogonov, "Triumph and Tragedy," *Oktyaber,* 1988, in Michel Heller, "Mr. Stalin, I Presume," 158.

12. See Conquest's seminal work, *The Great Terror,* and his *Inside Stalin's Secret Police: NKVD Politics, 1936–1939.* See the critique by John Arch

Getty, *Origins of the Great Purges: The Soviet Communist Party Reconsidered, 1933–1938;* also Walter Z. Laqueur, *Stalin: The Glasnost Years.* See also survival literature from the Soviet Union, such as the classic *In Stalin's Secret Service* by Walter G. Krivitsky; Alexander Uralov, *The Reign of Stalin;* and Boris Levytsky, *The Stalinist Terror of the Thirties.*

13. Peoples Commissariat of Justice, the USSR, *Report of Court Proceedings, Anti-Soviet 'Bloc of Rights and Trotskyites';* Dewey Commission, *Not Guilty: Report on Commission of Inquiry into the Charges Made Against Trotsky in Moscow Trials.*

14. John Erickson, *The Soviet High Command: A Military-Political History, 1918–1941.*

15. Ibid., 449–73.

16. See Richard Pipes, *A History of the Russian Revolution.*

17. See Edward Hallett Carr, *What Is History.*

18. See Klaus Jurgen Muller, *General Ludwig von Beck: Studien und Dokument zur Politisch-Militarischen Vortellungswelt und Tatigkeit des Generalstabschefs des Deutschen Heeres, 1933–1938.*

19. Sebastian Haffner, *The Ailing Empire: Germany from Bismarck to Hitler,* 225.

20. See Mikhail Heller and Aleksandr Nekrich, *Utopia in Power,* 323–25.

21. Ibid., 323.

22. Quoted ibid., 326; see also Krivitsky, *In Stalin's Secret Service,* 1–25.

23. Heller and Nekrich, *Utopia in Power,* 334.

24. Vojtech Mastny, *Russia's Road to the Cold War: Diplomacy, Warfare and Politics of Communism, 1941–1946,* 24.

25. Medvedev, *Let History Judge.*

26. Ibid., 728.

27. Interview with Berezhkov.

28. Quoted in Valentin Berezhkov, "Stalin's Error of Judgement," 13–22.

29. Watt, *How War Came,* 123.

30. Mastny, *Russia's Road,* 23–24, 25.

31. See Berezhkov, "Stalin's Error of Judgement," 20–21. Author's interview with Berezhkov, Moscow, summer, 1989.

32. See the writings of Oleg Rzheshevsky, Janghir Najafov, and Grigory Sevostianov in *Soviet–US Relations, 1933–1942,* 160–64, 228–42, 259–73.

33. Chalmers A. Johnson, *An Instance of Treason: Ozaki Hotsumi and the Sorge Spy Ring.*

34. Barton Whaley, *Codeword Barbarossa,* 12.

35. Ibid., 32.

36. Ibid., 35–36.

37. Heller and Nekrich, *Utopia in Power,* 365.

38. See Krivitsky's description of the purges in *In Stalin's Secret Service,* 181–243; see also Uralov, *The Reign of Stalin;* Alexander Orlov, *The Secret History of Stalin's Crimes,* 184–249; and Michael Bialoguski, *The Petrov Story.*

39. See Erickson, *The Road to Stalingrad* and *The Road to Berlin: Continuing the History of Stalin's War with Germany;* General A. Guillaume, *The German-Russian War;* Bryan I. Fugate, *Operation Barbarossa: Strategy and Tactics on the Eastern Front;* Albert Seaton, *The Russo-German War, 1941–45.*

40. Nikita Sergeevich Khrushchev, *Khrushchev Remembers: The Last Testament,* ed. and trans. Strobe Talbott, 160–62, 167–68.

41. Admiral Kuznetsov, in Seweryn Bialer, *Stalin and His Generals: Soviet Military Memoirs of World War II,* 198.

42. Ibid., 210.

43. Ibid., 179, 183.

44. Ibid., 171.

45. For more details on the early course of the war in the East, see Seaton, *Russo-German War* and *The Battle for Moscow, 1941–1942;* Fugate, *Operation Barbarossa;* and Col. E. Lederrey, *Germany's Defeat in the East: The Soviet Armies at War, 1941–1945.*

46. Albert Seaton, *Stalin as Warlord,* 129.

47. S. M. Shtemenko, *The Soviet General Staff at War, 1941–1945,* 1:181.

48. Ibid., 1:185.

49. Bialer, *Stalin and His Generals,* 43–44.

50. Ibid.

51. Ibid., 36.

52. Seaton, *Stalin as Warlord,* 78–98.

53. Bialer, *Stalin and His Generals,* 36.

54. Andreas Hillgruber, *Hitlers Strategie: Politik und Kriesfuhrung, 1940–1941.*

55. See Bernd Wegner, "The Road to Defeat: The German Campaign in Russia, 1941–1943," *Journal of Strategic Studies* 13 (December 1989): 107, 109.

56. Hitler's address to 250 generals, originally in Col. General Halder's diary, ibid., 108.

57. Quoted ibid.

58. Ibid., 109.

59. Ulam, *Stalin,* xxiv.

60. Kimball, "Crisis Diplomacy," 57.

7. Teheran: The Road to Yalta

1. Jeffrey Taylor Schwedes, "Winston Churchill's War Aims in Europe, 1940–1945," 9–14.

2. Churchill to Collville, in John W. Wheeler-Bennett, *Action This Day: Working with Churchill*, 83–84; quoted in Schwedes, "Churchill's War Aims," 14.

3. Sherwood, *Roosevelt and Hopkins*, 711–12; quoted in Schwedes, "Churchill's War Aims," 55.

4. Churchill to Eden, January 16, 1944, quoted in Schwedes, "Churchill's War Aims," 105.

5. Woodward, *British Foreign Policy*, 3:109–12; Schwedes, "Churchill's War Aims," 107–9.

6. Schwedes, "Churchill's War Aims," 106.

7. Carol Joyce Marion, "Ministers in Moscow," 2.

8. Standley and Ageton, *Admiral Ambassador to Russia*, 34.

9. Ministry of Foreign Affairs, the USSR, *Stalin's Correspondence with Roosevelt and Truman, 1941–1945*, vol. 2; hereafter cited as *Stalin's Correspondence*.

10. *FRUS: Soviet Union, 1943*, 534.

11. *Stalin's Correspondence*, 2:44, December 14, 1942.

12. Marion, "Ministers in Moscow," 79. See also *Stalin's Correspondence*, 2:131–32.

13. Marion, "Ministers in Moscow," 81.

14. *FRUS: Soviet Union, 1943*, 595–97.

15. Ernest R. May, "The United States, the Soviet Union and the Far Eastern War, 1941–1945."

16. For details, see Marion, "Ministers in Moscow," 130–42, 137, 141.

17. *FRUS: The Conferences at Cairo and Teheran, 1943*; see also *FRUS: The Far East, 1941*, 752; *FRUS: Europe, 1942*, 2:602–3, 605–6, 675–78; and *Stalin's Correspondence*, 2:22, 42–45.

18. *Stalin's Correspondence*, 2:51; *FRUS: Europe, 1942*, 2:582–83.

19. *Stalin's Correspondence*, 2:52; Soviet Foreign Ministry archives' documents.

20. *Stalin's Correspondence*, 2:73.

21. Ibid., 2:76.

22. Ibid., 2:109–37.

23. Paul D. Mayle, *Eureka Summit: Agreement in Principle and the Big Three at Teheran, 1943*, 42.

24. Quoted ibid., 43; from *FRUS: The Conferences at Cairo and Teheran, 1943*, 51–52.

25. Quoted in Mayle, *Eureka Summit,* 43.

26. Ibid.

27. Ibid.

28. Ibid., 45.

29. From "Conference Bits," *Newsweek,* December 13, 1943, p. 26; and Charles Wilson Moran, *Winston Churchill: The Struggle for Survival, 1940–1965,* 139, 146.

30. Churchill, in Mayle, *Eureka Summit,* 50.

31. *FRUS: The Conferences at Cairo and Teheran, 1943,* 383.

32. Sainsbury, *The Turning Point,* 84.

33. Keith Eubank, *Summit at Teheran,* 311; quoted in Forrest C. Pogue, *George C. Marshall: Organizer of Victory, 1943–1945,* 313.

34. Elliott Roosevelt, *As He Saw It,* 315.

35. Roosevelt to Stalin, *Stalin's Correspondence,* 2:110–11.

36. Roosevelt to Stalin, ibid., 2:112.

37. Hull, *Memoirs,* 2:1276–80; see also Benedict, "Roosevelt and Poland," 80–93.

38. *FRUS: The Conferences at Cairo and Teheran, 1943,* 487, 491, 494–95.

39. Ibid., 495.

40. William D. Leahy, *I Was There,* 245.

41. Quoted in Eubank, *Summit at Teheran,* 309; from Bryant, *Turn of the Tide,* entry for November 29, 1943.

42. Charles E. Bohlen, *Witness to History, 1929–1969,* 146.

43. Eubank, *Summit at Teheran,* 339.

44. Quoted ibid., 287.

45. Sainsbury, *Turning Point,* 226.

46. Quoted ibid., 274.

47. Ibid.

48. Ibid.

49. Ibid.

50. Eubank, *Summit at Teheran,* 445.

51. See Davies, *Heart of Europe,* 90–93; M. K. Dziewanowski, *The Communist Party of Poland;* and Coutouvidis and Reynolds, *Poland.*

52. Dziewanowski, *Communist Party of Poland,* 158.

53. Davies, *Heart of Europe,* 92.

54. Coutouvidis and Reynolds, *Poland,* 137.

55. Ibid., 148.

56. Ibid., 149.

57. Quoted ibid.

58. Zawodny, *Death in the Forest,* 15.

59. The most outstanding study of the Warsaw uprising is J. K. Zawodny's *Nothing But Honour: The Story of the Warsaw Uprising, 1944.*

60. Quoted ibid., 188.

61. Ibid., 221.

62. Quoted ibid.

63. Ibid.

64. Coutouvidis and Reynolds, *Poland,* 155.

8. Yalta: The Epitome of a Rooseveltian Utopia

1. Athan G. Theoharis, *The Yalta Myths: An Issue in U.S. Politics, 1945–1955,* 1.

2. See Robert Schulzinger, "Yalta" (review of Clemens and of Theoharis), *History and Theory* 2 (1973): 147–48.

3. Diane Shaver Clemens, *Yalta,* 286, 282.

4. Theoharis, *Yalta Myths,* 5–9; see also Schulzinger, "Yalta," 157–58.

5. See chart in Walker, "Roosevelt as a Negotiator," 142.

6. *FRUS: The Conference at Malta and Yalta, 1945,* 3–40.

7. Warren Kimball, "Naked Reverse Right: Roosevelt, Churchill and Eastern Europe from Tolstoy to Yalta and a Little Beyond," 14.

8. *FRUS: Soviet Union, 1943,* 3:729–31.

9. Jim Bishop, "In the Shadow of Yalta," *Roosevelt's Last Year, April 1944–April 1945,* 213, 220.

10. See Kimball, *Churchill and Roosevelt,* vol. 3.

11. William D. Hassett, *Off the Record with F.D.R., 1942–1945,* 314.

12. Moran, *Churchill,* 242–43.

13. Sherwood, *Roosevelt and Hopkins,* 843.

14. Ibid., 844–45.

15. Sir Winston Churchill, *Triumph and Tragedy,* 304–5.

16. David Dilks, ed., *The Diaries of Sir Alexander Cadogan, O.M., 1938–1945,* 702–3, 704–5.

17. Ibid., 206.

18. W. Averell Harriman and Elie Abel, *Special Envoy to Churchill and Stalin, 1941–1946,* 388, 391, 392.

19. Admiral C. E. Olsen, "Full House at Yalta," *American Heritage* (January, 1972): 21.

20. Dilks, ed., *Diaries of Cadogan,* 709.

21. Moran, *Churchill,* 249.

22. Walker, "Roosevelt as a Negotiator," 170.

23. *FRUS: The Conference at Malta and Yalta, 1945,* 728.

24. Walker, "Roosevelt as a Negotiator," 180.

25. *FRUS: The Conference at Malta and Yalta, 1945,* 779, 780–81, 780.

26. *FRUS: The Conference at Malta and Yalta, 1945,* 792–93, 803.

27. Walker, "Roosevelt as a Negotiator," 178–79.

28. *FRUS: The Conference at Malta and Yalta, 1945,* 846.

29. Clemens, *Yalta,* 195.

30. Kimball, "Naked Reverse," 15.

31. *FRUS: The Conference at Malta and Yalta, 1945,* 803–53.

32. George Frost Kennan, *Memoirs, 1925–1950,* 212.

33. Ibid., 204.

34. Ibid., 199–215.

35. Mastny, *Russia's Road,* 253.

36. Ibid., 137.

37. Ibid., 134.

38. Ibid., 136.

39. Ibid., 246.

40. Ibid., 248.

41. Ibid., 249.

42. *FRUS: The Conference at Malta and Yalta, 1945,* 64–66, 77.

9. Roosevelt and the Balance of Power in Europe

1. Range, *Roosevelt's World Order,* 105.

2. David Reynolds, "Roosevelt, Churchill, and the Wartime Anglo-American Alliance, 1939–1945, Toward a New Synthesis," 17.

3. Ibid., 18. Robert Hathaway, *Ambiguous Partnership: Britain and America, 1940–1947* (New York: Columbia University Press, 1981). Christopher Thorne, *Allies of a Kind: The United States, Britain, and the War against Japan, 1941–1945* (New York: Oxford University Press, 1978).

4. Stephen Roskill, *Naval Policy between the Wars, 1919–1929,* 20; see also James Leutze, *Bargaining for Supremacy: Anglo-American Naval Collaboration 1939–1941* (Chapel Hill: University of North Carolina Press, 1977); and Patrick Abazia, *Mr. Roosevelt's Navy* (Annapolis: Naval Institute Press, 1975).

5. Russell Davenport, "Open Letter to the British People," *Life,* October 31, 1942; quoted in Rand H. Fishbein, "From Sea to Shining Sea: Commerce, Conquest and the Collusion of British and American Empire in the Middle East, 1939–1945," 12.

6. Adapted from National Opinion Research Center, University of Denver, Table, April, 1943, in Fishbein, "From Sea to Shining Sea," 45.

7. See Levering, *American Opinion,* 87–89; Jordan Schwarz, *Liberal Adolph A. Berle: A Vision of an American Era,* 146–47; Fishbein, "From Sea to Shining Sea," 46–145.

8. Robert M. Hathaway, *Ambiguous Partnership: Britain and America, 1944–1947* (New York: Columbia University Press, 1981), 16–17.

9. Quoted ibid., 23–24.

10. Ibid., 28–29.

11. Schwarz, *Liberal Adolph A. Berle,* 114–74.

12. Ibid., 145.

13. Fishbein, "From Sea to Shining Sea," 60–69.

14. Quoted ibid., 65.

15. Don Lohbeck, *Patrick J. Hurley: An American* (Chicago: Henry Regnery Company, 1956), 210–11.

16. Quoted in Russell D. Buhite, *Patrick J. Hurley and American Foreign Policy,* 123.

17. Roosevelt, *As He Saw It,* 193, 204.

18. Lohbeck, *Hurley,* 5; quoted in Fishbein, "From Sea to Shining Sea," 112.

19. Lord Casey, *Personal Experience, 1939–1948* (New York: David McKay, 1962), 152.

20. Roosevelt, *As He Saw It,* 205.

21. Fishbein, "From Sea to Shining Sea," 138–43.

22. Alan J. Levine, "British, American and Soviet Political Aims and Military Strategies, 1941–1945," 463.

23. Julian G. Hurstfield, *America and the French Nation, 1939–1945,* 68.

24. Ibid., 74.

25. Churchill to Roosevelt, March 12, 1941, quoted ibid., 162.

26. *FRUS: The Conferences at Cairo and Teheran, 1943,* 255–56.

27. Hassett, *Off the Record,* 254–55.

28. Alfred Rieber, *Stalin and the French Communist Party, 1941–1947,* 59–62; Jean Lacouture, *De Gaulle: The Ruler, 1945–1970,* 3–126; Levine, "British, American and Soviet," 483.

29. From Bohlen's notes and *FRUS: The Conferences at Cairo and Teheran, 1943,* 484.

30. Ibid.

31. Ibid.

32. Peter Dunn, *The First Vietnam War,* 94.

33. *FRUS: The British Commonwealth, The Far East,* 300; quoted ibid., 94–95.

34. Quoted in Dunn, *Vietnam,* 96–97.

35. Ibid., 98.

36. Ibid.

37. Ibid., 99. On the question of whether or not Roosevelt supported the French forces, see ibid., 101–2.

38. Walter Le Feber, "Roosevelt, Churchill and Indochina, 1942–1945," 1279.

39. Ibid., 1290.

40. Jean Lacouture, *De Gaulle: The Rebel, 1890–1944,* 338.

41. Ibid.

42. Quoted in reference ibid., 350.

43. Warren F. Kimball, *Swords into Ploughshares,* 21.

44. All of the options are widely elaborated upon, ibid., 4–5.

45. Ibid., 7, 10.

46. Ibid., 34.

47. Ibid., 4.

48. Randall B. Woods, *A Changing of the Guard: Anglo-American Relations, 1941–1946,* 3.

10. President Roosevelt as a Diplomatic Failure

1. Kennan, "Comment," 31.

Appendix 3. USSR Foreign Affairs

1. On April 24, 1943, Welles told Litvinov that on April 26 an official announcement on the rupture of diplomatic relations with Finland would be made, and that a chargé d'affaires had stayed in Helsinki solely to report on the rupture.

Bibliography

Unpublished Documents, U.S. and Britain

National Archives, Washington, D.C., and Suitland, Maryland

RG–59, General Records of the Department of State: Decimal File; Lot File (1945)

RG–84, Records of the Foreign Service Posts of the Department of State: United States Embassy Moscow

RG–107, Records of the Office of the Secretary of War

RG–165, Records of the War Department General and Special Staffs, 1943–1947: Office of Strategic Services, Research and Analysis Branch Army Intelligence (G–2); G–2 Regional File, Iran; War Department Plans and Operations

RG–218, Records of the United States Chiefs of Staff: United States Chiefs of Staff; Combined Chiefs of Staff

RG–226, Records of the Office of Strategic Services

RG–319, Records of the United States Army Staff after 1947 (RG–165 and RG–319 sometimes overlap)

RG–331, Records of Allied Operational and Occupation Headquarters, World War II: Supreme Headquarters, Allied Expeditionary Force; Department of State Serial Files 740.0011 European War 1939–1945

OSS Archives

91, History of OSS in London
101, Miscellaneous: Yugoslavia, Greece, and Bulgaria; Special Teams

107, Survey of Foreign Experts

119, London Counter-Intelligence (CI) Files

139, Washington/Field Station: Cairo, Calcutta, Caserta, Honolulu, New York, Paris, Singapore, Stockholm, and Washington

147, OSS New York and London Office Records

148, OSS New York and Overseas Station Records: Chungking, Dakar, Holland, Istanbul, Kandy, Kunming, Lisbon, London, New York, Paris, Pretoria, Singapore, Stockholm, and Tangier

Library of Congress, Manuscripts Division

Papers of Joseph Alsop; Henry H. Arnold; Robert W. Bingham; Charles Bohlen; Raymond Clapper; Joseph E. Davies; Norman H. Davis; William E. Dodd; Herbert Feis; Cordell Hull; Harold Ickes; Frank Knox; William D. Leahy; Breckinridge Long; Laurence A. Steinhardt; Henry Wallace

Special permission granted by Mrs. Pamela Digby Churchill-Harriman: The Harriman Papers

Meikeljohn, R. P. "Report on Harriman's mission: March 1941-Oct. 1943." Harriman Papers, Container No. 166

Franklin D. Roosevelt Library, Hyde Park, New York

Franklin D. Roosevelt papers (President's Secretary's File, Official File, President's Personal File, White House Usher's diary); Adolph A. Berle Jr. Diary, Harry Hopkins papers, Henry J. Morgenthau Jr. presidential diary and diary.

Published Documents, U.S. and Britain

Cline, Ray S. *Washington Command Post: The Operations Division.* Washington, D.C.: Office of the Chief of Military History, Department of the Army, 1951.

Dewey Commission. *Not Guilty: Report on Commission of Inquiry into the Charges Made Against Trotsky in Moscow Trials.* New York: Harper's, 1938.

Foreign Relations of the United States: Japan, 1931–1941. 2 vols. Washington, D.C.: Government Printing Office, 1943.

Foreign Relations of the United States: The Conference at Malta and Yalta, 1945. Washington, D.C.: Government Printing Office, 1955.

Foreign Relations of the United States: The Conference at Quebec, 1944. Washington, D.C.: Government Printing Office, 1972.

Foreign Relations of the United States: The Conference at Washington, 1941–1942, and Casablanca, 1943. Washington, D.C.: Government Printing Office, 1988.

Foreign Relations of the United States: Soviet Union, 1941. Volume 1. Washington, D.C.: Government Printing Office, 1958.

Foreign Relations of the United States: Europe, 1942. Volumes 2–3. Washington, D.C.: Government Printing Office, 1961.

Foreign Relations of the United States: Soviet Union, 1943. Volume 3. Washington, D.C.: Government Printing Office, 1964.

Foreign Relations of the United States: The Soviet Union, 1944. Volume 4. Washington, D.C.: Government Printing Office, 1966.

Foreign Relations of the United States: Soviet Union, 1945. Volume 5. Washington, D.C.: Government Printing Office, 1968.

Foreign Relations of the United States: The Far East. Washington, D.C.: Government Printing Office, 1969.

Foreign Relations of the United States: The Near East and Africa. Volume 4. Washington, D.C.: Government Printing Office, 1964.

Foreign Relations of the United States: The Far East, 1941. Volume 4. Washington, D.C.: Government Printing Office, 1956.

Foreign Relations of the United States: The Conferences at Cairo and Teheran, 1943. Washington, D.C.: Government Printing Office, 1961.

Foreign Relations of the United States: The Conferences at Washington and Quebec, 1943. Washington, D.C.: Government Printing Office, 1970.

History of the Second World War Grand Strategy Series. Volume 1, by H. R. Gibbs. London, HMSO, 1976. Volume 2, by J. R. M. Butler. London: HMSO, 1957. Volume 3, part 1, by J. M. A. Gwyer. Volume 3, part 2, by J. R. M. Butler. London: HMSO, 1964. Volume 4, by Michael Howard. London: HMSO, 1972. Volumes 5–6 by John Ehrman. London: HMSO, 1956.

History of the Second World War, United Kingdom Military Series. London: HMSO, 1954.

Leighton, Richard, and Robert Coakley. *Global Logistics and Strategy 1940–1943.* Washington, D.C.: Office of the Chief of Military History, Department of the Army, 1955.

Matloff, Maurice. *Strategic Planning for Coalition Warfare, 1943–1944: United States Army in World War II.* Washington, D.C.: Government Printing Office, 1959.

Matloff, Maurice, and Edwin Snell. *Strategic Planning for Coalition Warfare, 1941–1942.* Washington, D.C.: Office of the Chief of Military History, Department of the Army, 1953.

Playfair, I. S. O. *The Mediterranean and the Middle East.* Volume 1. London: HMSO, 1954. Volume 2. London: HMSO, 1956. Volume 3, September 1940–September 1943. London: HMSO, 1960.

Pogue, Forrest. *The Supreme Command.* Washington, D.C.: Office of the Chief of Military History, Department of the Army, 1954.

Watson, Mark S. *Chief of Staff: Prewar Plans and Operations,* Washington, D.C.: Historical Division, Department of the Army, 1951.

Papers Relating to the Foreign Relations of the United States, 1933–1941. Washington, D.C.: Government Printing Office, 1955.

U.S. Department of State. *Documents on German Foreign Policy, 1918–1945.* Series C (1933–1937), Washington, D.C.: Government Printing Office, 1959–1966. Series D (1937–1941), Washington, D.C.: Government Printing Office, 1959–1964.

Unpublished Documents, USSR

I am the first Western scholar to examine previously unpublished Soviet Foreign Ministry archives in Moscow, which are being declassified for the first time, July 1989.

Published Documents, USSR

Ministry of Foreign Affairs. *Stalin's Correspondence with Churchill and Attlee.* Vol. 1. Moscow, 1957. *Stalin's Correspondence with Roosevelt and Truman, 1941–1945.* Vol. 2. Moscow, 1957. Taken from Correspondence between the Chairman of the Council of Ministers of the USSR and the Presidents of the U.S. and the Prime Ministers of Great Britain during the Great Patriotic War of 1941–1945.

Peoples Commissariat of Justice, the USSR. *Report of Court Proceedings, Anti-Soviet 'Bloc of Rights and Trotskyites.'* Moscow: Peoples Commissariat of Justice, the USSR, 1938.

Unpublished Manuscripts

Benedict, Blaine David. "Roosevelt and Poland, 1943–1945: Decision Making as a Choice Value Goals." Ph.D. dissertation, University of Pennsylvania, 1977.

Bennett, Edward M. "Franklin D. Roosevelt and Russian-American Relations, 1933–1939." Ph.D. dissertation, University of Illinois, 1965.

Bland, Larry I. "W. Averell Harriman: Businessman and Diplomat, 1891–1945." Ph.D. dissertation, University of Wisconsin, 1972.

Eagles, Keith David. "Ambassador Joseph E. Davies and American-Soviet Relations, 1937–1941." Ph.D. dissertation, University of Wisconsin, 1966.

Eubanks, Richard K. "The Diplomacy of Postponement: The United States and Russia's Western Frontier Claims during World War II." Ph.D. dissertation, University of Texas at Austin, 1971.

Fedron, Nona S. "Franklin D. Roosevelt: A Psychological Interpretation of His Childhood and Youth." Ph.D. dissertation, University of Hawaii, 1971.

Fishbein, Rand H. "From Sea to Shining Sea: Commerce, Conquest and the Collusion of British and American Empire in the Middle East, 1939–1945." Ph.D. dissertation, Johns Hopkins University, 1986.

Gaberding, William P. "Franklin Roosevelt's Conception of the Soviet Union in World Politics." Ph.D. dissertation, University of Wisconsin, 1959.

Langer, John D. "The Formulation of American Aid Policy toward the Soviet Union, 1940–1943: The Hopkins Shop and the Department of State." Ph.D. dissertation, Yale University, 1975.

Lazalier, James H. "Surrogate Diplomacy: FDR's Personal Envoys, 1941–1945." Ph.D. dissertation, University of Oklahoma, 1973.

LeBeau, John J. "Civil-Military Leadership in Wartime: Roosevelt, the Military and Second Front Decisions." Ph.D. dissertation, University of Massachusetts, 1978.

Levering, Ralph B. "Prelude to Cold War: American Attitudes toward Russia During WWII." Ph.D. dissertation, Princeton University, 1972.

Levine, Alan J. "British, American and Soviet Political Aims and Military Strategies, 1941–1945." Ph.D. dissertation, New York University, 1977.

Lewis, John M. "Franklin Roosevelt and the United States Strategy in World War II." Ph.D. dissertation, Cornell University, 1979.

Lindley, Christopher. "Franklin Roosevelt and the Politics of Isolationism, 1932–1936." Ph.D. dissertation, Cornell University, 1964.

McIlvenna, Don E. "Prelude to D-Day: American Strategy and the Second Front Issue." Ph.D. dissertation, Stanford University, 1967.

Marion, Carol Joyce. "Ministers in Moscow." Master's thesis, Indiana University, 1970.

Misse, Frederick, "The Loss of Eastern Europe, 1938–1946." Ph.D. dissertation, University of Illinois, 1965.

Schwedes, Jeffrey Taylor. "Winston Churchill's War Aims in Europe, 1940–1945." Ph.D. dissertation, University of Minnesota, 1977.

Walker, Gregg. "Franklin D. Roosevelt as a Summit Negotiator at Teheran, 1943 and Yalta, 1945." Ph.D. dissertation, University of Kansas, 1983.
Wilt, Alan. "The Significance of the Casablanca Decisions, January, 1943." Unpublished manuscript, 1990.

Books

Adams, Henry. *Harry Hopkins: A Biography.* New York: Putnam, 1977.
————. *The Letters of Henry Adams.* Edited by J. C. Levenson. 4 vols. Cambridge: Harvard University Press, 1988.
Barnard, Ellsworth. *Wendell Willkie, Fighter for Freedom.* Marquette: Northern Michigan University Press, 1966.
Bazhanov, Boris Georgievich. *Bazhanov and the Damnation of Stalin.* Translated with commentary by David W. Doyle. Athens: Ohio University Press, 1990.
————. *Stalin der rote Diktator.* Berlin: P. Aretz, 1931.
Bialer, Seweryn. *Stalin and His Generals: Soviet Military Memoirs of World War II.* New York: Pegasus, 1969.
Bialoguski, Michael. *The Petrov Story.* London: Heinemann, 1955.
Bishop, Jim. *Roosevelt's Last Year: April 1944–April 1945.* New York: William Morrow, 1974.
Bohlen, Charles E. *Witness to History, 1929–1969.* New York: Norton, 1973.
Bonch, Bruyevich. *From Tsarist General to Red Army Commander.* Moscow: Progress Publishers, 1966.
Bryant, Sir Arthur. *The Turn of the Tide: A History of the War Years Based on the Diaries of Field-Marshal Lord Alanbrooke, Chief of the Imperial General Staff.* Garden City: Doubleday, 1957.
Buhite, Russell D. *Patrick J. Hurley and American Foreign Policy.* Ithaca: Cornell University Press, 1973.
Bullitt, Orville H., ed. *For the President, Personal and Secret; Correspondence between Franklin D. Roosevelt and William C. Bullitt.* Boston: Houghton Mifflin, 1972.
Carlton, David. *Anthony Eden: A Biography.* London: A. Lane, 1981.
Carr, Edward Hallett. *What Is History?* New York: Knopf, 1961.
Charmley, John. *Chamberlain and the Lost Peace.* London: Hodder and Stoughton, 1989.
Churchill, Sir Winston. *The Second World War.* Volume 2, *Their Finest Hour.* London: Cassell, 1949. Volume 4, *The Hinge of Fate.* London: Cassell, 1951. Volume 6, *Triumph and Tragedy.* London: Cassell, 1954.
Clemens, Diane Shaver. *Yalta.* New York: Oxford University Press, 1970.

Cole, Wayne S. *Roosevelt and the Isolationists, 1932–45.* Lincoln: University of Nebraska Press, 1983.

Colville, John. *The Fringes of Power: 10 Downing Street Diaries, 1939–1955.* New York, W. W. Norton, 1985.

Conquest, Robert. *The Great Terror: Stalin's Purge of the Thirties.* London and Melbourne: Macmillan, 1968.

———. *Inside Stalin's Secret Police: NKVD Politics, 1936–1939.* Stanford: Hoover Institution Press, 1985.

Cooper, John Milton, Jr. *The Warrior and the Priest: Woodrow Wilson and Theodore Roosevelt.* Cambridge: Belknap Press of Harvard University, 1983.

Coutouvidis, John, and Jaime Reynolds. *Poland, 1939–1947.* New York: Holmes & Meier, 1986.

Dallek, Robert. *Franklin D. Roosevelt and American Foreign Policy, 1932–1945.* New York: Oxford University Press, 1979.

Davies, Joseph Edward. *Mission to Moscow.* New York: Simon and Schuster, 1941.

Davies, Norman. *God's Playground: A History of Poland.* 2 vols. New York: Columbia University Press, 1982.

———. *Heart of Europe: A Short History of Poland.* Oxford: Clarendon Press, 1984.

Davis, Kenneth S. *F.D.R.: The Beckoning of Destiny, 1882–1928.* New York: Putnam, 1971.

Dawson, Raymond H. *The Decision to Aid Russia, 1941: Foreign Policy and Domestic Politics.* Westport, Conn.: Greenwood Press, 1959.

DeSantis, Hugh. *The Diplomacy of Silence.* Chicago: University of Chicago Press, 1979.

Diggins, John P. *The American Left in the Twentieth Century.* New York: Harcourt Brace Jovanovich, 1973.

———. *Up from Communism: Conservative Odysseys in American Intellectual History.* New York: Harper & Row, 1975.

Dilks, David, ed. *The Diaries of Sir Alexander Cadogan, O.M., 1938–1945.* New York: Putnam, 1972.

Divine, Robert A. *The Illusion of Neutrality.* Chicago: University of Chicago Press, 1962.

———. *Roosevelt and World War Two.* Baltimore: Johns Hopkins University Press, 1969.

Dunn, Peter. *The First Vietnam War.* London: C. Hurst, 1985.

Dziewanowski, M. K. *The Communist Party of Poland.* Cambridge: Harvard University Press, 1959.

Eden, Anthony. *The Eden Memoirs: The Reckoning.* London: Cassell, 1965.

Erickson, John. *The Road to Berlin: Continuing the History of Stalin's War with Germany.* Boulder: Westview Press, 1983.

————. *The Road to Stalingrad.* New York: Harper & Row, 1975.

————. *The Soviet High Command: A Military-Political History, 1918–1941.* New York: St. Martin's Press, 1962.

Eubank, Keith. *Summit at Teheran.* New York: William Morrow, 1985.

Fitzgibbon, Louis. *Katyn: A Crime without Parallel.* New York: Scribners, 1971.

Friedel, Frank. *Franklin D. Roosevelt.* Volume 1, *The Apprenticeship.* Volume 2, *The Ordeal.* Volume 3, *The Triumph.* Volume 4, *Launching the New Deal.* Boston: Little, Brown, 1952.

Fugate, Bryan I. *Operation Barbarossa: Strategy and Tactics on the Eastern Front.* Novato, Calif.: Presidio Press, 1984.

Gaddis, John Lewis. *Strategies of Containment: The Post War American National Security Policy.* New York: Oxford, 1982.

————. *The United States and the Origins of the Cold War.* New York: Columbia University Press, 1972.

Getty, John Arch. *Origins of the Great Purges: The Soviet Communist Party Reconsidered, 1933–1938.* New York: Cambridge University Press, 1985.

Gilbert, Martin. *Winston Churchill: Road to Victory, 1941–1945.* Boston: Houghton Mifflin, 1986.

Gorodetsky, Sir Gabriel. *Stafford Cripp's Mission to Moscow, 1940–1942.* Cambridge: Cambridge University Press, 1984.

Greenfield, Kent Roberts. *American Strategy in World War II: A Reconsideration.* Westport, Conn.: Greenwood Press, 1963.

Greenville, J. A. S. *Lord Salisbury and Foreign Policy: The Close of the Nineteenth Century.* London: Athlone Press, 1970.

Gross, Jan Tomasz. *Polish Society under German Occupation.* Princeton: Princeton University Press, 1979.

————. *Revolution from Abroad: The Soviet Conquest of Poland's Western Ukraine and Western Belorussia.* Princeton: Princeton University Press, 1988.

Guillaume, A. *The German-Russian War.* London: War Office, 1956.

Haffner, Sebastian. *The Ailing Empire: Germany from Bismarck to Hitler.* New York: Fromm International Publishing Corporation, 1989.

Harriman, W. Averell, and Elie Abel. *Special Envoy to Churchill and Stalin, 1941–1946.* New York: Random House, 1975.

Harvey, John, ed. *The Diplomatic Diaries of Oliver Harvey, 1937–1940.* New York: St. Martin's Press, 1970.

————. *The War Diaries of Oliver Harvey, 1941–1945.* London: Collins, 1978.

Hassett, William D. *Off the Record with F.D.R., 1942–1945.* Westport, Conn.: Greenwood Press, 1958.

Healy, David F. *U.S. Expansionism: The Imperialist Urge in the 1890's.* Madison: University of Wisconsin Press, 1970.

Heller, Mikhail, and Aleksandr Nekrich. *Utopia in Power.* London: Hutchinson, 1986.

Herring, George C., Jr. *Aid to Russia, 1941–1946: Strategy, Diplomacy, the Origins of the Cold War.* New York: Columbia University Press, 1973.

Hillgruber, Andreas. *Hitlers Strategie: Politik und Kriesfuhrung, 1940–1941.* Frankfurt am Maim: Bernard & Graefe Verlag für Wehrwesen, 1965.

Hindus, Maurice Gerschon. *Hitler Cannot Conquer Russia.* Garden City: Doubleday, Doran & Co., 1941.

Hinsley, F. H., E. E. Thomas, C. F. G. Ransom, and R. C. Knight. *British Intelligence in the Second World War: Its Influence on Strategy and Operations.* New York: Cambridge University Press, 1979.

Howard, Michael Elliot. *The Mediterranean Strategy in the Second World War.* New York: Praeger, 1968.

Hull, Cordell. *The Memoirs of Cordell Hull.* 2 vols. New York: Macmillan, 1948.

Hurstfield, Julian G. *America and the French Nation, 1939–1945.* Chapel Hill: University of North Carolina Press, 1986.

James, Robert Rhodes. *Anthony Eden.* New York: McGraw-Hill, 1986.

Johnson, Chalmers A. *An Instant of Treason: Ozaki Hotsumi and the Sorge Spy Ring.* Stanford: Stanford University Press, 1964.

Keegan, John. *The Second World War.* New York: Viking Press, 1989.

Kennan, George Frost. *The Decision to Intervene.* Princeton: Princeton University Press, 1958.

———. *Memoirs, 1925–1950.* New York: Little Brown, 1967.

Kennedy, Sir John. *The Business of War.* New York: William Morrow, 1958.

Khrushchev, Nikita Sergeevich. *Khrushchev Remembers: The Last Testament.* Translated and edited by Strobe Talbott. Boston: Little Brown, 1974.

Kimball, Warren F. *Churchill and Roosevelt: The Complete Correspondence.* 3 vols. Princeton: Princeton University Press, 1984.

———. *The Most Unsordid Act: Lend-Lease, 1939–1941.* Baltimore: Johns Hopkins University Press, 1969.

———. *Swords into Ploughshares.* Philadelphia: J. B. Lippincott, 1976.

Kitchen, Martin. *British Policy towards the Soviet Union during the Second World War.* New York: St. Martin's Press, 1986.

Kleist, Peter. *Zwischen Hitler und Stalin, 1939–1945.* Bonn: Athen Aum-Verlag, 1950.

Konev, Ivan. *Year of Victory.* Moscow: Progress Publishers, 1969.

Koppes, Clayton R., and Gregory D. Black. *Hollywood Goes to War: How Politics, Profits, and Propaganda Shaped World War II Movies.* New York: Free Press, 1987.

Krivitsky, Walter G. *In Stalin's Secret Service.* New York: Harper and Brothers, 1939.

Kuniholm, Bruce R. *The Origins of the Cold War in the Near East.* Princeton: Princeton University Press, 1980.

Lacouture, Jean. *De Gaulle: The Rebel, 1890–1944.* New York: Norton, 1990.

————. *De Gaulle: The Ruler, 1945–1970.* New York: Norton, 1990.

Langer, William L. *Our Vichy Gamble.* New York: A. A. Knopf, 1947.

Laqueur, Walter Z. *Stalin: The Glasnost Years.* New York: Scribners, 1990.

Larrabee, Eric. *Commander in Chief: Franklin Delano Roosevelt, His Lieutenants, and Their War.* New York: Harper and Row, 1987.

Lash, Joseph P. *Roosevelt and Churchill, 1939–1941: The Partnership That Saved the West.* New York: Norton, 1976.

Leahy, William D. *I Was There.* New York: Arno Press, 1950.

Lederrey, Ernest. *Germany's Defeat in the East: The Soviet Armies at War, 1941–1945.* London: War Office, 1955.

Leslie, R. F., ed. *The History of Poland since 1863.* New York: Cambridge University Press, 1980.

Levering, Ralph B. *American Opinion and the Russian Alliance, 1939–1945.* Chapel Hill: University of North Carolina Press, 1976.

Levytsky, Boris. *The Stalinist Terror of the Thirties.* Stanford: Hoover Institution Press, 1974.

Loewenheim, Francis L., Harold D. Langley, and Manfred Jonas, eds. *Roosevelt and Churchill: Their Secret Wartime Correspondence.* New York: Saturday Review Press, 1975.

MacDonald, C. A. *The United States, Britain, and Appeasement, 1936–1939.* New York: St. Martin's Press, 1981.

McJimsey, George T. *Harry Hopkins: Ally of the Poor and Defender of Democracy.* Cambridge: Harvard University Press, 1987.

Maclean, Fitzroy. *Eastern Approaches.* London: J. Cape, 1948.

McNeal, Robert H. *Stalin: Man and Ruler.* New York: New York University Press, 1988.

McNeill, William H. *America, Britain and Russia: Their Cooperation and Conflict, 1941–1946.* New York: Johnson Reprint Corporation, 1970.

Maddux, Thomas R. *Years of Estrangement: American Relations with the Soviet Union, 1933–1941.* Tallahassee: University Presses of Florida, 1980.

Mastny, Vojtech. *Russia's Road to the Cold War: Diplomacy, Warfare and Politics of Communism, 1941–1946.* New York: Columbia University Press, 1979.

Mayle, Paul D. *Eureka Summit: Agreement in Principle and the Big Three at Teheran, 1943.* Newark: University of Delaware Press, 1987.

Medvedev, Roy Aleksandrovich. *Let History Judge: The Origins and Consequences of Stalinism.* Rev. ed. New York: Columbia University Press, 1989.

Meretskov, Kirill. *Serving the People.* Moscow: Progress Publishers, 1971.

Miner, Steven Merritt. *Between Churchill and Stalin: The Soviet Union, Great Britain, and the Origins of the Grand Alliance.* Chapel Hill: University of North Carolina Press, 1988.

Moran, Charles Wilson. *Winston Churchill: The Struggle for Survival, 1940–1965.* Boston: Houghton Mifflin, 1966.

Muller, Klaus Jurgen. *General Ludwig von Beck: Studien und Dokument zur Politisch-Militarischen Vortellungswelt und Tatigkeit des Generalstabschefs des Deutschen Heeres, 1933–1938.* Boppard am Rhein: H. Boldt, 1980.

O'Connor, Timothy Edward. *Diplomacy and Revolution: G. V. Chicherin and Soviet Foreign Affairs, 1918–1930.* Ames: Iowa State University Press, 1988.

Orlov, Alexander. *The Secret History of Stalin's Crimes.* London: Jarrolds, 1954.

Pipes, Richard. *A History of the Russian Revolution.* New York: Knopf, 1990.

Pogue, Forrest C. *George C. Marshall: Organizer of Victory, 1943–1945.* New York: Viking, 1973.

Possony, Stephen. *Lenin: The Complete Revolutionary.* New York: Henry Regnery, 1904.

Range, Willard. *Franklin D. Roosevelt's World Order.* Athens: University of Georgia Press, 1959.

Reynolds, David. *The Creation of the Anglo-American Alliance, 1937–41: A Study in Competitive Co-operation.* Chapel Hill: University of North Carolina Press, 1981.

Rieber, Alfred. *Stalin and the French Communist Party, 1941–1947.* New York: Columbia University Press, 1962.

Rock, William R. *Chamberlain and Roosevelt: British Foreign Policy and the United States, 1937–1940.* Columbus: Ohio State University Press, 1988.

Rokossovsky, Konstantin. *A Soldier's Duty.* Moscow: Progress Publishers, 1970.

Roosevelt, Eleanor. *This I Remember.* New York: Harper and Brothers, 1949.

Roosevelt, Elliott. *As He Saw It.* New York: Duell, Sloan and Pearce, 1946.

———, ed. *F. D. R.: His Personal Letters*. New York: Duell, Sloan and Pearce, 1947.

Roskill, Stephen. *Naval Policy between the Wars, 1919–1929*. London: Collins, 1968.

Ross, Graham. *The Foreign Office and the Kremlin: British Documents on Anglo-Soviet Relations, 1941–45*. Cambridge: Cambridge University Press, 1984.

Ruddy, Michael T. *The Cautious Diplomat: Charles E. Bohlen and the Soviet Union, 1929–1969*. Kent, Ohio: Kent State University Press, 1986.

Sainsbury, Keith. *The Turning Point: Roosevelt, Stalin, Churchill, and Chiang-Kai-Shek, 1943: The Moscow, Cairo, and Teheran Conferences*. Oxford: Oxford University Press, 1985.

Schwarz, Jordan. *Liberal Adolph A. Berle: A Vision of an American Era*. New York: Free Press, 1987.

Seaton, Albert. *The Battle for Moscow, 1941–1942*. London: Rupert Hart-Davis, 1971.

———. *The Russo-German War, 1941–45*. New York: Praeger, 1970.

———. *Stalin as Military Commander*. New York: Praeger, 1975.

———. *Stalin as Warlord*. London: Batsford, 1976.

Shapiro, Leonard. *The Origins of Command Autocracy*. Cambridge: Harvard University Press, 1961.

Sherwood, Robert Emmet. *Roosevelt and Hopkins: An Intimate History*. New York: Harper, 1948.

Shtemenko, S. M. *The Soviet General Staff at War, 1941–1945*. 2 vols. Moscow: Progress Publishers, 1975.

Soviet–US Relations, 1933–1942. Moscow: Progress Publishers, 1989.

Standley, William H., and Arthur A. Ageton. *Admiral Ambassador to Russia*. Chicago: Henry Regnery, 1955.

Stavrakis, Peter J. *Moscow and Greek Communism, 1944–1949*. Ithaca: Cornell University Press, 1989.

Stettinius, Edward R., Jr. *Lend-Lease: Weapon for Victory*. New York: Macmillan, 1944.

———. *Roosevelt and the Russians*. New York: Macmillan, 1949.

Stoler, Mark A. *The Politics of the Second Front: American Military Planning and Diplomacy, 1941–1943*. Westport, Conn.: Greenwood Press, 1976.

Taylor, A. J. P. *Beaverbrook*. New York: Simon and Schuster, 1972.

Terry, Sarah Mieklejohn. *Poland's Place in Europe*. Princeton: Princeton University Press, 1983.

Theoharis, Athan G. *The Yalta Myths: An Issue in U.S. Politics, 1945–1955*. Columbia: University of Missouri Press, 1970.

Tucker, Robert. *Stalin in Power: The Revolution from Above, 1928–1941*. New York: W. W. Norton, 1990.

Ulam, Adam Bruno. *Expansion and Coexistence: The History of Soviet Foreign Policy, 1917–1967.* New York: Praeger, 1968.

———. *Stalin: The Man and His Era.* New York: Viking Press, 1973.

Uralov, Alexander. *The Reign of Stalin.* London: Bodley Head, 1953.

Van Minnen, Cornelis, and John Sears, eds. *FDR and His Contemporaries: Foreign Perceptions of an American President.* New York: St. Martin's Press, 1992.

Van Tuyll, Hubert P. *Feeding the Bear: American Aid to the Soviet Union, 1941–1945.* New York: Greenwood Press, 1989.

Volkogonov, Dmitri. *Stalin: Triumph and Tragedy.* London: Weidenfeld, 1991.

Ward, Geoffrey C. *A First Class Temperament: The Emergence of Franklin Roosevelt.* New York: Harper and Row, 1989.

Watt, Donald Cameron. *How War Came: The Immediate Origins of the Second World War, 1938–1939.* New York: Pantheon Books, 1989.

Whaley, Barton. *Codeword Barbarossa.* Cambridge: MIT Press, 1973.

Wheeler-Bennett, Sir John W. *Action This Day: Working with Churchill.* London: Macmillan, 1968.

Williams, Robert Chadwell. *Russian Art and American Money, 1900–1940.* Cambridge: Harvard University Press, 1980.

Wilson, Theodore A. *The First Summit: Roosevelt and Churchill at Placentia Bay, 1941.* Boston: Houghton Mifflin, 1969.

Woods, Randall B. *A Changing of the Guard: Anglo-American Relations, 1941–1946.* Chapel Hill: University of North Carolina Press, 1990.

Woodward, E. L. *British Foreign Policy in the Second World War.* 3 vols. London: HMSO, 1971.

Xydis, Stephen George. *Greece and the Great Powers.* Thessaloniki: Institute for Balkan Studies, 1963.

Zawodny, J. K. *Death in the Forest: The Story of the Katyn Forest Massacre.* Notre Dame: University of Notre Dame Press, 1962.

———. *Nothing But Honour: The Story of the Warsaw Uprising, 1944.* Stanford: Hoover Institution Press, 1978.

Zhukov, M. K. *Reminiscences and Reflections.* 2 vols. Moscow: Progress Publishers, 1985.

Articles

"The Administrator: Harry Hopkins." *Time,* January 22, 1945, 17- 20.

Ambartsumov, E. E. "Osvobozhdenije ot Stalinisma [Freedom under Stalinism]." *Moscow News,* December, 1989.

"Babbit Bolsheviks." *Time,* March 15, 1937, 20–24.

Berezhkov, Valentin. "Stalin's Error of Judgement." *International Affairs* 9 (September, 1989): 13–27.

————. "Stalin and Franklin D. Roosevelt." In Cornelis Van Minnen and John Sears, eds., *FDR and His Contemporaries: Foreign Perceptions of an American President,* 45–61. New York: St. Martin's Press, 1992.

Berlin, Isaiah. "Roosevelt Through European Eyes." *Atlantic Monthly* 196 (July, 1955): 67–71.

Bland, Larry I. "Averell Harriman, The Russians and the Origins of the Cold War in Europe." *Australian Journal of Politics and History* 23 (1977): 403–16.

Blum, John M. "'That Kind of a Liberal': Franklin D. Roosevelt after Twenty-Five Years." *Yale Review* 60 (Autumn, 1970): 14–23.

Borg, Dorothy. "Notes on Roosevelt's 'Quarantine Speech.'" *Political Science Quarterly* 72 (September, 1957): 405–33.

Bullitt, William C. "How We Won the War and Lost Peace." *Life,* August 30, 1948, 83–97, and September 6, 1948, 86–103.

Butenko, A. P. "Realnaya Drama Sovetski Istorii [Real Drama in Soviet History]." *Nauka I Zhizn [Education Times],* February, 1989, 1–24.

Campbell, A. E. "Franklin Roosevelt and Unconditional Surrender." In *Diplomacy and Intelligence during the Second World War,* edited by Richard Langhorne, 219–41. Cambridge: Cambridge University Press, 1985.

Chandler, Harriette L. "The Transformation to a Cold Warrior: The Evolution of W. Averell Harriman's Polish Policy." *East European Quarterly* 10:2 (1976): 229–45.

Cole, Wayne S. "The America First Committee." *Journal Illinois State Historical Society* (Winter, 1951): 305–22.

————. "American Entry into World War II: A Historiographical Appraisal." *Mississippi Valley Historical Review* 43 (March, 1957): 595–617.

————. "Senator Key Pittman and American Neutrality Policies, 1933-1940." *Mississippi Valley Historical Review* 46 (March, 1960): 644–62.

Cowperthwaite, L. L. "Franklin D. Roosevelt at Harvard." *Quarterly Journal of Speech* 38 (February, 1952): 37–41.

Craig, Gordon A. "Dangerous Liaison." *New York Review of Books* 36:5 (March 30, 1989): 15–19.

Crowell, Laura. "Roosevelt the Gotonian." *Quarterly Journal of Speech* 38 (February, 1952): 31–36.

Dallek, Robert. "Allied Leadership in the Second World War: Roosevelt." *Survey, a Journal of East and West Studies* 21 (Winter–Spring, 1975): 1–10.

————. "Franklin Roosevelt as World Leader." *American Historical Review* 76 (December, 1971): 1503–13.

Dallin, Alexander. "Allied Leadership in the Second World War: Stalin."

Survey, a Journal of East and West Studies 21 (Winter–Spring, 1975): 11–19.

Doenecke, Justus D. "Non-interventionism of the Left: The Keep America Out of the War Congress, 1938–1941." *Journal of Contemporary History* 12 (April, 1977): 221–36.

Field, Henry. "How F.D.R. Did His Homework." *Saturday Review* 44 (July 8, 1961): 8–10.

Friedel, Frank. "Roosevelt's Father." *FDR Collector,* November, 1952, 3–10.

Gaddis, John Lewis. "Presidential Address: The Tragedy of the Cold War." *Diplomatic History* 17:1 (Winter 1993).

Haight, John, Jr. "Roosevelt and the Aftermath of the Quarantine Speech." *Review of Politics* 24 (April, 1962): 233–59.

Heller, Michel. "Mr Stalin, I Presume?" *Survey, a Journal of East and West Studies* 30:4 (June, 1989): 155–63.

Herring, George C., Jr. "Lend-Lease to Russia and the Origins of the Cold War, 1944–1945." *Journal of American History* 56 (June, 1969): 93–114.

Hilton, Stanley E. "The Wells Mission to Europe, February–March, 1940: Illusion or Realism?" *Journal of American History* 52 (January, 1971): 93–120.

Janczewski, George H. "The Origin of the Lublin Government." *Slavonic and East European Review* 50:120 (July, 1972): 410- 33.

Jonas, Manfred. "Review of Cole's Roosevelt and the Isolationists." *American Historical Review* 89 (April, 1984): 538–39.

Kahn, E. J., Jr. "Profiles: Plenipotentiary II." *New Yorker,* May 10, 1952, 36–57.

Kaiser, David E. "Churchill, Roosevelt, and the Limits of Power." *International Security* 10:1 (Summer, 1985): 204–21.

Kennan, George Frost. "Comment." *Survey, a Journal of East and West Studies* 21:1–2 (Winter–Spring, 1975): 29–36.

Kimball, Warren F. "Lend-Lease and the Open Door: The Temptation of British Opulence, 1937–1942." *Political Science Quarterly* 86 (January, 1971): 232–59.

———. "Naked Reverse Right: Roosevelt, Churchill and Eastern Europe from Tolstoy to Yalta and a Little Beyond." *Diplomatic History* 9:1 (1985): 1–24.

Kluckhohn, Frank L. "The Men Around the President." *New York Times Magazine,* March 29, 1942, 8–10.

Langer, John D. "The 'Red General' Philip R. Faymonville and the Soviet Union, 1917–1952." *Prologue* 8 (Winter, 1976): 209–21.

Le Feber, Walter. "Roosevelt, Churchill and Indochina, 1942–1945." *American Historical Review* 80 (1975): 1277–95.

Lowenthal, Mark M. "Roosevelt and the Coming of the War: The Search for United States Policy, 1937–1942." *Journal of Contemporary History* 16 (July, 1981): 413–40.

Lukas, Richard C. "Soviet Stalling Tactics in the Forties." *Aerospace Historian* (Spring, 1967): 51–56.

———. "The Velvet Project: Hope and Frustration." *Military Affairs* 28 (Winter, 1964): 145–62.

MacLean, Elizabeth Kimball. "Joseph E. Davies and Soviet-American Relations, 1941–1943." *Diplomatic History* 4:1 (1980): 73–93.

McNeal, Robert H. "Roosevelt Through Stalin's Spectacles." *International Journal* 18 (Spring, 1963): 194–206.

Mark, Eduard. "Charles E. Bohlen and the Acceptable Limits of Soviet Hegemony in Eastern Europe: A Memorandum of 18 October 1945." *Diplomatic History* 3 (Spring, 1979): 201–13.

Mastny, Vojtech. "Stalin and the Prospects of a Separate Peace in World War II." *American Historical Review* 77 (1972): 1365–88.

May, Ernest R. "Nazi Germany and the United States: A Review Essay." *Journal of Modern History* 41 (June, 1969): 207–14.

———. "The United States, the Soviet Union and the Far Eastern War, 1941–1945." *Pacific Historical Review* 24 (May, 1955): 153–74.

Moroz, O. "Posledni Diagnoz [Last Diagnosis]." *Literaturnya Gazeta,* September 28, 1988.

Neumann, William L. "Franklin D. Roosevelt: A Disciple of Admiral Mahan." *U.S. Naval Institute Proceedings* 78 (July, 1952): 713-19.

———. "Roosevelt's Options and Evasion in Foreign Policy Decisions." In *Watershed of Empire: Essays on New Deal Foreign Policy,* edited by L. Liggio and J. Martin. Colorado Springs: R. Myles, 1976.

Paterson, Thomas G. "The Abortive American Loan to Russia and the Origins of the Cold War, 1943–1946." *American Journal of History* (June, 1971): 70–92.

Perlmutter, Amos. "Shooting from the Lip: FDR's Cowboy." *Wall Street Journal,* May 13, 1987, 28.

Pratt, Julius. "The Ordeal of Cordell Hull." *Review of Politics* 28 (January, 1966): 76–98.

Reynolds, David. "Roosevelt, Churchill, and the Wartime Anglo-American Alliance, 1939–1945, Toward a New Synthesis." In *The "Special Relationship": Anglo-American Relations Since 1945,* edited by William R. Louis and Headly Bull. Oxford: Clarendon Press, 1986.

Rider, Frank J. "Harry L. Hopkins: The Ambitious Crusader." *Annals of Iowa* (February, 1977): 89–102.

Sbrega, John J. "The Anticolonial Policies of Franklin D. Roosevelt: A Reappraisal." *Political Science Quarterly* 101 (1986): 65–84.

Steele, Richard W. "Franklin D. Roosevelt and His Foreign Policy Critics." *Political Science Quarterly* 94 (Spring, 1979): 15–35.

———. "The Great Debate: Roosevelt, the Media, and the Coming of the War, 1940–1941." *Journal of American History* 71 (June, 1984): 69–92.

Urban, George. "Was Stalin (the Terrible) Really a Great Man" (A long conversation with Averell Harriman). *Encounter* 57 (November, 1981): 20–40.

Van Alstyne, Richard W. "The United States and Russia in WWII." *Current History* 19 (November–December, 1950): 257–60, 334–39.

Watt, Donald. "Roosevelt and Neville Chamberlain: Two Appeasers." *International Journal* 28 (1972–1973): 185–204.

Weinberg, Gerhard L. "Hitler's Image of the United States." *American Historical Review* 59 (July, 1964): 1006–21.

Chronology

1939–1945

Britain and France declare war on Germany (September 3, 1939).

"Phoney War," characterized by lack of action except at sea (September, 1939–March, 1940).

France falls (June, 1940).

Battle of Britain (July, 1940).

Destroyers Deal: British receive fifty World War I destroyers from U.S., and U.S. receives leases on land in British possession in the Caribbean in what Churchill calls "a decidedly unneutral act by the U.S." (August, 1940).

Four Freedoms: Weapons supplied to democracies (January, 1941).

U.S. Congress passes the Lend-Lease Act, providing $7 billion in appropriations to Britain (March 11, 1941).

Germany invades the USSR in Operation Barbarossa (June 22, 1941).

Atlantic conference, code name "Riviera" (August 9–12, 1941). FDR and Churchill meet aboard ships anchored in Placentia Bay, Newfoundland, issuing the Atlantic Charter.

Atlantic Charter is signed (August 14, 1941).

Neutrality Act is revised by U.S. Congress, arming U.S. merchant ships and setting restrictions on entering combat zones (November 13, 1941).

Pearl Harbor: Japanese forces bomb U.S. naval military and air bases in Hawaii (December 7, 1941). Japan declares war on U.S. and Britain; U.S. declares war on Japan (December 8, 1941). Germany and Italy declare war on U.S., and Congress declares war against both (December 11, 1941). The war is now global and total.

The first Washington conference, code name "Arcadia" (December 22, 1941–January 14, 1942). FDR and Churchill discuss U.S.-U.K. long-term strategy and European strategy. Churchill commits troops to North Africa. Marshall proposes a major invasion of France (Operation Sledgehammer) for 1942.

Japan invades the Dutch Netherlands and East Asia (January 10–11, 1942).

Singapore falls (February 15, 1942).

The Philippines surrenders (April 10, 1942).

Battle of Midway Island (June 4, 1942).

Tobruk falls (June 21, 1942).

Allied forces land in North Africa in Operation Torch (November 7–8, 1942).

Casablanca conference, code name "Symbol" (January 19–24, 1943). FDR, Hopkins, Leahy, Marshall, and Churchill, with his top military advisers, discuss formula for unconditional surrender and invasion of Sicily (Operation Husky).

German Army capitulates at Stalingrad (February 2, 1943).

Washington conference, code name "Trident" (May, 1943). FDR, Churchill, and their advisers discuss cross-channel invasion (Operation Overlord), planned for May, 1944, and atomic-bomb project, code name "Tube-Alloys."

Siege of Leningrad by German forces (June 1, 1943).

U.S. airborne troops and British paratroops land on Sicily (July 9–10, 1943).

Mussolini resigns and is arrested (July 25, 1943).

Quebec conference, code name "Quadrant" (August, 1943). FDR, Churchill, and their military advisers discuss Operation Overlord.

Allied forces land in Italy (September 3, 1943).

German forces capture Kiev (November 6, 1943).

The first Cairo conference, code name "Sextant" (November 22–26, 1943). FDR, Churchill, and Chiang Kai-Shek discuss Far Eastern issues.

Teheran conference, code name "Eureka" (November 27–December

2, 1943). The first and one of the three most significant meetings of the Allied leaders. FDR's first meeting with Stalin.

1. Participants form European commission for managing the occupation of Italy and Germany.
2. Participants debate and decide on the dismemberment of Germany and zones of occupation and to have no sphere of influence.
3. FDR proposes Four Policemen idea (U.S.-U.K.-USSR-China). Churchill objects to China as one of the four great nations.
4. Participants debate Operation Overlord. Stalin is impatient to have a second front. Churchill prefers the underbelly-Balkan rather than cross-channel invasion. U.S. Chiefs are furious. Participants keep Anglo-American-Soviet relationships vague.

Blockade of Leningrad lifted (January 27, 1944).
Allied forces carry out bombing raid over Europe. Out of 8,000 bombers, 6,000 deployed to Germany (March, 1944).
Anglo-American offensive at Anzio Beach (May 23, 1944).
Operation Overlord, the revised plan for cross-channel assault, is carried out in the invasion of Normandy (June 6, 1944).
Soviet forces attack on all fronts (July, 1944).
Hitler's generals unsuccessfully attempt to kill him (July 20, 1944).
Paris is liberated (August 23, 1944).
U.S. invades the Philippines (January 9, 1945).
Yalta Conference, code name "Argonaut" (Crimea, February 7–11, 1945). The second major tripartite meeting, and FDR's last meeting. Participants engage in furious debate over the fate of Poland and the question of territory. Stalin will not compromise, except to accept Churchill's Curzon Line, which the Poles adamantly oppose. No final decision is made on Poland. Major decisions made:

1. United Nations will be formed.
2. USSR will enter the war with Japan.

U.S. Army crosses the Rhine (March 7, 1945).
President Roosevelt dies (April 12, 1945).

San Francisco conference (April 25 – June 26, 1945). Fifty delegates complete U.N. Charter.

Mussolini is shot and killed (April 28, 1945).

Hitler commits suicide (April 30, 1945).

Unconditional surrender of the German armies (May 4, 1945) and of
  Germany (May 7, 1945).

VE Day (May 8, 1945).

Potsdam conference. Truman, Stalin, and Churchill discuss the treatment of Germany and the Poland controversy (July 17, 1945).

First atomic bomb is dropped, on Hiroshima (August 6, 1945).

USSR declares war on Japan (August 8, 1945).

Second atomic bomb is dropped, on Nagasaki (August 9, 1945).

Japan surrenders (August 14, 1945).

VJ Day (August 15, 1945).

Index